ABDULLAH AL-TALL
Arab Legion
Officer

ABDULLAH AL-TALL
Arab Legion Officer

Arab Nationalism and Opposition
to the Hashemite Regime

RONEN YITZHAK

sussex
ACADEMIC
PRESS
Brighton • Portland • Toronto

2 4 6 8 10 9 7 5 3 1

First published 2012 in Great Britain by
SUSSEX ACADEMIC PRESS
PO Box 139
Eastbourne BN24 9BP

and in the United States of America by
SUSSEX ACADEMIC PRESS
920 NE 58th Ave   Suite 300
Portland, Oregon 97213–3786

and in Canada by
SUSSEX ACADEMIC PRESS (CANADA)
8000 Bathurst Street, Unit 1, PO Box 30010, Vaughan, Ontario L4J 0C6

British Library Cataloguing in Publication Data
A CIP catalogue record for this book is available from the British Library.

Library of Congress Cataloging-in-Publication Data
Yitzhak, Ronen.
Abdallah al-Tall, Arab Legion commander : Arab nationalism and
   opposition to the Hashemite regime / Ronen Yitzhak.
   p. cm.
Includes bibliographical references and index.
ISBN 978-1-84519-408-6 (h/b : alk. paper)
   1. Tall, 'Abd Allah. 2. Soldiers—Jordan—Biography. 3. Governors
—Jordan—Biography. 4. Israel–Arab War, 1948–1949. I. Title.
DS154.52.T33Y58 2012
956.9504'3092—dc23
[B]
                                                            2011028429

Typeset and designed by Sussex Academic Press, Brighton & Eastbourne.
Printed by TJ International, Padstow, Cornwall.
This book is printed on acid-free paper.

Contents

Foreword by Professor Eyal Zisser

This story of the life of an officer in the Arab Legion, Abdullah al-Tall, is a fascinating narrative which could have been the subject of a thriller or detective novel. A young army officer, a hero of the 1948 war in Palestine, gets caught up in a conspiracy against his king, Abdullah I, is convicted of involvement in his assassination, and flees for political refuge in Egypt, where he continues his struggle against King Hussein and the Hashemite dynasty in Jordan. Ultimately, however, everything works out: Al-Tall is pardoned, returns to his homeland in 1965, and becomes a loyal supporter of the monarchy, having become a prominent member of the Jordanian Senate by the end of his political career.

The excellent account given in the book does not only provide us with a detective story based upon the personal life of its hero, however. The tale in fact encompasses all the major events of that period in Jordanian and Middle Eastern history – the establishment of the state and the monarchy in Jordan under the Hashemite dynasty; Britain's involvement in Transjordan and in the entire Middle East; the question of Palestine and the Arab-Israeli conflict; and finally, Israeli-Jordanian relations in their formative years.

Likewise, al-Tall's personal biography reflects the history of a whole generation of Arab youth who, like al-Tall, came to personal and political maturity at the end of the 1940s – a generation destined to play a key role in the region's history, bursting onto center stage in the military and the political and ideological arenas alike. Subsequently these young men also dominated the political stage of the various Arab states during the struggle for independence from Western powers, and later during the struggle for power in the independent Arab states.

It is no coincidence that Abdullah al-Tall was born in 1918, the same year as Gamal Abd al-Nasser and Muhammad Anwar Sadat, both of whom played a major role in shaping Egypt's fate during the 1950s, '60s, and '70s. Al-Tall's life, indeed, reflects and represents the story of a whole Arab generation born on the heels of the demise of the Ottoman Empire who grew up between the two world wars.

This period was one in which the region began to shape its features and fate, from Ottomanism to Arabism, under the shadow of a Western presence in the Middle East.

When al-Tall's public career ended, he was a member of the Jordanian Senate. In this respect, one cannot but recall another Jordanian hero of the 1950s, Suleiman al-Nabulsi, Prime Minister of the short-lived government which ruled between the end of 1956 and the beginning of 1957. Together with the then Jordanian Chief of Staff, Ali Abu Nuwar, al-Nabulsi found himself in opposition to the Hashemite dynasty and King Hussein. The two men fled to Damascus, where they continued their struggle against the Jordanian ruler. Eventually, however, they returned to Jordan and were pardoned, al-Nabulsi himself – like Abdullah al-Tall – being appointed to the Senate, an institution comprised of the kingdom's elders despite lacking any real political influence or power. In this sense, al-Tall's story – like that of al-Nabulsi – reveals King Hussein's art of survival and his regime's ability to contain the protest and subdue the flames of rebellion and revolt.

Al-Tall published his memoirs in the late 1950s, at a relatively early stage in his political career and before he had reached either maturity or his prime. Although he wrote extensively, the full picture of his life and an appraisal of the significance of the course he took and his activity has yet to be portrayed. The complex task of reconstructing his complete politico-military biography by placing his life-story within a broader context has been undertaken in this book by Ronen Yitzhak, a long-time scholar of the Jordanian kingdom whose ground-breaking works have illuminated numerous chapters in the history of Jordan – in particular the key events in its formative years: the establishment of the Arab Legion, and military-state relations during the formative period of Abdullah's reign. He has now provided us with another brick in the history of the Jordanian kingdom in this excellent account of Abdullah al-Tall.

Using al-Tall's own writings and memoirs and those of his colleagues, the book is based on extensive research in British, American, and Israeli archives and the Arab and Western press. All these sources unite to produce a masterful work which will undoubtedly deepen our understanding of critical chapters in the growth of the Jordanian kingdom and the formation and emergence of the Arab Legion in the 1940s and '50s.

The significance of this research is particularly striking in light of the time of its publication, just as the Arab Spring has erupted throughout the Middle East. The Arab Spring has yet to affect Jordan, the country thus demonstrating an immunity similar to that which it exhibited in the 1950s and '60s during the storm which broke over the Arab world in those decades. Study of the revolt of the young generation in the 1940s and '50s – to whom al-Tall served as a voice – is imperative for anyone seeking to trace the roots of the present protests sweeping the Arab world.

PROF. EYAL ZISSER
Dean, Faculty of Humanities,
The Yona and Dina Ettinger Chair of
Contemporary Middle Eastern History,
Tel Aviv University

Preface

There are few officers who receive compliments and praise from their enemies. Abdullah al-Tall, an Arab Legion officer, was one of the few Arab officers, if not the only one, to receive such. Despite fighting against the Jews during the 1948 war, he quickly endeared himself to those with whom he had contact as he attempted to make political arrangements with Israel as a special messenger of King Abdullah. However, shortly after this diplomacy he changed his position regarding Jews and Israel – a typical turnaround that reflected his personality. He was a volatile officer who changed his opinion depending on circumstances as he perceived them. Al-Tall had received a British education and cooperated with British officers in the Arab Legion, but he hated them and for what they stood for. He was close to King Abdullah and was promoted in the Arab Legion with the assistance and blessing of the king, but he was later to become involved in a plot to assassinate him.

In March 1950, Abdullah al-Tall caused a sensation in the Arab world when he began to publish his memoirs from the 1948 war. He laid bare, for the first time, the secret ties and contacts between Israel and Jordan during the war, thus laying the foundation for the "conspiracy myth" that would develop later. The memoirs, which were published in the important Egyptian newspaper *Akhbar al-Youm,* beginning on 18 March 1950, gave rise to much anger in Jordan whose government confiscated all the issues of the paper distributed in Jordan. Fearing a worsening of the already tense relations between the two countries, at the request of Jordan the Egyptian authorities ordered a halt to the publication of Abdullah al-Tall's memoirs shortly after they appeared.

Nine years later in 1959, when he was in political exile in Cairo, his complete memoirs of the 1948 war were published in a book titled *Karithat Filastin* (The Catastrophe of Palestine). The work is generally considered as one of the most fundamental and important books on the war. Beyond providing political and military facts related to the conduct of the war, al-Tall's goal in writing the book was to clear his name after it had been discovered that he sought to make political contact with Israel and had become a "personal friend of Moshe Dayan, the Israeli commander", as General Glubb Pasha claimed. Al-Tall wrote his memoirs in an attempt to discredit the name of King Abdullah and the commander of the Arab Legion, General Glubb Pasha. He accused both of them as being traitors to Arab nationalism.

In addition to his book *Karithat Filastin*, Abdullah al-Tall wrote five other books on various subjects. The first of these was *Rihla ila Britaniya* (Journey to Britain), which he wrote in 1947 when he was serving as an officer in the Arab Legion. In the book he describes his military training and that of his fellow Arab officers in Britain. The book is not anti-British; in fact there is an appreciation of the British culture he encountered there.

While he was in Cairo endearing himself to the Arab public at large, and after he had published his book *Karithat Filastin*, he wrote another book entitled *Filastin Waba'ath al-Qawmiya al-Arabiya* (Palestine and the National Arab Ba'at). It was published in a series of national Arab books with the support of the Egyptian government. The main theme of the book was that Palestine had always belonged to Arabs and that the Jews had no legitimate part in it. He accused Britain of betraying the Arab collective with the Balfour Declaration of 2 November 1917.

In later years he grew closer to Islam and studied at al-Azhar University, receiving a master's degree in 1965. He intended to continue his studies to doctoral level, but stopped when he returned to Jordan that same year. On the basis of his studies at al-Azhar, al-Tall published three anti-Semitic Islamic books, which tried to prove that Jews were dangerous to the world because of their bad qualities. The first of this trilogy was *Khatar al-Yahudiya al-Alamiya Ala al-Islam wal-Masihiya* (The Danger of World Jewry to Islam and to Christianity), which was published in 1964. The second, *Judhur al-Bila* (Roots of the Evil), was published in 1970. And the last, *al-Af'a al-Yahudiya fi Ma'aqil al-Islam* (The Jewish Viper in Islamic Mentality), was published in 1971. All three books expressed similar ideas, primarily claiming that the Jews intended to control the world and would not stop at any means to do so, including worldwide prostitution and corruption. He tried to prove that all the disasters in the world occurred because of the Jewish people and discussed their supposed innate negative characteristics, which he claimed included cowardice, cruelty and deception.

Abdullah al-Tall not only wrote books but also liked to be interviewed. He was contacted by the international press constantly. General Glubb Pasha disliked al-Tall's contact with the press and said: "To be made a hero and daily reported in the Press is heady wine for a young man". Media reception was a deliberate strategy of Abdullah al-Tall. He wanted to establish himself as a young leader in a short time and believed in the power of media to do so. Daily media exposure served his purpose well: to become a popular and well-known figure in the Arab world.

I encountered many stumbling blocks in the research and writing of this book. Historical research on the Arab military mind is problematic for any researcher, let alone an Israeli researcher seeking to extract information from various sources, including Arab countries. Unfortunately, I was unable to write this book with sought for collaboration with Jordanian officials and my efforts to reach unofficial Jordanian sources were also unsuccessful. The al-Tall family also refused to cooperate with me. However, the wide variety of sources used – including archives, newspapers and secondary sources in three languages (English, Hebrew and Arabic) – provide the reader with insights into Abdullah al-Tall's background as well as his political and religious views. This is not just a biography of al-Tall in the classical meaning of the word. "Biography is the only true history", said Thomas Carlyle more than 150 years ago. For this book does not only deal with Abdullah al-Tall himself, but is an in-depth look at a wide-range of important military and political events that took place in the Middle East at the time he was active, involved and about which he wrote.

The book opens with a chapter describing the general circumstances surrounding the establishment of Transjordan and the Arab Legion and illuminates the relationship between Britain and the Hashemite regime, as well as Abdullah's connections with the Zionists. This chapter is essential to understanding the political reality in which Abdullah al-Tall lived and acted, and which he tried to change. The chapter also looks at the al-Tall family, one of the most important families in Jordan. It reviews his activities in his first years of service in the Arab Legion. The chapter ends with the first victory achieved by Abdullah al-Tall in the 1948 war – the attack on the Etzion Block. This attack, which he commanded, proved his military skill and his ability to command the Arab Legion for the first time.

The second chapter focuses on Abdullah al-Tall's activities in Jerusalem. It discusses the military background of the Arab invasion of Palestine in May 1948, and King Abdullah's decision to send the Arab Legion into Jerusalem. It examines military operations under his command to occupy the Jewish Quarter, the negotiations with the Jews and the surrender agreement. The chapter then deals with al-Tall's activities as military governor of Jerusalem under the Hashemite regime and his relationship with the Palestinians. Much of the chapter is devoted to the negotiations between Israel and Jordan, and the role al-Tall played in these negotiations until an armistice agreement was reached in Rhodes in April 1949.

The third chapter opens with a look at the status of the army in the Arab world after the 1948 war, Abdullah al-Tall's attempt to carry out a military coup in Jordan, and his decision to leave Jordan for Egypt. The chapter continues with his activities against the Hashemite regime in Jordan – his accusations and claims against King Abdullah and General Glubb Pasha – and examines them in the light of historical facts. Finally, the chapter describes the background to the assassination of King Abdullah in Jerusalem in July 1951, and discusses Abdullah al-Tall's part in this attack.

The final chapter describes the political activities of Abdullah al-Tall in Egypt, his contacts with Arab nationalists and his relationship with Algerian rebels. It continues the discussion of his anti-Semitic concepts, examining the books he wrote in the 1960s. The chapter ends with an explanation of the circumstances that enabled al-Tall to return to Jordan in April 1965, and examines his position after his return and repentance.

As stated, in writing the book I have used a wide variety of Arabic sources. The translation from Arabic to English is my own. Although some Arabic sources have been translated into English, such as King Abdullah's memoirs or Nasser's famous book, I preferred to use authentic Arabic versions which are more precise, and therefore the translation of these Arabic sources to English was done in the light of my interpretation of them.

To facilitate easier reading by those not familiar with Arabic sources, I utilized the English transliteration of Arabic names common in the English press. For example, I write Abdullah and not 'Abdallah, which is used by academic professionals, and Hussein not Husayn, etc.

A number of people have helped me during the writing of this book to whom I give grateful thanks: Western Galilee College, for their financial aid and Yehudit Lahav, who read the book carefully, made comments, and edited it professionally. Also, I would like to thank the Archives staff, particularly the IDF Archive staff, who allowed me to use a number of important documents and gave me permission to use the image for the book's cover. In addition, I would like to thank Anita Grahame, Marketing Director at Sussex Academic Press, for assistance throughout the publication process. I am deeply grateful to Prof. Zisser for providing a Foreword, which puts the historical narrative presented here in contemporary context.

Finally, I would like to thank my dear family, my parents and my wife Limor for their support, encouragement and patience for all the time I spent on writing this book when I should have been with them.

List of Abbreviations

ACSP	Arab Collective Security Pact
ALA	Arab Liberation Army
CENTO	Central Treaty Organization
CO	Colonial Office (London)
DEFE	Ministry of Defence (London)
DFLP	Democratic Front for the Liberation of Palestine
FO	Foreign Office (London)
HA	Haganah Archive
IDF	Israel Defence Forces
IDFA	Israel Defence Forces Archive
ISA	Israel State Archive
IZL	Irgun Zvai Leumi (National Military Organization)
MEC	Middle East command
MEJ	*Middle East Journal*
MELF	Middle East Land Forces
MER	*Middle East Record*
MES	*Middle Eastern Studies*
NA	National Archives (London)
NATO	North Atlantic Treaty Organization
PCC	Palestine Conciliation Commission
PFLP	Popular Front for the Liberation of Palestine
PLO	Palestine Liberation Organization
PREM	Prime Minister's Office papers (London)
RAF	Royal Air Force
TJFF	Transjordan Frontier Force
UAR	United Arab Republic
UNRWA	United Nations Relief and Works Agency
WO	War Office (London)

Abdullah al-Tall: Chronology

17 July 1918	Born in Irbid.
October 1937	Recruited into the TJFF.
June 1942	Recruited into the Arab Legion.
12 May 1948	Commander of the attack against the Etzion Bloc.
18 May 1948	Commander of the attack against the Old City.
July 1948	Commander of the 6th Regiment in the Arab Legion.
20 March 1949	Appointed as civilian governor of Jerusalem
26 July 1949	Resigned from the Arab Legion.
5 October 1949	Left Jordan for Egypt.
January 1950	Opened the campaign against King Abdullah of Jordan.
20 July 1951	Took part in the assassination of King Abdullah.
February 1958	Took part in the establishment of the Revolutionary Council.
March 1959	Published his book on the 1948 war (*Karithat Filastin*).
April 1960	Established the Arab Brigade to fight in Algeria.
13 April 1965	Returned to Jordan from Cairo.
9 December 1971	Joined the Jordanian Senate.
13 August 1973	Al-Tall dies.

1

The First Years in the Arab Legion

Abdullah Yousef al-Tall was born on 17 July 1918 in Irbid in northern Jordan, about three years before the official formation of the Transjordan emirate by the British. In those days, shortly before the end of the First World War, the British forces advancing from Egypt under the command of General Edmund Allenby conquered southern Palestine, the coastal cities of Palestine and Jerusalem and after the breaking of the Ottoman front at the battle of Megiddo on 19 September 1918, the road north towards Syria was opened to them.[1] Simultaneously an Arab army column commanded by Faysal, son of Hussein the Sharif of Mecca, also advanced north in Transjordan toward Damascus. On 1 October 1918 the Arabs entered Damascus after the British had overcome Ottoman resistance and taken control of the city. Although Faysal ruled Syria for a short period (1918–1920), he was deported with the start of French mandatory rule on 24 July 1920.[2]

Four months later, on 21 November 1920, Faysal's brother, the Amir Abdullah, arrived from Hijaz at Ma'an on the border of Hijaz-Transjordan with about 300 men and six machine guns.[3] His declared goal was to fight the French in order to depose his brother Faysal from the throne in Syria. However, by doing so, Abdullah also sought to wrest control of Transjordan from the British. His elder brother, Ali, now ruled Hijaz and his younger brother, Faysal, who left Syria for Europe, was about to rule Iraq; he, Abdullah, remained crownless.[4] On 21 August 1920, the High Commissioner to Palestine, Herbert Samuel, in the spirit of the British policy which sought to form a friendship with the Arabs in the Middle East, declared in Salt, west-central Jordan, his plan to separate Transjordan from the British Mandate in Palestine. And instead of one central command over Transjordan, Samuel called for the formation of local governments in Karak, Salt and Irbid with the help of British officers.[5]

The three local governments, established under the leadership of prominent Jordanians, Rufayfan al-Majali (Karak), Mazhar Raslan (Salt) and Ali Khalqi al-Sharayri (Irbid), and under the supervision of British officers,[6] found it hard to establish normal everyday life in Transjordan, because of the population's refusal to pay taxes, Bedouin raids on settled residents and traditional tribal hostilities.[7] The only solid achievement during the three governments' term of office (August 1920–April 1921) was the establishment of a local military force in Amman under British command to protect the settled residents, mainly the Circassian, from Bedouin raids. Although this force is generally identified with its first commander, Colonel Frederick Gerard Peake, the idea of establishing such a force was submitted to High Commissioner Samuel by the British officer in Amman, Captain Dunbar Brunton, on 20 September 1920. The force established under Brunton's command a month later was known as the Reserve Force and comprised only around 200 men from Faysal's army who had stayed in the Transjordan after Faysal's ejection from Syria. In December after Brunton left Amman, Colonel Peake, commander of the Imperial Camel Corps during First World War, took command of the Reserve Force.[8]

From Ma'an, Abdullah formed contacts with different nationalist Arab elements including the tribal heads who had had contact with the Hashemite family during the Arab revolt, Arab leaders who had served alongside Faysal in Damascus and municipal Arab leaders who now opposed both the British and French Mandates. He called on them to join him in the national fight against the French in Syria. It appears that he even made contact with Mustafa Kemal (Ataturk), the nationalist Turkish leader who sought the return of territories lost during the First World War (including skenderun) to Turkey. Abdullah also requested Ataturk's assistance because he believed that they saw eye to eye on the matter of ridding Syria of French rule.[9]

Abdullah used Islamic and national slogans to incite the people in the Middle East to join his combat against France and restore rule in Syria to the Arabs. In a proclamation addressed to the "people of Syria" two weeks after he arrived in Ma'an, he declaimed French imperialism and the intention to destroy Arab and Islamic heritage. He said that he knew Syrians would defend themselves against French imperialism and expressed his belief that they would eventually be victorious.[10]

This proclamation turned Amir Abdullah from a local Hijaz leader into a regional leader. He gained support from nationalist and traditional Arab leaders from Transjordan, Syria and Palestine, who started going to Ma'an to express their support for his aims and to donate money to help him realize them. Among them were Sa'id al-Mufti, the leader of the Circassian community in Amman and Mithqal ibn Fayiz, leader of the Bani Sakhr tribe.[11] However, not all in Transjordan supported Amir Abdullah. For instance, Sultan al-Adwan, leader of the Adwan tribe which resisted Abdullah, refused to welcome him. The head of the local government in Salt, Mazhar Raslan, also opposed Abdullah's plan and even sent him a furious telegram regarding his arrival: "The government has heard of your intention to visit in Transjordan. If your visit is a private one, we will welcome you. If it is for political purposes, the government will do all within its means to stop it".[12]

British policy pertaining to Amir Abdullah was unclear. Despite stating his intention to fight the French, the British did little to prevent his advance north into Damascus; they just warned the local residents not to join him. Thus, in January 1921 Abdullah, heading a force of some 2,000 men, advanced toward Karak which was inside Transjordan. The British adviser in Karak, Alec Kirkbride, asked the Palestine High Commissioner, Samuel, what he was to do should Abdullah enter Transjordan, but the answer he received showed that the British did not believe he would. Samuel therefore replied that: "It was considered most unlikely that the Amir Abdullah would arrive into territory which was under British control." After it became clear that Abdullah was indeed heading toward Karak and without any orders from Samuel, Kirkbride decided (without approval from his superiors) that the best policy was to meet Abdullah; thus, when he appeared about three days later in Karak, Kirkbride met him and said: "Sir, welcome to Transjordan".[13]

With no British resistance, Abdullah continued north according to his original plan and on 2 March 1921 he entered Amman. This increased concern among the British that he would draw them into a conflict with the French because Transjordan, along with Palestine, was part of the British Mandate according to the resolution of the San Remo conference in April 1921. The British had a solution to the Abdullah problem. In a conference which took place in Cairo on 12 March, led by Winston Churchill (then Secretary of State for the Colonies), the Palestine and Iraq High Commissioners,

Herbert Samuel and Percy Cox, and with the participation of T. E. Lawrence (Lawrence of Arabia, Churchill's adviser on Arab affairs), it was decided to let Faysal rule in Iraq and to leave Transjordan under Abdullah's control for an experimental period of six months on the condition that he abandon the idea of attacking the French in Syria.[14]

At the end of March, Churchill met Abdullah in Jerusalem and submitted the British proposal to establish an independent government in Transjordan under his rule, in return for his recognition of British control over Transjordan as part of the Palestine mandate and acknowledging the British representative in Amman as adviser to his government. Amir Abdullah would receive a monthly British subsidy of £5,000 for six months to organize the security forces to maintain law and order. Abdullah agreed not to act against the French. At the end of the six months, after visiting Transjordan, Lawrence advised Churchill to extend Abdullah's rule indefinitely. Thus, without any premeditated by the British, the Transjordan Emirate was established and the regime of Amir Abdullah, son of Hussein Sharif of Mecca, began and lasted for 30 years.[15]

The British decision to appoint Abdullah to rule Transjordan was an indication of the close links already forged between the Hashemite family, to which Abdullah belonged, and the British. On the eve of First World War, political ties had been formed between the father of the modern Hashemite family, Hussein ibn Ali, the Sharif of Mecca, and the British. Hussein's political ambition was to form one great Arab state under his sons' leadership: the oldest son Ali in Hijaz, Abdullah in Iraq and Faysal in Syria. He hoped that with British help he could realize that dream. On 5 June 1916 following successful negotiations with the British High Commissioner to Cairo, Henry McMahon (the McMahon-Hussein correspondence), over the establishment of an independent Arab state led by him, Hussein organized the Arab revolt against the Ottoman Empire in the Middle East, the success of which is doubted by modern historians, despite T. E. Lawrence's input. However, it is clear that the opposition of the Hashemite family to other Arabs, no matter how dubious its motives, was an expression of its alliance with the British.[16]

Historical Background: Transjordan from Emirate to Kingdom

Amir Abdullah immediately started to organize the Emirate and confirmed his rule over the entire Emirate territory. On 11 April 1921 he appointed Rashid Tali, a Druze originally from Mount Lebanon who had held office as the Internal Minister of Faysal's government in Damascus, to be the first Prime Minister of Transjordan in what was officially called a Council of Consultants. A few days later, in accordance with the agreement between Abdullah and Churchill, Albert Abramson, the military governor of Hebron, was appointed the first British representative in Transjordan (April 1921–November 1921).[17] The British Liberal government under Lloyd George which was responsible for the new order in the Middle East (which meant the formation of the two Hashemite countries, Iraq and Transjordan), continued to nurture relations with Amir Abdullah and reinforce his position both internally and regionally, in order to ensure stability in the area and thus promote British interests. In Churchill's White Paper of 3 June 1922, Transjordan was to be separated from Palestine to create a new independent Emirate under Amir Abdullah's rule. A month later, the League of Nations recognized this when it handed the Palestine mandate to Britain (Article 25).[18]

Furthermore, at the end of that year, Abdullah was invited to London to discuss Transjordan's status. During the official meetings held in October and November 1922, the Emirate's borders were agreed as was British financial support for Transjordan to the sum of £150,000 for the year starting on 1 April 1923. However, during Abdullah's visit to London Lloyd George's government fell and with it, Abdullah's patron Winston Churchill. Despite this, Abdullah managed to get a commitment from the British government to "recognize the existence of an independent government in Transjordan under the rule of His Highness the Amir Abdullah ibn Hussein". On 25 May 1923 the Palestine High Commissioner Samuel arrived in Amman and declared this publicly. Abdullah thanked Britain for granting "independence" and emphasized the close relations between the Arabs and Britain. "There is no doubt that the Arabs had proven in all terms and conditions their loyalty and friendship to their great ally", Amir Abdullah declared.[19]

Despite Britain's efforts to establish Amir Abdullah, his appointment encountered heavy resistance from both the traditional tribes in Transjordan and from his enemies in Arabia, Ibn Saud and the Wahhabis. They had opposed Hashemite rule over Transjordan and Iraq ever since the Hashemite family had fought them in Arabia and they intended to overthrow Abdullah's rule in Transjordan.[20]

One of the most pressing problems Abdullah had to deal with in his new Emirate was tax collection. Transjordan residents refused to pay taxes to the central regime in Amman because they saw it as an expression of subordination to that regime. In May 1921 about two months after Abdullah was appointed, a rebellion broke out around the village Kura, in northwestern Transjordan, which darkened the start of Abdullah's regime in Transjordan.

The villagers, led by Kulayib al-Shurayda, claimed it was unfair that only settled residents were obliged to pay taxes, while Bedouin tribes were exempt.[21] In fact, the Kura tribes had a tradition of resistance and rebellion in Transjordan. The tribe leader, Kulayib al-Shurayda, was not represented in the local government in Irbid and he therefore opposed the new regime established in Transjordan by the British. Instead, he established an autonomous regime in the area of Irbid with French support and the encouragement of Damascus.[22] In order to collect taxes, a special force of about 100 cavalry from the Reserve Force, commanded by Fuad Salim, was sent under order of the Amman government on 12 May. "The result was disastrous", Peek wrote later. When the untrained force arrived at the village, it was surrounded; 18 men died, the rest surrendered and lost their horses and arms. It was a severe blow, not only to Amir Abdullah, but also to the short-lived Reserve Force which was almost eradicated. The government negotiated with Kulayib for the captives' release and only after Abdullah's personal involvement, promising gifts and unconditional pardons, did they release the prisoners. The tribe continued to refuse to pay taxes.[23]

Although the rebellion in Kura ended in a harsh military failure for Abdullah, it showed his determination to strengthen his rule over Transjordan and helped him to subdue other rebellious tribes. Following this rebellion, in December 1921 he reached an agreement with the Karak tribes on tax collection and shortly thereafter with the Tafila tribes as well.[24] However, it was clear that without an efficient and credible military force, the Amir's position would be weak. Thus, the British decided to re-form the Reserve Force in Amman under Peek's command with the help of the two Arab officers, Fuad Salim and Muhammad Ali Ajluni. It was to be increased to 750 soldiers and officers and would be the primary force for maintaining Abdullah's regime in Transjordan. Although its main objective was to maintain order and security, repress tribal insurgencies and raids and so on, it would also collect taxes to fill the Transjordan Emirate treasury.[25]

It should be noted that as well as the rebellion in Kura, the British had another consideration in re-forming the Reserve Force. This was the understanding concluded with the French during the San Remo conference for taking control of the Turkish Petroleum Company (TPC) on the condition that the French received 25 per cent of the company shares.[26] This was validated in the Treaty of Sèvres in August 1920 and was realized in tandem with the British receiving mandate over Iraq and the coronation of King Faysal in August 1921. Because of the strategic importance of the area and the British army's need of oil, it was essential to form an efficient military force that would not only maintain the Hashemite regime in Jordan, but would also secure the safe passage of oil in the area. This explains why the British increased the intensive supervision over the Reserve Force and during 1921–1922 slowly started to appoint more British officers who served alongside the Arab officers to form special units.[27]

Abdullah's territory was small and desert-like and lacked any resources. It compromised 99,000 square kilometers, divided into three districts: Ajlun, Balqa and Karak, which together amounted to 119 villages, encompassing a population of 225,380. The biggest city at that time was Salt, in northeastern Transjordan, with 20,000 residents, which had been used as an administrative center during Ottoman times. Abdullah, however, chose Amman as the new Emirate capital.[28] Amman was a small town of about 2,400 residents, mainly Circassian, who had revitalized the town at the end of the 19th century when they were deported by the Russian Empire from the Caucasus. In contrast to most of the other locals, the Circassian residents of Amman welcomed Abdullah with open arms and their leader, Sa'id al-Mufti, who had welcomed Abdullah in Ma'an, received him into his own home. One cannot help but conclude that its high geographic position overlooking the entire area, its position on the route to Damascus and the participation of the Circassian residents in the Reserve Force were the main considerations for choosing Amman as the capital city.[29]

Despite Abdullah's efforts to reach an understanding with the Jordanian tribes, his position during 1922–1924 was unstable. The main threat was from Sultan al-Adwan, the prominent leader of the

Adwan tribe, who challenged his regime and gained support from nationalist Arabs. A tradition of hostility had existed between al-Adwan and Abdullah even before he arrived at Ma'an.[30]

In August 1923 a rumor started that taxes collected from the Adwan tribe were being transferred to their enemies, the Bani Sakhr tribe, and that the latter had also been granted lands in the district of Balqa in northwestern Transjordan. The rumor was not without foundation. Abdullah did indeed try to keep the Bani Sakhr tribe, who were a target of the Wahhabis' attacks and were under their influence, close. In order to keep their loyalty and fearing that they would follow the Wahhabis, Abdullah's enemies, he gave them bribes which included land and money, some of which had been collected from the Adwan tribe. He even gave them jobs in the Jordanian government.[31] Because of the hostility between the two tribes, the Bani Sakhr refused to participate in the local government of Salt because of the Adwan presence and instead formed an alternative government in Amman under the leadership of Mithqal ibn Fayiz, who supported the Hashemite family and Abdullah.[32]

The crisis worsened when Sultan al-Adwan, leader of the Adwan tribe, instructed the tribal council to give Abdullah an ultimatum, which included administrative reforms (such as casting out strangers – Syrians, Iraqis, Palestinians – from key positions in the government) and demanded the participation of their own representatives in the government, calling for "Transjordan for the Transjordanians".[33] The government rejected these demands. With the support of the majority of the residents and with encouragement from nationalist Arab elements, Sultan al-Adwan decided to advance on Amman. In an effort to prevent British intervention, he sent a warning to the British representative in Amman, John Philby notifying him that this was an internal matter and not an anti-British one. He claimed that if Philby interfered he would report him to the Colonial Office. Philby was not deterred and warned al-Adwan not to proceed, but al-Adwan was determined to act.[34]

On 16 September 1923 Sultan al-Adwan, leading the tribal force, advanced from Sulayh towards Amman. However, when they reached Amman, the Reserve Force and two armored cars commanded by Fuad Salim ambushed the Adwan and fighting broke out. Eighty-six tribal people were killed (including 13 women), while the rest of the rebels fled to Jabel Druze in Syria.[35] Philby and Peake used the momentum gained from repressing the rebellion to arrest other Arab nationalists in the army and the government who were opposed to Amir Abdullah. Among those arrested was Abdullah al-Tall's uncle, the famous Jordanian poet Mustafa Wahbi al-Tall, who was close to the Adwan. He was put on trial for "conspiracy against the state", and was later deported to Karak.[36]

There is no doubt that the Adwan rebellion had been a great threat to Abdullah's regime. Following the repression of the insurgency, all security forces were united with the Reserve Force to form a new army, commanded by Peake. It was called "The Arab Legion" or "The Arab Army", after the army led by Sharif Hussein which had revolted against the Ottoman Empire during the First World War, and was increased in strength to 1,200 officers and soldiers.[37] Beyond the symbolism of the name, intended to express the legacy of the Arab army, it seems that Abdullah also sought to hint at his political ambitions towards Syria. These ambitions should have ended with his meeting with Churchill in March 1921, but may have continued as long as he ruled Jordan, and they comprised part of his official foreign policy.

Though the Arab Legion was formed to protect Amir Abdullah's regime from internal enemies, opposition to his regime also came from the Hashemite family's enemies in Arabia Ibn Saud and the Wahhabis, who renewed their conflict at the end of the First World War. T. E. Lawrence was sent to Arabia in order to settle the conflict between the two rulers but he did not succeed. During 1921–1922, the Wahhabis took over Tima and Khaybar as well as more territory towards Wadi Sirhan, which was under Ibn Rashid's control. After the formation of Transjordan, the Wahhabis increased the number and severity of their raids, not only for financial-agricultural reasons as was usually the custom during the summer, but also for religious and political reasons, hoping to cause the collapse of Abdullah's regime in Transjordan.[38]

Such an attempt by the Wahhabis took place on 15 August 1922 when some 1,500 Wahhabis went west through Wadi Sirhan into Transjordan and attacked the Bani Sakhr villages neighboring Amman during the night. The attack was bloody and brutal. Most of the Reserve Force was located in the north, fighting the Kura tribes who still refused to pay taxes. However, the Wahhabis quickly fled when they saw an RAF airplane. "By the time news of this event reached Amman and aeroplanes had been sent over", wrote Peake, "they had completely disappeared and were never to be seen again".

By the end of the attack, there were 300 Wahhabi casualties and 61 Jordanian casualties, including one woman.[39]

A much more serious Wahhabi raid took place two years later. On 14 August 1924, about 5,000 Wahhabis invaded Transjordan and this time they penetrated about eight kilometers into Amman before they were discovered. During their advance near the village of Kaf, they ran into an Arab Legion convoy making its way to Karak and massacred all 18 men in the convoy. Arab Legion armored cars and a squadron of RAF planes from Jerusalem attacked and defeated the Wahhabis, who had 500 casualties. The Transjordans had 130 dead and wounded, primarily from the Bani Sakhr. Abdullah reported that those Wahhabis who were not killed by the British fled into the desert and were either hunted down by Transjordanian tribesmen or died of thirst or hunger.[40]

The raids proved to Abdullah that his regime did indeed depend on the British army, which protected him from external threats as well as internal insurgencies. Knowing this, the British used it to widen their control in Jordan. Two days after the raid, when Abdullah returned to Amman from his pilgrimage to Mecca (*Hajj*), he was "requested" by Palestine High Commissioner Samuel to agree to all Samuel's demands. Abdullah was forced to acquiesce. "From that moment", Peake wrote, "started a new era in the history of Transjordan", meaning tight British supervision over Transjordan, or in other words, Abdullah's total dependence on the British and Jordan's transformation into a British stronghold in the Middle East.[41] Abdullah had no choice but to agree to the terms because Britain was the key to Abdullah's continued regime in Transjordan. There were "tears in his eyes", Mary Wilson wrote, when Abdullah signed the ultimatum submitted by the British.[42]

The Wahhabi invasion of Transjordan was part of Ibn Saud's strategy to conquer Hijaz and remove the Hashemite family. Ten days after the invasion on 24 August, the Wahhabis and Ibn Saud attacked Taif on their way to Mecca. About six weeks later, on 3 October, Hussein resigned in favor of his oldest son, Ali, and fled to Jeddah. From Jeddah, he went to Aqaba where he stayed until June 1925, when the British ordered him to leave, fearing that his presence so near to Transjordan would encourage the Wahhabis to attack. Hussein eventually went to Cyprus, where he died in 1931; he was buried on Temple Mount in Jerusalem. On 14 October 1924 the Wahhabis entered Mecca and Ali also fled to Jeddah; he appealed to the British, who refused to intervene. After he left

Jeddah, on 19 December 1925, the Wahhabis marched in and a week later Ibn Saud announced the end of the war. On 8 January 1926 he declared himself King of Hijaz.[43]

Before the official fighting between the Hashemite family and Ibn Saud and the Wahhabis ended, in May 1925 Abdullah had announced that "the Aqaba and Ma'an districts are part of the Transjordan emirate", thus officially annexing these districts. It seems that annexing the territory between Hijaz and the Transjordan was done with the support of the British, who sought to strengthen their position on the route to the Red Sea and Aqaba gulf. However, it led to a political debate between Transjordan and Saudi Arabia, which lasted for years, about the legitimacy of the annexation to Transjordan because the territory had been an inseparable part of Hijaz for years.

Ibn Saud refused to recognize the annexation, claiming that since the area was an inseparable part of Hijaz, when he took control of Hijaz he was entitled to this area as well.[44] Abdullah's attempt to present the annexation as legitimate, because his Hashemite family transferred the area to his responsibility before they were deported from Hijaz, did not succeed. However, Ibn Saud managed to portray Abdullah as an illegal conqueror. He gained support from the Muslim states which, at the end of the World Islamic Conference held in Mecca in 1926, agreed a resolution that stated that Aqaba and Ma'an were part of Hijaz and called for the reversal of their annexation to Transjordan. The British, who supported Abdullah, had admitted in the 1925 official Mandate report to the Council of the League of Nations that the area was part of Hijaz and "was brought under the administration of the Transjordan government in the course of the year" without explaining why it was transferred and under what circumstances.[45]

By annexing Aqaba and Ma'an to Transjordan, Abdullah unilaterally set the border with Hijaz – a border Ibn Saud repudiated. With the help of British mediation, an agreement was reached regarding the Transjordanian borders with Syria and Iraq. The British also managed to reach an understanding with Ibn Saud over the border around Najd,[46] but because he did not recognize the annexation, the British continued to worry about a renewal of war between Ibn Saud and Abdullah. At the end of March 1926 the second High Commissioner to Palestine, Lord Herbert (Viscount) Plumer, ordered the formation of a new security force to take effect on 1 April 1926. The new force, which was called the Transjordan

Frontier Force (TJFF), was in fact a British imperial force under the command of the High Commissioner in Palestine, but it was stationed within the Transjordanian borders in an attempt to prevent raids on Transjordan, especially from Syria and the Arabian Peninsula. Despite Peake's objection (he did not see the need to form another security force), its very presence is what probably dissuaded Ibn Saud from attacking Transjordan and eventually left Aqaba and Ma'an in Abdullah's hands.[47]

Following the formation of the new force, the Arab Legion was reduced from about 1,600 officers and soldiers to only 900. The artillery, machine-gun and signal units were disbanded and those officers and soldiers were transferred to the new force. The new British representative in Amman, Henry Fortnam Cox, had replaced Philby in April 1924 and he led an expense-saving policy for the Transjordanian government, which included reducing the size of the Arab Legion. The TJFF comprised four companies that amounted to a total of 723 officers and soldiers; it was based in Zarka. About half of the officers were British and the rest were Muslim, Christian Arabs and Jews.[48]

On 20 February 1928 the first in a series of Anglo-Transjordanian agreements was signed in Jerusalem by the High Commissioner to Palestine, Lord Plumer, and the Transjordanian Prime Minister, Tawfiq Abu al-Huda. The agreement did not bring Transjordan nearer to independence; on the contrary, it expressed Transjordan's dependence and the dependence of Amir Abdullah himself on Britain's government. The agreement validated his special status in the Emirate and stated his rights. Even though it specifically recognized Abdullah as the Amir of Transjordan, the agreement stated: "His Highness the Amir agrees to be guided by the advice of His Britannic Majesty tendered through the High Commissioner to Transjordan in all matters concerning foreign relations of Transjordan, as well as in all important matters affecting international and financial obligations . . . " (Article 5); the agreement also stated that "His Britannic Majesty may maintain armed forces in Trans-Jordan and may raise, organize and control in Trans-Jordan such armed forces as may in his opinion be necessary for the defense of the country . . . " (Article 10). The agreement, which was seen as a humiliation in Transjordan, aggravated and increased opposition to Abdullah. In all of the 21 articles included in the agreement, Britain committed to nothing other than ensuring that "nothing shall prevent the High Contracting Parties from reviewing from time to time the provisions of this agreement" (Article 20).[49]

About two months later, on 16 April 1928, an Organic Law was published (al-Qanun al-Asasi) which was the Emirate's first constitution. This gave unlimited power to the Amir and stated that he would have responsibility for legislating and appointing members of the government, as well as the dispersal of parliament. The regime was to be a constitutional one presided over by a legislative council (Majlis al-Tashri'i) of 16 members, of which the ethnic composition would be set in advance (9 Muslim Arabs, 3 Christians, 2 Circassian and 2 Bedouins). For elections purposes, Transjordan was divided into three districts: Ajlun, Balqa and Karak, and the right to vote was given to Jordanian citizens (male only) aged 18 or over. On 2 April 1929 the parliament convened its first meeting during which it approved the Anglo-Transjordanian agreement.[50] Simultaneously, the Transjordanian government approved the citizenship law which stated that all residents who had lived in the Emirate before 1924 were considered citizens of Transjordan. This law allowed the deportation of foreign nationals who had come to the Emirate during 1921–1924 and had tried to undermine Transjordan's stability.[51]

A significant development in the Arab Legion occurred in November 1930, when John Bagot Glubb Pasha, who was known by his Arabic nickname Abu Hunaik (of the little jaw) joined its ranks. Glubb Pasha, a British intelligence officer who specialized in relations with the Bedouin tribes in Iraq, was appointed Peake's deputy and was in charge of dealing with the Bedouin tribes of Transjordan and preventing raids from Arabia. His first action was to form a new company whose task was to patrol and guard the areas in the eastern Emirate. The new company was known as the Desert Patrol and included 150 soldiers from the Bedouins themselves.[52]

Glubb's success in getting the Bedouins into the Arab Legion, in contrast to Peake who thought it would be better to increase the number of settled residents, was noteworthy. Not only did the Bedouins who had earlier objected to joining the Arab Legion and had even denied its existence now join it, but the rivalries between the tribes also ended and the number of recruits increasingly grew until in the 1940s the Bedouins became the bedrock of the Arab Legion.[53] Even though Transjordan's financial situation at the beginning of the 1930s contributed to the recruitment of the Bedouins, who realized they could earn a living in the Arab Legion, it is doubtful whether, without Glubb's intervention, the Bedouins would have been recruited. An expression of the close links in those days between Glubb Pasha and the Bedouins can be found in one of the Arab Legion Bedouins' description of Glubb Pasha as "the second Lawrence" for his actions on behalf of the Arabs and also as a *Sahib* (friend), because of the intimacy he had forged with the Bedouins.[54]

Because of the Arab revolt in Palestine during 1936–1939, in the lead up to the Second World War, the Arab Legion grew. Abdullah tried to keep the violent events away from Transjordan and to avoid any connection with the Arab gangs in order to maintain his relationship with the British. The British on their part increased the Arab Legion by two companies of cavalry and a mechanized force, a total of 800 soldiers, to prevent infiltration into Palestine and weapon smuggling and to guard the borders. However, at the beginning of the Arab revolt, a number of extremist Arabs from Palestine managed to infiltrate the Ajlun district. They blew up the oil pipeline killing some civilians and only escaping after the Arab Legion had attacked them with some persistence.[55]

Abdullah's good relations with the British, which had become stronger, can be seen in the conclusion of the Peel Commission, the British Royal Commission's inquiry into this revolt. The commission, which came to Palestine in December 1936 to investigate the reasons for the outbreak of the Arab revolt and to recommend ways to solve the conflict, recommended in its report, published in July 1937, that Palestine should be divided into three parts that formed two states: Jewish, Arab and international. However, in contrast with the independent Jewish state, the Arab-Palestinian state would not be independent, but rather it would be united with Transjordan under Abdullah's regime. It was the first time that Abdullah had gained British political support and without a doubt it expressed the warm relationship between him and the British which lasted until his death.[56]

Abdullah also had cordial relations with the Zionists in Palestine. Unlike most Arab nationalists, Abdullah and the Hashemite family were generally not hostile towards the Zionist movement. They had had dealings with them in the past. When Hussein was still in Mecca during the First World War, he supported Jewish immigration to Palestine and he did not oppose the Balfour Declaration. In January 1919 Abdullah's brother, Faysal, signed the Chaim Weizmann agreement (the Faysal–Weizmann Agreement), which stated that

Palestine would be separate from Hussein's planned Arab country and the Jews would form a national home according to the Balfour Declaration. During Faysal's rule in Iraq he cultivated good relations with the Jews of Iraq and one of them, Sassoon Eskell, was appointed the first Minister of Finance. An expression of the warm relations between the Zionist movement and the Hashemite family can also be seen in the presence of representatives from the Jewish Agency and the Chief Rabbinate at Sharif Hussein's funeral in Jerusalem in June 1931 and in the telegram of condolence sent by them both after the death of King Faysal in 1933.[57]

The relationship between Abdullah and the Zionists was only natural and with the outbreak of the tough economic crisis in Transjordan during the 1930s it grew stronger. Abdullah was willing to lease about 70,000 dunams of soil around Ghur al-Kibd, east of the Jordan River, about 50 kilometers north of the Dead Sea, to the Jewish Agency. On 7 January 1933 the agreement was signed and the Jewish Agency paid Abdullah about 500 Palestinian pounds for the lease. According to the agreement, the Jewish Agency was granted a six-month option for leasing Ghur al-Kibd lands for three periods of 33 years each, at a price of 2,000 Palestinian pounds per annum. Abdullah's motive was mainly an economic one but he also wanted to extricate himself from British patronage. Relations between the Zionists and elements in Transjordan improved and additional figures expressed willingness to support the leasing of lands for Jewish settlement, including from Mithqal ibn Fayiz, leader of the Bani Sakhr tribe.[58]

This economic relationship was the result of Abdullah's political ambitions. Even in his meeting with Churchill in March 1921 he requested that his territory should include Palestine as well as Transjordan, but Churchill rejected the idea. Abdullah's ambitions towards Palestine and rumors at the beginning of the 1920s that he intended to reach an agreement with the British (and possibly the Jews as well) concerning uniting Palestine with Transjordan led him into conflict with the leader of the Palestinian national movement, the Mufti of Jerusalem Hajj Muhammad Amin al-Husayni. Al-Husayni had sought to establish an independent Palestinian country in Palestine since the beginning of the 1920s and therefore objected to a union between Palestine and Transjordan. The Mufti was an extremist leader who did not only object to the idea of establishing a Jewish state in Palestine, but also worked to prevent any political understanding between the Arabs and the Jews and incited

Palestinian extremists against Jewish settlement in Palestine. Abdullah thought that the Zionists' objections to the extremist Mufti would help him to reach an agreement with them regarding the annexation of Palestine to Transjordan in return for autonomy for the Jews. This was the basis of the relations that developed between Abdullah and the Jews in Palestine in the end of the 1920s and the beginning of the 1930s.[59]

The Second World War put the relationship between Abdullah and the British to the test. While the Arab world in general wanted Britain to be defeated and Germany victorious so that it could liberate itself from British imperialism, Abdullah hoped for his British patron's victory.[60] He was the only Arab leader, apart from the leaders of Hashemite Iraq, who stood clearly with Britain and offered it military support even though on the eve of the war eve the command of the Arab Legion was given to General Glubb Pasha after Peake retired. The British thought it pointless to seek help from the Arab Legion because they did not value its military strength but also because they did not want to be indebted to Abdullah.[61]

However, during 1941 the British position in the Middle East worsened day by day. In June 1940 with the French surrender to Germany, its colonies fell into the hands of the pro-German Vichy government. In April 1941 Germany invaded Greece and a month later they arrived in Crete. In North Africa, Erwin Eugen Rommel (the Desert Fox) advanced with his forces at the beginning of February 1941 from Libya towards Egypt and surrounded the British forces in Tobruk. In Iraq, the pro-British Hashemite regime fell and a group of extremist officers (The Golden Square)[62] seized power and appointed the anti-British politician Rashid Ali al-Kilani as Prime Minister. The British loyalists in Iraq were headed by the regent Abd al-Ilah, the young King Faysal II, and the former Prime Minister Nuri al-Sa'id, who fled Baghdad in fear of their lives.[63] In his speech to the Iraqi people, Ali al-Kilani said: "The criminal Britain, enslaver of the weaker nations, hurt our independence by flooding our country with its soldiers. As a protection for our homeland I am now declaring war on Great Britain. The day of liberation of all Arab nations is here; our enslavement will not last long".[64]

The British felt that they were losing their political influence in the Middle East and that they might lose Basra – Iraq's most important port in the Persian golf – to pro-German elements and thus they decided to act swiftly. This is not the place to describe Britain's military maneuvers in Iraq and in the Middle East in general during the Second World War, but from 18 April 1941 Britain sent infantry and artillery forces from India to Basra. Because of Iraq's strategic importance Britain decided to reinforce its forces in the two RAF bases (Habbaniya about 90 kilometers west of Baghdad and Shaibah about 20 kilometers southwest of Basra) which it maintained as part of the Anglo-Iraqi Treaty of 1930.[65]

Although the landing of military forces in Iraq and reinforcement of the military presence in the RAF bases was carried out according to the Anglo-Iraqi Treaty, Ali al-Kilani's extremist government refused to recognize that and decided to act with force, probably after being promised help from the Germans. On 30 April, Iraqi forces started to surround the Shaibah RAF base in the area of Basra and on 2 May, after futile and useless negotiations under Turkish mediation, fighting began between the Iraqi and British army which was surrounded inside the base. British aerial bombing of Iraqi positions in the area began at the same time as the British prepared reinforcements from Egypt and Palestine.[66]

The Arab Legion's participation in the war was incidental and unplanned despite British consent to get aid from the Transjordanians during Foreign Secretary Anthony Eden's visit to Amman shortly after the French surrender to Germany.[67] At the same time, an irregular Iraqi force led by Fauzi al-Qawuqji took over the Rutbah Castel on the Iraq-Transjordan border on 2 May and opened fire on the British workers there. At first, the British tried to use a platoon of the TJFF to repel them, but when they refused to participate, it was decided to use the Arab Legion.[68] The Legion's initial task was to take control of Rutbah Castel. Though the force commanded by Glubb Pasha indeed attacked al-Qawuqji, it did not manage to take control of the castle. Only after armored reinforcements arrived on 9 May did the British capture the castle; the Arab Legion entered it the next day.[69]

Despite the Arab Legion's failure in Rutbah, the British acceded to Glubb's request to allow him to attach about 350 soldiers from the Desert Patrol of the Arab Legion to a force organized by the British at Habbaniya.[70] It seems that the British agreement for Glubb and the Legionnaires' attachment to the Iraqi expedition was mainly to use his specialist knowledge of Iraq's Bedouin tribes. Indeed, after Glubb Pasha and his soldiers arrived in Iraq with the column commanded by Brigadier James Kingstone, he made contact with the Bedouin tribes especially in al-Jazera (between the

Tigris and Euphrates rivers) in order to encourage them to rebel against Rashid Ali al-Kilani's government.[71]

The Kingol column under the commanded of Kingstone, which joined the Arab Legion, arrived at Habbaniya on the evening of 17 May and entered the RAF base the next morning. From there, the British advanced to Faluja and took control of it on 19 May. On 22 May, they repulsed an Iraqi counter-attack on Faluja and continued on to Ramadi and Baghdad. On 31 May, the Iraqi government surrendered to the British, Prime Minister Rashid Ali al-Kilani and the nationalist military officers escaped from Baghdad and the road for the return of the Hashemite family, who were loyal to the British, was laid.[72]

Quite a few stories have been told and many legends woven about the Arab Legion's activities in Iraq which embellish the important role it played during the war. The most prominent among these is, without a doubt, Glubb Pasha's famous book *The Story of the Arab Legion*. However, other authors exaggerated the legion's importance: the author Lias Godfrey in his book, *Glubb's Legion*, claims that without the Arab Legion the Germans would have won the war. According to Godfrey, the Germans, with the help of Rashid Ali al-Kilani, would have won the battle in Iraq and would then have succeeded in taking over the entire Middle East. If the Middle East had fallen into their hands, they would have continued to India, and the fall of India would have brought about the end of the British Empire. The famous Jordanian historian, Sa'ad Abu Diya, also wrote in his book *Ta'arikh al-Jayish al-Arabi 1921–1946* (The History of the Arab Legion 1921–1946) that without the Arab Legion the British would have been helpless because they did not know the desert and that it was only thanks to the Legionnaires' special knowledge of the roads that they managed to arrive safely; thus the Arab Legion made a huge contribution to the repression of the Rashid Ali Al-Kilani rebellion.

These and other similar descriptions were intended to divert attention from the Arab Legion's lack of significant participation in the battles in Iraq. The Arab Legion's main role was to give the fighting British forces assistance with security, patrols, interrogation of prisoners, navigation in the desert, etc. However, it should be noted that during some of their patrols, they did exchange fire with Iraqi soldiers and came under German aerial bombardment.[73]

A much more significant role was played by the soldiers of the Arab Legion who stood alongside the British in Syria to fight the forces under the pro-German Vichy government's regime. The Arab Legion forces that joined the British attacking the city of Palmyra in Eastern Syria in June 1941 took over 200 captives. Later, they continued with the British forces toward Seba Bivar and went with them all the way to Sukhna. After the conquest of Syria on 11 July 1941, the Arab Legion was only involved in policing and propaganda activities for the Transjordanian government.[74]

On the eve of the war, especially as Faysal had died in 1933, it seemed that Abdullah was not satisfied with annexing Palestine to Transjordan. Instead, he sought to realize a plan to unite Syria, Lebanon and Palestine with Transjordan under his rule, known as the "Greater Syria" plan. Abdullah started a propaganda campaign to convince the Arabs that this was the aim of the Arab revolt of 1916. "We came out of Hejaz for the sake of Syria, Transjordan, Palestine and Lebanon which are one entity – Greater Syria".[75] The political situation in Syria encouraged him that it was possible. When France surrendered to Germany its colonies in the Middle East and North Africa fell into the hands of the pro-German Vichy government. On 1 July 1940, Abdullah hurried to send a letter to Churchill in which he again raised again his request from March 1921 to rule Syria. Churchill, who preferred to strengthen his relations with the "Free French" forces led by General Charles de Gaulle and also because the Arabs themselves opposed it, rejected the request.

Despite this, in the mid-1940s Abdullah continued to try to realize the plan, while also attempting to foil efforts made by the National Bloc, led by Shukri al-Quwatly in Syria, for independence. Syria and Lebanon were granted independence at the end of the Second World War after the allied forces withdrew and the commander of the Free French forces in the Middle East, General Georges Catroux, declared the end of the French Mandate. Abdullah sought to realize his "Greater Syria" plan while establishing the Arab League in 1944–1945.[76]

Transjordan's support of Britain during the Second World War and the Arab Legion's participation with the allies did not leave much doubt about the political and strategic relations between the two countries, as Glubb Pasha admitted.[77] The Arab Legion under Glubb's command turned into an efficient and operative army now trained for fighting and was granted a budget and military supplies that Britain had earlier refused. After the war, the Arab Legion became part of the British forces in the Middle East.[78] However, both inside and outside Transjordan, Arab criticism for Abdullah's pro-Western policy increased. The Mufti Amin al-Husayni's attempts to cause the collapse of the Hashemite regime in Transjordan grew and there was an initial attempt to assassinate Abdullah and British officers in the Arab Legion .[79]

After the war and the rise of the Labour party in Britain in July 1945, a new era in the Middle East and Europe in general, had begun. Although the Labour party, led by Clement R. Attlee, had a policy of preserving the British Empire, this was contrary to the party's traditional principles and since the 1930s it had expressed objections to British imperialism. However, the difficult economic situation and the need to reduce the government's expenses in parallel with the strengthening of relations with the United States against Soviet ambitions in the Middle East brought Attlee's government to political concessions and a new military-strategic assessment in the area.[80] From the mid-1940s a new tendency in the British government began: removal of direct British rule reaplced by the formation of a friendly native government to keep that country under British influence.

In accordance with this policy, Abdullah was invited to London in February 1946 to discuss a new treaty between the two states. A month later, on 22 March 1946 the Anglo-Jordanian Treaty (Treaty of London) was signed, which ended the British mandate over Transjordan and recognized it as an "independent" kingdom. In return, Britain kept the right to maintain armed forces without any limitation in Transjordan and to build military bases in Transjordanian territories. Britain thought that by doing so it could also strengthen Abdullah's position among the Arab rulers in the area and more importantly have Transjordan join the United Nations as a British satellite. Although the United Nations recognized the treaty on 18 April, the Transjordanian demand to join the United Nations was rejected because of a veto from the Soviet Union. Only in December 1955 after winning the Soviet Union's consent did Jordan join the United Nations. Following Jordan's independence, Abdullah declared himself King on 25 May 1946. The coronation was held in Amman with representatives from Britain and a number of Arab countries.[81]

On 1 February 1947 Transjordan presented its new constitution. The Parliament (*Majlis al-Umma*) consisted of two houses: the lower house, the Chamber of Deputies (*Majlis al-Nuwab*), would have 20 members to be elected for a four-year term. The upper house, the Chamber of Notables (*Majlis al-Ayan*) or the Senate, would have ten members appointed by the King for a term of eight years. Half the members of the Chamber of Notables were to be appointed every four years.[82]

The al-Tall Family: The Most Prominent Family in Jordan

There are several versions regarding the origin of the al-Tall family and its name. The most popular version claims that the family descends from the Bani Zayidan family from Arabia, one of the most respected and influential families because of its connection to the Prophet Muhammad.[83] During the 17th century, under unclear circumstances the family went to Palestine and settled in the Galilee area. Some of the family stayed there, but one, Yousef Abbas, went to Transjordan and settled in Amman, close to the citadel, called by the local residents *al-Tall*, meaning the "hill". About 30 years later, when the family decided to move away from Amman and settle in the city of Irbid, about 70 kilometers north of Amman, it took the nickname al-Tall which later became the family name of Yousef's four sons: Hussein, Hassan, Abd al-Rahman and Abd al-Rahim. This also became the family name of their descendants. To preserve the name of the father of the family, family members usually add the name "Yousef" to their first name and "al-Tall" as the last name.[84]

Because of its strategic importance between Damascus and Jerusalem and because the land is fertile, the city of Irbid has been settled since the Bronze era, about 3,000 years B.C.E. Modern Irbid was founded by the Ottoman governor Tahir Badirkhan in 1882 when he rebuilt the old city, a mosque and an elementary school. In 1867 the Ottomans formed a central government in the city, but the first direct elections for mayor took place in 1903.[85] When Transjordan was founded in 1921, the population of Irbid was 3,500 and it was a part of the district of Ajlun.[86] The al-Tall family was one of the city's most respectable families, but according to Ali Khalki, it was not the oldest family there. Other families, which had arrived in Irbid before the al-Tall family, were Sharayri, Dalkamani, Abduh, Rashidat and al-Kharisat.[87] However, even today, the al-Tall family is identified with the city of Irbid because the family held public office in the Ottoman period. Among them were Abd al-Qadir al-Tall who served as Irbid's delegate to the Ottoman council of the Syria district from 1908 and later as the Minister of Finance in the Irbid local government and Ali Nayazi al-Tall who served as the governor of Mosul in Iraq, and later as the governor of Arabkir in Turkey (today in Armenia).[88]

The whole al-Tall family played an important role in the establishment of the Transjordanian Emirate. Both British and Arab sources show that some of the family supported Abdullah's moves against the French and even cooperated with him. Khalaf Muhammad al-Tall (Abu Hajem) and Ahmad al-Tall (Abu Sa'ab) were the first to welcome Amir Abdullah in Ma'an.[89] Khalaf went to northern Transjordan on Abdullah's behalf in order to publicize Abdullah's intentions against the French and recruit support.[90] When Abdullah was appointed ruler of Transjordan, the al-Tall family supported him: first Khalaf and Ahamd and later Abd al-Qadir al-Tall, the Minister of Finance in the Irbid local government.[91] Khalaf and Ahmad al-Tall's loyalty to the Amir Abdullah's regime was expressed by their becoming officers in the Reserve Force. In May, 1921 when the rebellion in Kura against Abdullah's regime took place, they were part of the force sent to suppress the rebellion.[92] Khalaf Muhammad al-Tall held public office, initially as mayor of Irbid from 1932–1936, afterwards for a short period as the Interior Minister in the Transjordanian government (1938–1939) and then as the Consul of Amman in Baghdad, where he died in 1943.[93]

However, not all the members of the al-Tall family agreed with Abdullah's regime. Abd al-Qadir al-Tall, Abdullah al-Tall's uncle, changed his opinion toward Emir Abdullah very quickly because of his pro-British policy and became a strong supporter of the Syrian fight for independence. He published a number of articles in the press opposing Abdullah's aggressive policy toward the Jordanians and the arbitrary arrests made by his regime. At the beginning of 1925, the Jordanian government arrested him together with other opposition activists and imprisoned him for "cooperating with the Syrian rebels and forming gangs to attack the French".[94] At the end of the 1920s, Abdullah secured his release from prison; he was reconciled with the Hashemite regime and was mayor of Irbid from 1929–1932. In 1936, he was elected once again and held office until 1939.[95] In 1947, Abd al-Qadir al-Tall was appointed as the chairman of the Jordanian Parliament for a short period, and then seems to have fallen out with Abdullah again and retired from political life.[96]

Another opponent, maybe the most prominent, was his uncle, the famous Jordanian poet Mustafa Wahbi al-Tall (Arar), the father of Wasfi al-Tall who would become Prime Minister of Jordan during King Hussein's rule. Wahbi al-Tall rebelled during his high school studies in Damascus. There he joined the Arab Nationalist Movement and took part in anti-Turkish activity. He was exiled from Damascus, but returned shortly after. In February 1920 he was exiled to Alep for his activities against the French, where he finished high school. His activities in favor of Arab nationalism and his opposition to Abdullah's regime because of his pro-British stance made him a prominent opponent in Jordan. Due to his status as a journalist and a poet, he was given jobs in public service, for example, as school principal in various areas of Transjordan. However, the Jordanian authorities did not hesitate to act harshly against him and arrested him occasionally when they thought that he crossed the line and criticized Abdullah's policy excessively.[97]

Abdullah Yousef al-Tall was born on 17 July 1918 in the city of Irbid. He finished elementary school in his hometown, but because Irbid didn't have a high school he completed his education in the larger city of Salt. He excelled in English, a rarity at the time among the Arabs. His knowledge of English influenced his later advancement in the Arab Legion. When he finished high school in October 1937, he was recruited to the TJFF and served as a customs officer. It was an easy job which paid 3.5 pounds a month, considerably more than the average salary in the Transjordanian public service, and was welcome considering the high level of unemployment Transjordan then endured. Despite his diligence and good interpersonal relationships, he was not promoted in the TJFF. His quick promotion would only occur with his recruitment to the Arab Legion.[98]

With the outbreak of the Second World War, Britain increased its support of the Arab Legion both financially and militarily. The Arab Legion grew and more young Arabs were recruited and new units were formed. Among the new recruits to the Arab Legion was Abdullah al-Tall who joined in June 1942 as a second lieutenant and served in the first Brigade.[99] After less than a year, in May 1943 al-Tall was promoted to first lieutenant and in September 1944 was made captain. He was the personal assistant to the Arab Legion's training base commander in Sarafand, near Ramle. In March 1948, after finishing the staff officer course, he was promoted to major and three months later in June, after having commanded the battle to conquer Jerusalem, he was promoted to lieutenant colonel. Abdullah al-Tall's quick promotion in the Arab Legion, five ranks in seven years, was unprecedented in the Arab Legion and was also unusual in other modern Arab armies.[100]

Towards the end of the war in 1944, Abdullah al-Tall married Asia Ahmad Mismar from Salt. They had five sons called al-Muntasir, Salah al-Dain (Saladin), Osama, Khaled, Hamza and a daughter Inas; all were born in Cairo after he defected there from Jordan at the end of the 1948 war. The names of his children indicate al-Tall's regard for Muslim history because they are all names of well-known Muslim heroes. Ahmad, Abdullah's brother, claimed that the name of his first born, al-Muntasir (the victor), who was born in February 1950, points to his victory over the Israelis in the battle of Jerusalem during the 1948 war.[101]

In mid-December 1946, while serving as staff officer of the second regiment, al-Tall joined 12 Arab Legion officers who went to Britain for military training. Their official goal was to learn about a weapon which the Arab Legion was supposed to receive from Britain,[102] but from al-Tall's memoirs published in his book, *Rihla ila Britaniya* (Journey To Britain), it appears that the course also included visits to many tourist attractions, including Madame Tussaud's Waxworks Museum, London Zoo, Oxford University, the Imperial War Museum, the Houses of Parliament, Buckingham Palace and more. The course, which lasted about eight weeks, was meant to show the Arab officers of the Arab Legion some British culture and history in order to strengthen the ties between Arab and British officers.[103] "The British tried to make me English", al-Tall claimed later about his military training in Britain while speaking critically about the cooperation between the two states.[104] However, no critical tone toward the British regime or society or even British control over the Arab Legion or the cooperation between the two states can be seen in al-Tall's memoirs published about a year after this military training. Instead, his positive comments compliment the British. This strengthens the claim that at the beginning of his military service in the Arab Legion, al-Tall was not anti-British; rather he supported them even though he knew of the British involvement in Jordan.

The Arab Legion officers' training in Britain was only one of the ways the British army trained the Legion as part of the treaty between the two states. As the UN's involvement in the Palestine problem grew, so too did the cooperation between the Arab Legion and the British army. In March 1948 the Anglo-Jordanian Treaty, which had been signed two years earlier, was modified in order to reinforce the Arab Legion in light of the British army's withdrawal from Palestine. As long as the British army was in Palestine, it supplied the Arab Legion with logistical and administrative services. Upon its withdrawal, there was a need to reinforce the Arab Legion and prepare it as an independent army, with offensive weapons instead of only defensive ones in order to assist Britain in the event of a third World War.[105]

Thus, with the signing of the Anglo-Jordanian Treaty in March 1948, Britain increased military supplies to the Arab Legion, encouraged recruitment, and seconded its officers and British sergeants to technical professions. Moreover, the weapons and ammunition held by the TJFF which had been disbanded on 1 March 1948, as well as those found in their ammunition warehouse, were given to the Arab Legion by the British before they left Palestine. The preparations for the forthcoming war with the Jews in Palestine and the need for additional manpower beyond what the British could supply led to the Arab Legion enlisting the help of additional foreign officers including Germans, Italians, Yugoslavians and Poles.[106]

On the eve of the 1948 war, the Arab Legion consisted of four regiments in two brigades (the First and the Third), 15 guard companies and two security companies, according to Glubb Pasha amounting to about 6,500 officers and soldiers. Most historians however, claim that it had more than 7,000 soldiers and there are those who say that it had even more.[107] In any case, the Arab Legion became the largest Arab army relative to population size. This is not coincidental. The high unemployment rate and the difficult economic conditions in Jordan motivated many to join the Arab Legion and thus enjoy a high salary, free medical care, pension, vacations, and more.[108]

The senior command of the Arab Legion remained in the hands of the British officers and out of the 44 senior officers (major and above), who served in the Arab Legion during the 1948 war, only seven were Arabs; Abdullah al-Tall was among them. The others were Abd al-Qadir al-Jundi, Ahmad Sidqi al-Jundi, Habis al-Majali, Abd al-Halim al-Sakit, Muhammad al-Muaita and Ali al-Hiyari.[109] Al-Tall however, was much more prominent, not only because of his quick promotion, but also because he was the most-decorated officer in the Arab Legion. According to the Jordanian newspaper *al-Dustour*, he won four decorations between the time he joined the Arab Legion and the 1948 war. It also explains why he was considered one of the most prominent Arab officers in Jordanian military history.[110]

The First Victory: Abdullah al-Tall and Conquering the Etzion Bloc

On 29 November 1947 the General Assembly of the UN accepted the Partition Plan and decided to establish two independent states in Palestine: an Arab-Palestinian state and a Jewish state. The UN's decision resulted in angry reactions in the Arab world and led to the convening of the Arab League in Cairo on 8 December 1947. All the heads of government who were members of the Arab League except for the Prime Minister of Yemen went to Cairo to participate in the conference.[111] The Prime Minister of Iraq, Salih Jabr, demanded the involvement of regular Arab armies in Palestine, because "The Zionists cannot be subdued with the use of irregular forces" and called for the establishment of a joint Arab command for that purpose. However, the other Arab leaders refused to involve the regular armies in Palestine as long as the British Mandate continued. Samir al-Rifai, the Prime Minister of Transjordan, said during the conference that the Arab Legion would be involved in Palestine only after the end of the Mandate "and not a minute before".[112]

Under these circumstances, the Secretary General of the Arab League, Abd al-Rahman Azzam, with the support of the Arab leaders, decided to avoid regular military involvement in Palestine for fear of provoking the UN and bringing about sanctions. There was also a fear of complicating relations with Britain, which made it clear to the Arab League generally and the leaders of each country personally, that it would maintain law and order in Palestine until its final withdrawal and would prevent a regular Arab military invasion of Palestine. Instead, the League made two important decisions: the first, to call on Britain to extend the Mandate in Palestine and the second, to adopt the recommendation of Syria President Shukri al-Quwatly to establish a volunteer force that would be recruited, equipped and armed by the Arab League and sent to fight the Jews in Palestine instead of the regular armies.[113]

This volunteer force was known as the Arab Liberation Army

(ALA) and its commander was Fauzi al-Qawuqji, a prominent Arab nationalist and one of the commanders who had fought in Palestine in the Arab revolt in 1936–1939. The establishment of such a volunteer force was opposed by Hajj Amin al-Husayni, who sought to prevent the involvement of Arab countries in the Palestine problem – an involvement which had begun during the Arab revolt in 1936, but increasingly grew as war approached. Instead of an ALA set up by the Arab League, al-Husayni wanted a Palestinian force, under his leadership, so that he could control it and direct its activity as he saw fit. His fear was that the ALA would promote foreign interests that would damage his ambitions of forming a Palestinian state in Palestine. Al-Husayni's suggestions were not accepted by the Arab League, so he decided to form an independent Palestinian force and make his cousin Abd al-Qadir al-Husayni its commander. This force, which was named *Jihad al-Muqaddas* (Holy Jihad), was not connected to the Arab League, nor did it cooperate with the ALA during the 1948 war.

While the two irregular forces were acting in Palestine against the Jews, al-Tall, then a captain, was attending the staff officer's course which was being held at the British army base of Fayid, about 20 kilometers south of Ismailia. The course lasted about three months and with its completion in mid-March 1948 al-Tall was promoted to major and assigned to serve in the second garrison group in Sarafand, under the command of Bahjat Tabbara.[114] The second garrison group, along with the first garrison group under the command of Ahmad Sidqi al-Jundi, whose HQ was based in Haifa, was part of 15 guard companies and two security companies that formed the Arab Legion's infantry corps. About two weeks later, at the beginning of April 1948, al-Tall was appointed commander of the convoy guard of the Arab Legion, which was responsible for the convoys transporting equipment and ammunition to the Arab Legion from the British base at Rafah to the Arab Legion base at Amman via Jerusalem. He had two companies (one armored and one infantry) as well as a mortar platoon. The HQ was based in Jericho.[115]

Al-Tall claimed in his memoirs that when he was appointed to this position, the commander of the Arab Legion, Glubb Pasha, ordered him to "avoid taking any active part in the battles between the Jews and the Arabs in the Palestine".[116] He accused Glubb Pasha of favoring the Zionists in the Palestine, a claim expressed throughout his entire book. However, Glubb's order was not unusual and was part of King Abdullah's policy. Indeed, while the British were in Palestine, they banned foreign forces from taking any active part in the battles between the Jews and the Arabs in Palestine. The commander of the British army in Palestine, General Gordon Macmillan, stated clearly and unequivocally his opposition to seeing any aggression from the Arab Legion against the Jews: "As long as the Arab Legion is in Palestine under our instructions it mustn't fight the Jews".[117] Since the Arab Legion was under British command, the British commanders prevented their soldiers from participating in the hostile activity against the Jews. Indeed, the Arab Legion did not get involved in the battles against the Jews and was generally neutral as Arab sources maintained.[118]

The British directive suited King Abdullah's policy and Abdullah feared that any active involvement of his soldiers before the end of the Mandate would worsen his relations with Britain. It might hinder the signing of a new Anglo-Jordanian Treaty to be signed in March 1948, which would supply additional military and financial assistance to the Arab Legion upon Britain's withdrawal from Palestine. He also feared that worsening relations with Britain might foil his political ambitions of conquering the Arab territories of Palestine which he would attempt should the British show any inclination to support it.[119]

The Arab officers of the Arab Legion protested against the British decision not to involve the Legion in the war. These officers felt that they, too, were obligated to join the general Arab struggle. According to them, it was a task which would be easy to carry out since they were already located in the area of combat. In their eyes, there was no difference between an army soldier and an Arab irregular, both of whom wanted to protect Palestine.[120] For that reason, al-Tall claims, Arab officers initiated provocations against the Jews. They hoped for retaliation by the Jewish troops which in turn would provide the Arab Legion with a legitimate reason to join the war.[121] Most of the provocative actions were carried out in the Haifa area where there were two infantry companies of the Arab Legion. Legion troops kidnapped Jews and assassinated them inside the Arab Legion camps, intentionally crashed into Jewish-owned cars, opened fire against Jews, and threw grenades at them from inside the Arab Legion camp. The Jewish Agency protested against the many acts of terror taking place in Haifa for which the Arab Legion was responsible and in February 1948 General Macmillan removed the Arab Legion companies from areas of Jewish settlement and stationed them elsewhere in order to avoid further clashes between the Arab Legion and the Jews.[122]

However, actions against Jews did not end there. From Arab historians we learn that a significant number of the Arab officers serving in the Arab Legion preferred to resign from the service in order to volunteer in the irregular Arab forces, mainly Fauzi al-Qawuqji's ALA.[123] The most prominent of those officers was Muhammad Ahmad al-Haniti, who resigned from the Arab Legion in February 1948 and was appointed the ALA commander of Haifa. Two other officers – Amin Jamian and Sari al-Fanish – resigned and also joined the ALA and were given command over the city of Safed.[124] There is documentation indicating other instances in which Arab officers resigned from the Arab Legion for the same reason and joined the Mufti's forces (*Jihad al-Muqaddas*).[125] Defection from the Arab Legion grew over time and reached "large proportions", as claimed by a British officer serving in Palestine at that time.[126] These officers operated openly against the Jews, as in the case of the ALA's attack on the Yehiam convoy at the end of March 1948.[127] One hundred and fifty of those who had defected from the Arab Legion took part in this attack. In contrast to those officers who defected, resigned or assisted the Palestinians, there is no evidence that al-Tall took any independent military action against the Jews during the irregular forces' activities, despite the fact that his book emphasizes that he "decided to act and grant the Palestinians the help they needed against the Jews".[128]

Al-Tall's military activities against the Jews only began on the eve of the end of the British Mandate when he commanded the Arab Legion, with the irregular forces' attack on the Etzion Bloc (Gush Etzion) on 12 May 1948. The Bloc included four Jewish settlements (Kfar Etzion, Massuot Yitzhak, Ein Tzurim and Revadim) and was located alongside the Hebron-Jerusalem road. Since the partition resolution in November 1947, the Bloc had been under massive Arab attack mainly from the Mufti's force *Jihad al-Muqaddas*, which was active in the area. Jewish convoys to and from the Bloc were damaged to such an extent that the Jews stopped the convoys in the beginning of 1948.

Al-Tall claimed he himself decided to destroy the four Jewish settlements in the Bloc for fear that this road, which was used as the Arab Legion's main military supply route from British military bases in Suez (Suez-Gaza-Hebron-Jerusalem-Amman), would be closed by the Jews. If that were to happen, the Arab Legion would not be able to get supplies for the coming war. Al-Tall, as commander of the convoy guard, was concerned that the Jews would block the Legion's main supply route on the eve of the Mandate's end.

Indeed, the attacks on the Arabs from the Jewish side grew from 6 May when the Jews, who controlled the al-Sha'ar monastery (Russian monastery) next to Kfar Etzion which dominated the Hebron-Jerusalem road, opened fire on Arab vehicles. On the same day, a civilian Arab convoy in the area, which included 30 cars and was accompanied by the Arab Legion, was fired upon from the monastery. In the attack, two soldiers of the Arab Legion and three civilians were killed. The commander of the convoy, Qasim Muhammad, informed al-Tall of the attack and he went to the assistance of the Arab Legion soldiers who were injured. That same day, he decided to attack the Bloc, but the attack was poorly organized and it failed. On 10 May he secretly convened with Hikmat Mahyer, the commander of the 12th company of the Arab Legion, which was stationed in Hebron, and both decided to provoke the Jews to cause a concerted attack on the Bloc which, according to al-Tall, was "to destroy the Jewish settlement there".[129]

According to the plan, on 12 May the attack began with artillery and mortar fire with cooperation from Arab irregulars from Hebron and the surrounding area. The Arab Legion soldiers took control of the positions around the Bloc and cut off Kfar Etzion (the largest settlement in Bloc) from the other settlements, but did not succeed in subduing the Bloc. Therefore, Hikmat Mahyer asked for military reinforcement from Glubb Pasha. Glubb, who was concerned about the situation in the area, ordered al-Tall to immediately send "a complete infantry platoon commanded by an officer".[130] He sent a platoon commanded by First Lieutenant Muhammad al-Sahih, but the military situation did not improve for the Arabs. Now Glubb Pasha had no choice and he called al-Tall again expressing his fear about Hikmat Mahyer's inability to command the attack, for he was "a police officer and not a military officer". He asked al-Tall to come to the battlefield and take the command of the attack because he had the most operational experience and the highest rank.[131]

Al-Tall's plan succeeded as he had intended: "what I want – is what happened", al-Tall wrote in his book. When al-Tall arrived in the morning with military reinforcements and took over command of the battle, he reorganized the Arab Legion forces. Massive fire increased the pressure on the Bloc and prepared the ground for the infantry advance. However, al-Tall's first assault failed. Despite this, he did not give up. He knew that the Jews could not hold out very long nor could they get reinforcements or supplies because the roads were blocked by Arab residents while the only airport nearby, from which the Haganah HQ had transported supplies, was also already controlled by the Arab Legion.[132]

After the Jews ran out of ammunition and their resistance was weakened, at noon on 13 May, the armored cars advanced to Kfar Etzion followed by the infantry troops commanded by al-Tall who cleared the settlement house by house. The Jews had no choice but to surrender. However, when they congregated in the center of Kfar Etzion and handed their weapons to the Arab Legion soldiers, the Arabs opened fire massacring 127 people, including 21 women. Only four Jews survived: three men and one girl.[133] The next day, after the Arab Legion increased its attack on the three remaining settlements and after Red Cross intervention, the Jews agreed to surrender to the Arab Legion according to the Red Cross terms, handing over weapons to the Arabs, the men being taken captive and the women, elderly, children, and the badly wounded being handed over to the Red Cross and returned to the Jewish Agency.[134]

Thus, on the eve of Israel's independence, al-Tall won his first battle against the Jews. He received many congratulatory telegrams; among them was one from Glubb Pasha. It was the first attack al-Tall had commanded and it ended with victory for the Arab Legion and many Jewish casualties: 233 Jewish dead (including the 127 people who were massacred in Kfar Etzion) and 320 people surrendered. The Arab Legion had only six dead. The irregular Arab forces which joined the attack, mainly residents of Hebron, broke into the Bloc after the Jews' surrender and looted their belongings. In an attempt to stop them, Arab Legion soldiers shot at them and killed over a hundred.[135]

There is no doubt that the Jewish presence in the Bloc endangered the Arab Legion and therefore Arab Legion HQ felt it was necessary to remove this "obstacle". Glubb Pasha and his deputy, Abd al-Qadir al-Jundi, also claimed that the attack on the Bloc was meant to remove the Jewish threat and ensure the free passage of military supplies to the Arab Legion until the end of the British Mandate.[136] However, the question is was it really al-Tall's independent decision which brought the HQ of the Arab Legion to join an attack which he commanded, or was al-Tall just acting on orders from HQ? Al-Tall's claim is not based on any other source and therefore it seems that he was not the one to initiate the attack on the Etzion Bloc. On the other hand, archive sources point to the intention of the Arab Legion to attack the Etzion Bloc from the end of April 1948. On 24 April, reliable intelligence was received in the Haganah HQ: "About 500 Legionaries have arrived from Jericho and these forces came in order to attack the Etzion Bloc". Two days later, intelligence confirmation was received that did not leave any doubt regarding the intentions of the Arab Legion plan to attack the Bloc.[137]

Al-Ja'abri, the mayor of Hebron, was close to Abdullah and supported the annexation of the Arab territories of Palestine to Transjordan. Thus, he allowed Arab Legion soldiers to base themselves in his city and encouraged them to attack the Etzion Bloc, claiming it was "a sharp thorn stuck in the heart of a purely Arab area".[138] As part of the preparations for the attack, Glubb Pasha visited Hebron on 10 May and met with the mayor. Glubb updated him on the planned attack and promised him that Arabs from Hebron and other Arab villages in the area would participate in the attack on the Bloc. In light of this, it would seem that there was prior intent to attack the Bloc planned by Glubb Pasha and the mayor of Hebron with Abdullah's knowledge; this was intended not only to ensure the Arab Legion free passage on the supply road, but also to ensure the Legion's takeover of this area upon the Arab invasion of Palestine in order to annex this and other Arab territories to Transjordan.[139]

Despite this, al-Tall's part in conquering the Etzion Bloc must not be underestimated. Even though he did not initiate the attack, he conducted it with determination and firmness while preventing the Red Cross's involvement in the battle until Arab Legion supremacy was ensured in order to have greater leverage against the Jews. According to Israeli intelligence reports, the Legion's attack was carefully organized and planned: the Legion commanders had maps of the Bloc (possibly received from the British), which assisted them in preparing the attack. They knew where to concentrate fire-power and how to break into the village avoiding the mines. Al-Tall, having been trained by the British army, knew how to make good use of the firepower available to him. The armored cars and the artillery softened the Bloc, after which the armored cars led the assault while the infantry took cover behind them. At the end of the battle, al-Tall received a certificate of commendation from the commander of the Arab Legion, General Glubb Pasha, for the "heroism and courage" he had shown during the battle.[140]

The Jews who surrendered were transferred under heavy Legion guard to the police station in Hebron while the Arab populace tried to attack them. The Arab Legion broke the surrender agreement and did not hand over women and the badly wounded to the Red Cross. They too were transferred to Jordan as prisoners of war together with the rest of the Jews. They were only released in mid-June after the Israeli government and the Red Cross put pressure on Jordan. The remaining prisoners were released towards the end of the war in February–March 1949.[141]

Preparations by the Arab countries to invade Palestine increased. On 21 April the Iraqi government officially announced its intention to go to war in Palestine, and a few days later the Transjordanian government also decided to send the Arab Legion to Palestine for the war against the Jews. "All attempts to try and solve the Palestine problem in peaceful ways ended with failure. The only option left is war", King Abdullah declared on 26 April during a press conference.[142] Despite King Farouk of Egypt's refusal to declare his country's intentions, the Arab League decided to convene in Amman on 30 April in order to prepare the Arab invasion plan. Apart from concluding that the war in Palestine demanded no less than five full-strength divisions, six squadrons of fighter planes and bombers, and that the armies would be put under a unified command, the Arab League did not reach any other agreement. Up until a few days before the invasion it was unclear who would be command the Arab armies. Abdullah demanded to be appointed to this position, but the Arab leaders initially refused, probably for fear that he would exploit the military situation in Palestine to promote his political ambitions. The decision to appoint Abdullah as commander was made only four days before the invasion.[143]

Indeed, fear of King Abdullah's political ambitions in Palestine was well based. He had not abandoned his "Greater Syria" plan and saw the partition resolution of November 1947 as an opportunity to realize it. Moreover, Abdullah maintained contact with the Zionists. In August 1946, Moshe Shertok (Sharett), then head of the political department of the Jewish Agency, reached an agreement with King Abdullah on the partition of Palestine into two parts: a Jewish part in which a Jewish state would be formed and an Arab part annexed to Jordan. Although Abdullah was excited about the agreement claiming, "partition . . . was the only practical solution to

Palestine problem", he had to withdraw his support shortly after he became aware that the British opposed the agreement.[144]

However, closer to the partition resolution and the British withdrawal from Palestine, it would seem that Abdullah had abandoned the idea of partitioning Palestine, preferring a complete annexation of Palestine to Transjordan. In his secret meeting with Golda Meyerson (Meir), then head of the political department of the Jewish Agency, in Naharayim on 17 November 1947, King Abdullah suggested forming an independent Hebrew republic in a part of Palestine "inside a Transjordanian country that would include both sides of the Jordan" ruled by him.[145] Abdullah repeated his offer to form a Hebrew republic under his rule on the second meeting with Golda in Amman on 11 May 1948. "Why are you in such a hurry to proclaim your state?" Abdullah asked Golda. She answered that "a people who had waited 2,000 years should not be described as being 'in a hurry'". Abdullah warned Golda that if the Jews insisted on declaring a state, he would be forced to join the other Arab countries and fight against them.[146]

In contrast with al-Tall's claim that the two parties had agreed that "the king will send a governor to rule over the Arab territories of Palestine according to the partition resolution"[147] and in contrast with the myth that has developed over the years, not only did the two sides not agree on partitioning Palestine into two parts, they did not reach any agreement whatsoever at that meeting. An interesting detail was recorded by al-Tall in his book, stating that King Abdullah gave Golda his promise that the Jordanian and the Iraqi armies would not go to war with the Jews. It is interesting because no other documents mention it, although Moshe Dayan mentioned it a few years later in a conversation he had with Israeli students in 1975.[148] Since Moshe Dayan was not in office, nor did he take any part in the contact with the Jordanians on the eve of the war, it is possible that he heard it from al-Tall himself in one of their meetings during the war. Dayan probably believed it to be true and therefore declared that it was.

Even though the British knew in general of King Abdullah's intentions to occupy all of Palestine (or at least the Arab parts of it) according to the partition resolution and maybe even supported these intentions; British approval or agreement was given orally only about three months before the Arab countries invaded Palestine. At the beginning of February 1948, the Jordanian Prime Minister, Tawfiq Abu al-Huda, went to London to meet with the British

Foreign Secretary, Ernest Bevin. During the meeting, Abu al-Huda described the possible scenarios following the British withdrawal from Palestine: either the Jews would ignore the UN resolution, take control of Palestine and establish the State of Israel over all of it; or the Mufti, Hajj Amin al-Husayni would enter Palestine and make himself the leader of an Arab country. Since neither of the two possibilities was acceptable, not to Britain or to Transjordan, Abu al-Huda suggested that the Arab Legion would enter Palestine and take control over the territories allocated to the Arabs according to the partition resolution. "It seemed the obvious thing to do", Bevin agreed, but added a warning that the Arab Legion must not enter any territory allocated to the Jews; Abu al-Huda agreed.[149]

The British agreed to the Arab Legion's occupation of Arab territories in Palestine in the belief that by doing so bloodshed in Palestine could be reduced. A British intelligence report received by Haganah HQ at the time stated: "In a time in which the riots in the Palestine are heading towards a total clash, Abdullah's policy has a chance to prevent chaos".[150] Despite this, the fact that the British decision was made out of political considerations to prevent the formation of an Arab Palestinian state cannot be denied. The two parties (the British and the Jordanians) had no interest in establishing an Arab Palestinian country. In 1946, Abdullah admitted specifically that he intended "to take over Arab Palestine in order to prevent the creation of an unwanted Palestinian state" and Abdullah repeated his refusal to form such a state in a meeting with Golda in November 1947 when he said "I do not wish to create a new Arab country that will disrupt my plans".[151] The British refused because they believed that the leadership of the Mufti, Hajj Amin al-Husayni, would destabilize the area politically. The Mufti was considered by many to be an uncompromising and extremist leader who would not be deterred from violence in order to realize his political goals. He had cooperated with Germany against the British during the Second World War which, claimed some Palestinian leaders, was another reason why the British objected to his regime.[152]

With British agreement, as well as confidence in the Arab Legion's military capability to take over Palestine, King Abdullah could go to war on 15 May to realize his "Greater Syria" plan – as many in the Arab world believed he intended to do.[153]

2

Conqueror of Jerusalem

"An indication of Abdullah's intentions is his concern about Jerusalem's holy places", was written in a Haganah intelligence report just a few days before the termination of the British Mandate in Palestine.[1] This report was one of many sent to Haganah commanders on the eve of Britain's withdrawal from Palestine. These reports strengthened the Haganah's conviction that despite the UN Partition Plan, approved on 29 November 1947 (Resolution 181), which stipulated that Jerusalem would be an international territory under UN supervision, the Arab Legion, intended to invade the city as part of an Arab invasion of Palestine, which they did on 15 May 1948.

The future of Islamic holy sites in Jerusalem concerned King Abdullah especially after the decision to end the Mandate was made at the end of 1947. In mid-February 1948, Abdullah declared his intention of protecting the holy sites and two months later he was quoted in an interview he gave to United Press International that "at the first opportunity he would send Glubb Pasha to conquer Jerusalem". At the beginning of May, he asked the British once again to allow him to send Arab Legion troops to Jerusalem to protect Islamic holy sites. Simultaneously, an Arab source reported to Haganah HQ that "Abdullah aspires to be the 'ruler of the dome' [Dome of the Rock], and therefore he is eager to march into Jerusalem and rule it".[2] However, all Abdullah's requests about ruling Jerusalem were rejected by the British who claimed that the city would be governed according to the UN Partition Plan: it would be an international territory under UN supervision.

As the Arab League's involvement increased in Palestine during May 1948, King Abdullah decided to intensify his campaign to take over Jerusalem. On 11 May, the Arab chiefs of staff met in Damascus to plan the invasion of Palestine when the British mandate ended. The Syrian and Lebanese armies were to enter

Palestine through the Malkiya Gate on the Palestine-Lebanon border, conquer Safed and Tiberius, and move on to Nazareth. The Iraqi force, along with the Arab Legion, was to cross the Jordan River at Naharayim, conquer all the territories from there to Afula, continue moving towards Nazareth and join the Syrian and Lebanese forces. Simultaneously, the Egyptian army was to march from the south towards Tel Aviv and delay Jewish troops in order to assist the Arab efforts in the north. The final goal of all Arab armies was Tel Aviv – the most important city of the Jewish settlement in Palestine.[3]

The invasion plan was unpopular with both King Abdullah, for political reasons, and with Glubb for military ones. Both worried that fighting the Jews in the Naharayim area – from which the Arab Legion was supposed to launch its invasion – would trap the Legion's soldiers and delay their invasion efforts. Their main concern was that while the Legion fought the Jewish forces, the Mufti Amin al-Husayni would exploit the situation to exert his influence over the Arab territory of Palestine, mainly Jerusalem, which as the Arab League had agreed in January 1948 would be under the Mufti's military force *Jihad al-Muqaddas*; indeed, the Mufti had even allowed his troops to deploy in the area.[4] Therefore, with the support of the Egyptians who wanted to secure their army's position, the Jordanians decided to revise the invasion plan to secure their proximity to Jerusalem in order to protect it from the Mufti's possible manipulations.[5]

Although the new plan that Glubb Pasha devised on 13 May did not include a war in Jerusalem, it guaranteed an invasion route into the Arab territories that was convenient, short and safe, without potentially colliding with the Jewish forces. This new plan stipulated that rather than the Arab Legion invading Palestine via Naharayim alongside the Iraqi army, it would advance in two columns: one from the Damiya Bridge towards Jenin, Tul-Karem and Nablus; and the other from the Allenby Bridge towards Jericho, the Judean Hills and the area of Ramallah. This route would guarantee a swift conquest of the Arab territories of Palestine without encountering any Jewish forces and would also grant the Arab Legion a strategic advantage over the other Arab forces, setting the scene for the Arab Legion's invasion of Jerusalem when the time was right.[6]

It was no coincidence that Jerusalem was not directly mentioned as a possible target by the Arab Legion (or any other Arab army for that matter). Glubb Pasha wanted to avoid fighting in Jerusalem for political and military reasons: politically, because of the proposed internationalization of Jerusalem according to the UN partition resolution, as well as possible clashes with the UN and Britain. From 8 May a ceasefire had been declared in Jerusalem and it was to last until the British withdrawal from the city early on the morning of 14 May. When Glubb was devising his plan, the truce in Jerusalem was still in effect and it would seem that Glubb was worried about violating a truce orchestrated by the British High Commissioner to Palestine, Sir Alan Gordon Cunningham.[7] Militarily, Glubb feared the Arab Legion soldiers' lack of experience and training in urban warfare. Fighting in residential areas would have resulted in many casualties. The Arab Legion was a relatively small standing army with no reserve units. "If we move to Jerusalem", claimed Glubb Pasha "we shall use up to half of our army. Then, we cannot hold the rest of the country. If the Jews occupy the rest of the country, Jerusalem itself would be outflanked and fall".[8]

In order to avoid invading Jerusalem, the Arab Legion commanders decided to use a route around the city from Jericho to Bittin (north of Ramallah). If Glubb had genuinely not intended the Arab Legion to participate in the battle over Jerusalem, but had still decided to position it near the city, it must mean that Glubb and King Abdullah had reached a compromise. King Abdullah wanted to stipulate that the Arab Legion would invade and conquer Jerusalem in order to realize his ambition to take over the Moslem holy sites, despite Glubb having refused to do so.

"Go save Jerusalem": Abdullah al-Tall in Jerusalem

Following the invasion plan, the Arab Legion avoided entering Jerusalem and most of the soldiers arriving at Jericho continued on to Ramallah via the bypass route. Two Legion companies remained in Jericho as reserves, under the command of Abdullah al-Tall. The companies were deployed along the Jericho-Jerusalem road, about 17 kilometers from Jerusalem, with the mission of securing the road and keeping it open.[9]

Haganah HQ, inside Jerusalem, had learned that High Commissioner Sir Cunningham had decided to leave the city on the morning of 14 May, earlier than expected. Consequently, the Haganah immediately decided to launch Operation *Kilshon* ("pitchfork") designed to take over strategic locations controlled by the

British and create territorial continuity with the besieged Jewish quarters in both northern Jerusalem (Mount Scopus) and southern Jerusalem (Talpiyot and Ramat Rachel).[10] Coordinating with *IZL* ("Irgun Zvai Leumi" – National Military Organization) troops, Haganah forces quickly took over the British security zone ("Bevingrad") located in the Russian Compound, as well as Sheikh Jarah, Talbiya and Bak'a Arab quarters, the German Colony, the Italian Hospital on Hanevi'im Street, Notre Dame Monastery, the Allenby Camp, the al-Alamein camp, the central post office building, and others. Capturing the Sheikh Jarah quarter was crucial to the Jews because it enabled them to communicate with two of the most important institutions on Mount Scopus which had been isolated since the beginning of 1948 – Hadassah Hospital and the Hebrew University.[11]

The swift capture of the core British locations and Arab quarters by Haganah and IZL troops caused the enemy great concern. The irregular Arab armies situated in Jerusalem at the time, mostly the Mufti's military force *Jihad al-Muqaddas* and the Arab Liberation Army troops, were helpless. Although Operation *Kilshon* was not supposed to take over the Old City, the Arabs were concerned that the Jews intended to take over Islamic holy sites on the Temple Mount, as al-Tall claimed in his book.[12]

The frustration of the Arabs in Jerusalem was growing because two Arab Legion companies were stationed right outside the city, but had not yet received orders to enter Jerusalem. General Glubb Pasha describes the difficult situation of the Arabs in Jerusalem in his book *A Soldier with the Arabs*: "The Jews are advancing everywhere. The city is in confusion! Everywhere the noise of shooting is deafening! All Arabs will be massacred! For God's sake, come and save us! Come! Come! Quickly!" Israeli intelligence reports also confirmed this feeling among the Arabs.[13]

While Glubb was firm that the Arab Legion should avoid fighting in Jerusalem, King Abdullah, who had already asked the British during the mandate period to allow him to take over Jerusalem, felt that the moment to fulfill that wish had come. "I am an Arab King of an Arab state with an Arab army", he explained to the *Times* correspondent, John Phillips, explaining why he should invade Jerusalem.[14] Circumstances smoothed his way. Criticism among the Palestinians and in the Arab world about the two Arab Legion companies stationed outside the city, but "not stirring or moving", as described in the Egyptian newspaper *al-Misri*, increased. Added to this, the Arab officers in the Arab Legion protested that the Legion was unable to stand aside any longer and had to fight the Jews in Jerusalem. They also defamed Glubb Pasha and other British officers in the Legion as "British agents" who were on the Jews' side. These factors brought King Abdullah to accept the Arab demand to "save" Jerusalem, which in reality was a demand to conquer it.[15]

King Abdullah met the Arab delegations in Amman and agreed to order the Arab Legion to enter Jerusalem. The Secretary General of the Arab League, Abd al-Rahman Azzam, who also went to Amman on 16 May to voice his concerns over the Arab Legion's refusal to assist the Arabs inside the city, promised to do so as well. Abdullah said to Azzam: "Ya Azzam . . . I'm not aiming for just the Old City or just the new city . . . .with Allah's help, I will get to Tel Aviv as well".[16] The same day, it was clear that King Abdullah has already decided to enter Jerusalem. "I fully realize my national duties and religious motives toward Palestine as a whole and Jerusalem in particular", wrote King Abdullah to the British on 16 May to justify his invasion to Jerusalem.[17]

The next day, on 17 May at 11:30 a.m., when Glubb Pasha was in First Division HQ in Ramallah, he received a telegram from the King Abdullah with a direct order to send Legion soldiers from Ramallah into Jerusalem. About 30 minutes later, Glubb received another telegram from Jordanian Defense Minister Fauzi al-Mulqi commanding him to follow the King's orders and to send Arab Legion soldiers with artillery "to attack the Jewish quarter in Jerusalem". "Report quickly that the operation has commenced!" ordered the Minister.[18] Despite this, Glubb Pasha still insisted on not sending soldiers to Jerusalem, insisting it was better to wait for the UN to arrange a truce in the city.[19] When King Abdullah learned that his orders had not been carried out, he decided at 2:00 a.m. (the night between 17–18 May) to give a direct order to al-Tall to enter Jerusalem with his soldiers. "We cannot wait any longer," said King Abdullah to al-Tall, "Go save Jerusalem!" King Abdullah had completely ignored the Arab Legion chain of command. Al-Tall claimed in his book that action clearly demonstrated his fear of the Old City being conquered by the Jews.[20] About an hour later, the first of the Arab Legion soldiers entered the Old City and started taking positions against the Haganah and IZL troops. Abdullah's choice of al-Tall was deliberate: he was the highest ranking Arab officer near Jerusalem and two of his companies had been stationed near the city on the Jericho-Jerusalem road since the Arab Legion invasion. Therefore, it seemed only natural that he would carry out the order to attack the city.[21]

After Glubb was informed of the Arab Legion's attack on Jerusalem, he had no choice but to honor the king's decision. "The die was cast," said Glubb and therefore decided on 18 May to send the entire Arab Legion into the city to conquer it.[22] Glubb claimed that a war over Jerusalem could no longer be avoided, "since the fall of the Old City to the Jews would mean that virtually nothing could prevent their advance on the Jerusalem-Jericho road to cut off the Legion's units from their base," wrote Glubb.[23] As part of the decision to conquer Jerusalem, Glubb also sent the 4th Regiment under the command of Habis al-Majali to Latrun, to block the road to Jerusalem so the Arab Legion could easily occupy the city.[24]

The outbreak of the war between the Arab Legion and the Jewish forces in the city, which had been declared international territory, and in which a truce was declared on the eve of the British withdrawal, prompted the Jordanians to claim that they were coerced into battle over Jerusalem because the Jewish forces had violated the truce agreement and launched Operation *Kilshon*. According to Glubb Pasha and other official Jordanian historians, the Legion's invasion of Jerusalem was intended to prevent the conquest of the city by the Jews, to prevent them turning it into a Jewish city. They claimed the Arab invasion was aimed at protecting Islamic holy sites in Jerusalem.[25] This claim, which essentially declared Israel as the aggressor in the war in Jerusalem, was corroborated by British officials and even by several Israeli historians. "We are confident the attack would not have taken place if the Jews had accepted the truce for Jerusalem," was written in a British Foreign Office report on 22 May 1948. According to the British authorities the Legion's invasion was a result of the violation of the ceasefire by the Jews. Similar statements were made by the British High Commissioner to Palestine, Sir Cunningham, just a few months after he left Palestine.[26]

However, it is clear that it was not the Jews' violation of the truce that caused the Legion to invade the city. While Operation *Kilshon* did violate the truce, so too did the Arab forces, mainly in the Old City. Both sides wanted to take over the Jewish Quarter. In his memoirs, Fauzi al-Qawuqji, Commander of the ALA, admitted that he ordered the commander of the ALA's company in Jerusalem, Fadel Abdullah Rashid, to ignore the truce and continue the fight against the Jews in Jerusalem because, in his opinion, the truce in the city did not serve Arab interests. Al-Qawuqji felt that hunger and thirst resulting from the siege on the city would weaken the Jewish forces and that an ensuing truce would have allowed them time to regroup.[27] Several irregular Arab armies were fighting in Jerusalem including the ALA, the Muslim Brotherhood, and Palestinian volunteers. In light of their ongoing defeat they asked for a regular, trained army to come to their aid. According to Israeli historian Avraham Sela, the commanders of the irregular Arab armies could have brought about a truce before the Arab Legion ever arrived in Jerusalem, but the Arab leadership refused, intentionally dragging its feet over the truce because it wanted the Legion to invade Jerusalem.[28]

Abdullah couldn't resist fulfilling his ambitions to take over the city. What Abdullah really wanted to do, explained the French ambassador to Amman, was play "Saladin . . . in this twentieth-century crusade".[29] By this he meant conquering Jerusalem in order to make it a religious center for the Hashemite kingdom under his leadership. Because he saw the role of the Hashemite family as protectors of Islamic Holy sites, it is quite possible that this played an important part in his decision to conquer Jerusalem – the third most holy city to Islam.[30]

The Arab Legion's invasion of Jerusalem had important implications for the balance of military forces in the city. The Arab Legion was systematic, disciplined, well-armed and equipped, and it contributed significantly to the Arab forces in the city. It also affected the balance of Jewish and Arab forces inside the city, both in quantity and in quality. The members of the UN Consular Committee sent to maintain the truce in Jerusalem were growing increasingly concerned that the Arab Legion's participation in the battle over Jerusalem would bring about the city's total ruin. They were worried that as a result of the shift in balance in favor of the Arabs, they would then refuse to end the battle and a truce would no longer be possible.

Because of this the committee decided to do everything in its power to convince King Abdullah to prevent the fighting in Jerusalem; two committee members, Belgian Jean Nieuwenhuys and Spanish Pablo de Azcarate, were sent to Amman to meet with him. According to the consuls, they met with a very nervous, irate Abdullah who refused to even discuss a truce in Jerusalem. When they raised the issue of food and water supplies to the city and asked that he intervene, "The King replied sharply that there would be no water and no food." The only issue the King was willing to discuss was an immediate and unconditional Jewish surrender.[31]

Al-Tall as commander of the Arab Legion in Jerusalem was among the Jordanian officers who participated in the meeting and was described as an unrelenting man, who would not compromise and demanded immediate surrender. He also threatened that if the Jews did not surrender by 5 p.m., the Legion would start to bombard the city. According to the surrender conditions presented by al-Tall, all Jewish troops would be taken as prisoners of war, women and children would be handed over to the Red Cross, and the Legion would take control of the holy sites. Because the Jews refused to yield to the Legion's demands, King Abdullah rejected all Jewish truce proposals. British Consul to Jerusalem Beaumont in his telegram to the Foreign Office claimed that war in Jerusalem had become inevitable.[32]

As fighting began in the Old City on 15 May, the irregular Arab armies managed to take over the Zion and Dung Gates (the two gates closest to the Jewish quarter in the Old City) thus intensifying the siege of the Jews of the Old City. The attacks on the Jews grew stronger and more frequent. The two sides fought over the Beit El and Beit Yaacov (Churva) synagogues and the Porat Yosef seminary which all managed to stand their ground despite Jewish ammunition and supplies running dangerously low. On the next day, 16 May, the Jews in the Jewish quarter began sending telegrams to Haganah HQ describing the dire conditions and expressing their desire to surrender to the irregular Arab armies. The Haganah command encouraged them to hold on and promised they would "soon be rescued".[33]

A failed attempt by Haganah forces to enter the Old City took place on the night between 16–17 May. A force of Haganah soldiers from the *Etzioni* Brigade, which was supposed to break through Jaffa Gate and arrive at the Jewish quarter, was late in reaching its target. The force arrived at dawn rather than under cover of dark thus losing the element of surprise. The next night, another attempt was made to break through the Jaffa Gate, but this attempt also failed, as Israeli armored cars could not drive through the narrow alley leading to the gate.[34]

Before the Legion's invasion, the soldiers of the *Harel* Brigade had managed to break into the Old city via Zion Gate, contact the residents of the Jewish quarter, and provide medical assistance, ammunition, and provisions. However, when the *Harel* Brigade soldiers arrived at the Jewish quarter, the Zion Gate had been captured once again by the Arab forces and contact with the Jewish quarter was again severed.[35] At the same time the Arab Legion started to deploy within the Old City. The first infantry company, under command of Captain Mahmud al-Musa, entered the city on 18 May, the 8th Garrison Company, under the command of Captain Abd al-Razq Abdullah, arrived the following day and on 20 May the 6th Garrison Company, under command of Captain Daghram al-Falih, also entered the Old City.[36]

The three companies stationed in Jerusalem were combined into one regiment – the 6th Regiment – under al-Tall's command; it comprised 730 soldiers and officers. The Regimental headquarters was in the al-Rauda School in the Old City. Though al-Tall stationed his soldiers in various locations within the Old City, including Malha, Shu'afat, Beit Safafa, Abu Dis and others, he focused most of his efforts on guarding the gates of the Old City to prevent possible infiltration by Israeli forces.[37] In addition to the new regiment, al-Tall also had the irregular Arab armies at his disposal. According to Jordanian historian Arif al-Arif, they comprised about 500 troops, including the Arab Liberation Army, the Muslim Brotherhood, and Palestinian volunteers (some of whom were in the Mufti's military force), who were subject to the Arab Legion's command and who fought side by side with them in an effort to take the Jewish quarter.[38]

From 20–23 May, Legion forces intensified the siege on the Jewish quarter after taking several Jewish posts and a few synagogues within the Jewish quarter, including Or Haim, Succat Shalom and Beit Hillel. Attempts by Haganah forces to break through the Zion Gate into the Jewish quarter failed on both the nights of 21 May and 25 May.[39] Consequently, the Arab Legion decided to reinforce its soldiers in the Old City to prevent any further attempts. And so, on the morning of 25 May, the 5th Company arrived in Jerusalem from Ramallah with three armored cars and deployed inside the Old City and around the Jewish quarter.[40]

The Legion continued to bombard the Jewish quarter as the Arab Legion's infantry corps, with the support of the Palestinian volunteers, focused their efforts on taking the Churva synagogue which was sheltering Jews. The Legion commanders claimed that the synagogue was used as a shooting post from which to target their men and was therefore a legitimate tactical target. This claim was supported by British Consul to Jerusalem Beaumont and Dr. Otto Lehner from the International Red Cross. On 27 May, the Arab forces succeeded in conquering the synagogue and decided to blow it up.[41]

Conditions for the Jews blockaded in the Old City were ominous. They had run out of food and their ammunition was also running dangerously low. The failed attempts by Haganah forces to break through the Arab barricades crushed their already low morale and attempts by the Israeli Air Force to drop supplies from the air also failed with the supplies falling into the hands of the Arabs. The local Jewish residents no longer trusted the national leadership and decided to surrender.[42] On 28 May, at 11:00 a.m. two rabbis, Rabbi Reuven Hazan and Rabbi Zeev Mintzberg, advanced to the Legion post carrying a white flag to discuss surrender terms. However, the Legion wanted to discuss terms with the chairman of the committee of the Old City, Rabbi Mordechai Weingarten. Rabbi Hazan returned alone and Rabbi Mintzberg stayed in the Legion post as a hostage. The commander of the 6th Company, Mahmud al-Musa, told his commander, al-Tall, of the Jew's desire to surrender. Rabbi Weingarten and Shaul Tawil (Tuval), commander of the intelligence department of the Haganah in the Old City, who spoke Arabic, went out to negotiate. In the meantime, al-Tall had also arrived.[43] The terms of surrender presented by al-Tall in Jerusalem were similar to the ones he presented in the Etzion Block, namely handing over all weapons and ammunition, all men able to carry a weapon would be taken as prisoners of war, and women, children and the wounded would be transferred outside the Old City under the supervision of a UN representative. The surrender agreement was signed on the afternoon of 28 May between al-Tall, commander of the Arab Legion in Jerusalem and Moshe Rusnak, commander of the Haganah force in the city.[44]

The Arab Legion had taken 290 Jewish prisoners of war and later transferred them to a camp in Mafraq. Al-Tall did not keep his promise and took 150 lightly-wounded soldiers and non-combatants, including 30 elders, prisoner.[45] Later, al-Tall explained that "those were orders from Amman", meaning that he was supposed to take all residents of the Jewish quarter as prisoners without distinction. However, it seems likely that it was he himself who was disappointed at the small number of Jewish prisoners and therefore wanted to increase that number by taking non-combatant Jewish residents captive.[46] Al-Tall did attempt to ensure the Jewish prisoners' safety on their way through the Old City alleys by announcing a curfew which started immediately after the surrender and continued until 4 a.m. The curfew not only prevented the Jews from being attacked, but also prevented the looting which the Arabs had planned inside captured Jewish houses, according to testimony by an Arab renegade.[47]

There is no doubt that al-Tall made a significant contribution to the Arab Legion's success in conquering the Old City in Jerusalem. He claimed that upon his arrival in the city he met with the commanders of the irregular Arab forces to coordinate military operations against the Jews.[48] Indeed, both Arab historians and some Israeli sources emphasize the fact that al-Tall managed to unite all the Arab forces against the Jews.[49] This cooperation was important to the Legion's success. The same thing happened in the Latrun area, where the Arab Legion commander, Habis al-Majali, also succeeded in uniting the irregular Arab forces.[50] As a result of this cooperation, they were the only Arab Legion commanders who succeeded in defeating IDF soldiers during the 1948 war.

According to the report of the Old City's fall written by the IDF shortly after, al-Tall insisted on arming his units fully in preparation for the attack on the Jewish Quarter.[51] Every soldier was given a rifle, every squad a Bren LMG, every platoon 2- or 3-inch mortars as well as armored cars with 2-pound guns, in accordance with British military standards. This allowed him to lead a more effective assault and use all the firepower available. In conclusion, and as confirmed by IDF commanders, al-Tall not only commanded his men, but also showed true leadership by ensuring the attack was led in exemplary military order according to British military norms.[52]

After the conquest of the Old City, King Abdullah arrived for a victory visit in Jerusalem, where he met al-Tall and heard about the battle's progress in the city from him. Although the visit's purpose was mainly political – strengthening the connection between the two banks of the Jordan River and enforcing Jordanian rule in Jerusalem, as in the other territories in Palestine occupied by the Jordanians – it also had a military aspect.[53] King Abdullah congratulated Glubb on his military accomplishment in Jerusalem saying: "the victory of the Arab Legion in the battles over the Old City is the second most important victory for the Legion, after the conquest of Kfar Etzion and the adjacent settlements. If the first victory was vanquishing the Jews in the Hebron region, then the second is eradicating them and leaving the Old City for Arab inhabitance only".[54]

From al-Tall's point of view, the visit had far more significance. As Glubb recorded in his book, during the visit King Abdullah looked at al-Tall's shoulder and saw his rank as a major. "I'm making you a lieutenant colonel," said King Abdullah to al-Tall. Glubb Pasha was opposed al-Tall's promotion because he had only been promoted to major two months earlier. However, King Abdullah pressured Glubb who was forced to promote al-Tall shortly afterwards.[55]

On 19 May 1948, at the same time as the battle in the Old City, the Arab Legion tried to take over Mount Scopus which had become isolated from Jewish settlement after the Legion took over the Sheikh Jarah quarter in north Jerusalem. The Legion attacked with artillery and destroyed the Jewish Hadassah Hospital and Hebrew University. One of al-Tall's forces took part in the attack. He saw the significance of the attack on Mount Scopus as eliminating the Jewish presence in Jerusalem.[56] As a result of pressure by the truce committee's president on King Abdullah, on 22 May the King ordered that military actions on Mount Scopus be suspended for 24 hours to allow the Jews to evacuate their wounded from the hospital. The next day, the truce was lengthened indefinitely in the face of al-Tall's request to renew the fighting and capture Mount Scopus. The place remained under Red Cross supervision. Al-Tall heavily criticized the King's submission to international pressure, calling it "The Mount Scopus Disaster".[57]

During the first truce on 7 July 1948, both the Jordanians and Israelis, with UN mediation, reached the "Mount Scopus Agreement". Under its terms, the entire Mount Scopus area, including the Jewish Hadassah Hospital and Hebrew University – as well as Augusta Victoria Hospital and the Arab village of Isawiya – was to be demilitarized and come under UN supervision. Additionally, all armed forces would withdraw from the area the same day and a civilian Jewish and Arab police force would operate on behalf of the UN. The Jewish force, according to the agreement, would not exceed 85 police officers, and the civilian staff would not exceed 33 men. The number of Arab police officers in Augusta Victoria was set at 40. The agreement between both parties was fixed until the end of the hostilities or until the signing of a new agreement. It was signed by Norman Lash, the first Brigade's commander of the Arab Legion, and David Shealtiel, the Israeli commander of Jerusalem.[58]

Commander and Politician: Al-Tall Commander of Arab Jerusalem

On 29 May, one day after the surrender of the Jewish quarter, the UN Security Council with the help of the United States and Britain called for a truce in Palestine and threatened the Arab nations and Israel that if they refused to accept a truce, they would be accused of breaking the peace in the region and sanctions would be directed against them. The Security Council also called for a general arms embargo on all parties involved in the war in the Middle East. On 20 May, the UN appointed Swedish diplomat Count Folke Bernadotte as a mediator for Palestine.[59]

The Israeli government announced its acceptance of the truce, but the Arabs had doubts. In the Arab League session, which took place in Aly, Lebanon at the beginning of June, the Jordanian Prime Minister, Tawfiq Abu al-Huda, pressured the other Arab states to support the truce. He threatened that "If the League does not accept the truce, Jordan will discard her membership in the Arab League and in the war in Palestine."[60] Eventually on 9 June the Secretary General of the Arab League, Abd al-Rahman Azzam, declared on behalf of the Arab governments that the Arab states accepted the truce, "in order to give the UN an opportunity to resolve the problem of Palestine peacefully." The truce went into effect on 11 June at 06:00 GMT and was to last for four weeks.[61]

Jordan's acceptance of the truce, as well as the pressure it put on the Arab League to accept it, aroused strong criticism both inside and outside Jordan. Led by al-Tall, the Arab officers who served in the Arab Legion felt they were close to defeating Israel in light of the Jews' defeat in Latrun on 30 May, the conquest of the Jewish Quarter by the Arab Legion and the prisoners taken – more than by any other Arab country. They felt that the Jordanian government's agreement to uphold the truce was not just a mistake, but "a crime which cannot be atoned for," as claimed by Azat Hassan, an Arab officer.[62] According to Lapierre and Collins, al-Tall used his good relations with King Abdullah to try to convince him to reject the truce, which he described as "the biggest mistake in the history of the wars in the Middle East." "How can I stop these men?" al-Tall asked the King. "They feel victory is within reach." He tried to continue but the King refused to listen and told him: "You are a soldier and I give you an order . . . you must order a ceasefire."[63]

The real reason Jordan insisted on the ceasefire however was because of the poor status of the Arab Legion as a result of the UN arms embargo which froze the British subsidy to the Arab Legion and the ammunition shortage caused by the war "which lasted for a few days only," as estimated by Israeli Intelligence.[64] Glubb's offer to withdraw from the war was understood by the British Defense Office to be due to the shortage of ammunition.[65] The unfreezing of the subsidy to the Arab Legion and transfer of weapons were conditional on the acceptance of the ceasefire by the Jordanian government. Thus, the pressure Jordan put on the Arab League to accept the truce offered by Bernadotte can be understood.

The intention of the truce, as explained by Bernadotte, was "to ensure that no military advantage will accrue to either side during the period of the truce or as a result of its application." Therefore, no fighting personnel would be introduced into any of the Arab states or into any part of Palestine (subparagraph one). Jewish immigrants to Israel during the truce would not be given military or paramilitary training (subparagraph two). The International Red Cross Committee would administer relief to the populations of both sides in municipal areas which had suffered severely from the conflict (subparagraph eight). The result of this subparagraph was to open the Tel Aviv-Jerusalem road and allow Israel to transfer supplies (under Red Cross supervision) to besieged Jerusalem.[66]

The issue of supplying water to Jerusalem aroused controversy between Israel and Jordan. Israel claimed that supplying food and water to the Jews of Jerusalem was a humanitarian matter and therefore did not give any a military advantage to Israel. Jordan, on the other hand, claimed that supplying water to Jerusalem constituted a change in the status quo because the Jews could conserve the water thereby giving them a military advantage in opposition to the truce conditions. Al-Tall was deeply opposed to Jordan allowing the transfer of water to Jerusalem (including using the main water pipe from Ras al-Ain, as requested by the UN mediator Bernadotte). He claimed that it might "save the Jews from surrendering."[67] He intervened with the Arab commanders in the Latrun area, in order to make it difficult for the Israelis to transfer food and water supplies via the Tel Aviv-Jerusalem road until the Arab Legion HQ ordered him to "not report on issues outside of Jerusalem."[68] From archival sources, it is not clear exactly what part al-Tall had in the events in the Latrun area. However, the Arab Legion did all it could to disrupt Israeli convoys passing through the Arab Legion barriers around

Latrun despite the truce conditions and under the supervision of the Red Cross.[69]

Jordan took advantage of the first truce politically and militarily. Politically, the Jordanian government began to organize those in the conquered territories and prepare them for future annexation to Jordan. Military governors were appointed to important cities in the West Bank, relations were tightened between the two banks, and King Abdullah increased his visits to Jerusalem both to impress and capture the hearts of the people after the victory over the Jews.[70] He also took time to visit Cairo and Riyadh to examine the possibility of uniting the Arab armies. King Abdullah assumed that such a union would increase the pressure on the Jews and would bring about the conquest of all Jerusalem: "We could create a successful plan for a big attack with the Arab Legion, the Iraqi, and the Egyptian forces in Jerusalem and we would conquer the whole city," said King Abdullah after the meeting with King Farouk at the end of June.[71] However, Farouk, King of Egypt, refused the offer, fearing that Abdullah would eventually take over all of Jerusalem and annex it to Jordan. He also rejected Abdullah's suggestion to cease fighting and divide the Arab territories between them.[72]

The Arab Legion HQ recruited more soldiers, organized the soldiers' training, reinforced its posts, withdrew companies who had fought on the front back to their bases, and replaced them with fresh troops. Al-Tall played an important role at the time. He commanded his soldiers in the Old City to strengthen their posts and made sure they were fully supplied with guns and ammunition – purchased via the black market. In addition, the Arab Legion commanders went on combat tours near IDF posts in order to collect intelligence for the continuation of the conflict. This was done mainly around Latrun and in the Old City. According to Israeli intelligence reports, the two commanders, Habis al-Majali and al-Tall, used local villagers to get near IDF posts.[73]

An important step taken during the truce was to complete the formation of the two Regiments raised on the eve of the invasion on May 1948: the 5th Regiment and the 6th Regiment. When al-Tall received the command of the 6th Regiment it comprised just three companies: the first infantry company, under the command of Captain Mahmud al-Musa, the 6th Garrison Company, under the command of Captain Daghram al-Falih, and the 8th Garrison Company, under the command of Captain Abd al-Razq Abdullah. However, with the battle in the Old City, a support company, under the command of Lieutenant Ghalib Radiman, which included four armored cars, four 3-inch mortars, four 6-pounder guns and three Bren LMG, and an HQ Company were attached to the regiment, thus making it a proper infantry regiment. Al-Tall needed to turn the 6th Regiment into an infantry regiment to ensure his success in the Old City in Jerusalem. The Arab Legion had two types of regiments: one which was mainly infantry forces, found generally in concentrated population areas like Jerusalem, and the other consisted of armored cars and artillery, found around Latrun. Therefore, al-Tall's regiment, whose job was to defend the Old City – a densely populated urban area – consisted mainly of infantry troops rather than armored cars and artillery.[74] Al-Tall also had command of a Jordanian volunteer company, Manko Company, which was positioned in Jerusalem before the Arab armies' invasion of Palestine. The company comprised about 150 volunteers and was under the command of Barakat al-Tarad.[75]

At the end of the truce, al-Tall agreed to meet with Rabbi Weingarten, the former chairman of the committee of the Old City, who was sent on behalf of the Israeli government to discuss with al-Tall the problems created after the surrender of the Jewish Quarter. The meeting was held on the last day of the truce, 9 July 1948, at the 6th Regiment HQ in the al-Rauda School and it dealt with three issues: the Jewish dead, who were yet to be buried, the release of the non-combatant Jews captured by the Arab Legion, and the return of Torah scrolls stolen from synagogues in the Jewish Quarter. According to a report given by Rabbi Weingarten after the meeting, al-Tall was attentive to the Jews' problems and was willing to do his best to solve them.[76]

Despite this, he solved only the problem regarding burial of the dead, allowing them to be buried inside the Old City with special permission from the Chief Rabbinate of Israel. This was necessary because it is against Jewish religious law which states that no dead will be buried inside the walls. (After the Six Day War in June 1967, when the IDF captured Jerusalem, the dead were moved to a special common grave on the Mount of Olives.) Non-combatant Jewish prisoners were not released until February–March 1949. Al-Tall did not succeed in solving the mystery of the fate of the Torah scrolls stolen from the synagogues and even today their location is unknown.

The truce enabled al-Tall, in cooperation with the Military Governor of Jerusalem, Ahmad Hilmi, to start organizing civilian life in the Old City as part of the Hashemite regime in Palestine. Their goal was to improve the conditions of the local population which on the eve of the Legion invasion suffered from a substantial lack of basic commodities, paralysis of the civil administrative system in the city, as well as disease and poverty which was worsened by the arrival of 30,000 Palestinian refugees who had fled from battles in the previous month and found shelter in the Old City.[77] Al-Tall and Hilmi needed to establish law and order and an administrative system that would provide civilian services for the residents. A local militia was formed to replace the Palestinian police who remained loyal to the Mufti Amin al-Husayni, and its job was to enforce law and order in the city. With the assistance of ex-public servants, the administrative system was rehabilitated and municipal services began to be resumed. In addition, al-Tall only allowed civilians minimal weapons and vehicles were monitored.[78]

An improvement in conditions was essential not only to al-Tall, but also to the Hashemite regime in Palestine in general. Shortly after the Legion's invasion of Palestine, on 19 May it established military rule and appointed Ibrahim Hashim as Military Governor "of all parts of Palestine now effectively occupied by the Arab Legion." He was to restore law and order; he also started to minimize the influence of Palestinian fighters who were the Mufti's followers with the intention of annexing the territories to Jordan. Thus, East Jerusalem, like the other cities in the West Bank, would receive support from the Hashemite regime which was interested in establishing its rule in Palestine. Towards the end of May, postal and bank services were renewed between the West Bank and Jordan, the broadcasting station in Ramallah renewed activity, civilian and religious courts were built, and trade between East Jerusalem and West Bank cities and Amman was renewed. Food was brought to East Jerusalem to relieve the severe shortage.[79]

Even so, the population's situation remained poor, and according to an Israeli intelligence report many of them abandoned the Old City to live in Arab villages outside the city, probably fearing an Israeli counter-attack.[80]

Abdullah al-Tall and the Jews – Round Two: The Ten Day Battles

With the renewal of the battle on 9 July, Israel concentrated its efforts on conquering the two largest Arab cities, Lydda and Ramle, in Operation *Dani* (formerly operation *Larlar*) to remove the Arab threat against Tel Aviv and relieve Arab Legion pressure in Jerusalem. Besides conquering the two cities, IDF forces intended to take Latrun so they could open the Tel Aviv-Jerusalem road and continue on to Ramallah where the Arab Legion's First division HQ was stationed.[81] Within three days (10–12 July) IDF forces conquered Lydda and Ramle with no significant Arab opposition. Moreover, the 5th Garrison Company of the Arab Legion, stationed in the police station between Lydda and Ramle, retreated during the night of 11–12 July without even fighting.[82] Although the operation resulted only in the conquest of two cities, it was considered a big success for Israel.

The quick conquest of both cities or "the Lydda and Ramle Disaster" as al-Tall referred to it, and the withdrawal of the Legion aroused much anger among the Arabs and especially the Palestinians, who blamed the British officers in the Arab Legion for abandoning cities and conspiring with the Jews.[83] Al-Tall repeated the allegation and claimed that "giving Lydda and Ramle to the Jews is considered the heaviest disaster ever to occur in Palestine because the giving was done by the Arab Legion."[84] He maintained that the Legion acted as it did because both cities had a large concentration of Palestinian followers of Mufti Amin al-Husayni who opposed King Abdullah's political ambitions to annex the Arab territories to Jordan, and therefore the Arab Legion preferred to give away the area to prevent Palestinian opposition to the Hashemite regime.[85]

Glubb rejected al-Tall's accusation of a conspiracy with the Jews and claimed that military considerations only led him to withdraw from the two cities. He maintained that even before the war broke out, he had informed Jordanian Prime Minister Abu al-Huda that because of insufficient manpower in the Arab Legion he would not be able to hold both cities in addition to holding the Latrun area, and that he would need to give them up if they were attacked. Since the Latrun area was of higher strategic importance than the two cities of Lydda and Ramle, Glubb clearly decided that it was better to concentrate the main force in the area of Latrun than to split it into different sectors, which would allow IDF forces to take any sector separately and break through to Jerusalem.[86]

But al-Tall's claim about the Mufti's men in both cities would appear to have some substance. Israeli intelligence reports confirmed that Lydda and Ramle had a high concentration of Mufti followers who sided with Egyptian army supporters to prevent the establishment of Hashemite rule in the area. Their influence on the local population was so great that the residents themselves demanded the Jordanian government evacuate Arab Legion forces and agents from both cities. Therefore, even if there was not a conspiracy between Jordan and the Israelis, as al-Tall claimed, it is clear that there was Jordanian consent to an Israeli takeover of both cities – which explains the withdrawal of the Legion force from the area without a battle in order to prevent their annexation with other territories to Jordan.[87]

The battle continued in the north Jerusalem sector in the Sheikh Jarah quarter from the end of the first truce until the start of the second truce on 18 July 1948. The goal of the 3rd Regiment of the Arab Legion, under the command of William Newman stationed in that sector, was to take over the Jewish Mea Shearim quarter to capture the main transportation routes to Ramallah and Mount Scopus currently under IDF control. On 16 July 1948, one of the most important battles in the sector started during which Arab Legion forces succeeded in taking a number of Jewish buildings in the area.[88] According to Israeli historian Avraham Sela, the attack was initiated by al-Tall who tried, with the help of a number of Arab officers from the 3rd Regiment, to force the British commander to take a more significant part in the battle. Al-Tall sent a number of soldiers and officers from his regiment, together with a number of irregular fighters, to reinforce the 3rd Regiment. The IDF had succeeded in a counter-attack that same day to regain control over some of the buildings captured by the Legion. The other buildings stayed under the Jordanian control until the Six Day War in June 1967.[89]

The Legion attack on Mea Shearim preceded IDF HQ's intention of attacking the Sheikh Jarah quarter and the areas near Mount Scopus in order to reconnect Hadassah Hospital and the Hebrew University, which had been cut off since the Arab Legion takeover of Sheikh Jarah on 19 May. The order to conquer the Sheikh Jarah quarter was carried out on 16 July by the head of the operations branch, Yigael Sukenik (Yadin), commander of *Etzioni* Brigade and the Israeli commander in Jerusalem, David Shealtiel: "You need to take into consideration," the order said "what you can do at night. The possibilities seem to be: the Sheikh Jarah quarter or the Old City. In case just one is possible before the truce – it is to be Sheikh Jarah."[90] Shealtiel also laid the groundwork for an operation to conquer the Old City.

On 17 July, one day before the second truce started, in cooperation with IZL troops, Shealtiel ordered an attack on the Old City
through the Zion Gate and the New Gate. The attack failed. When
it proved to be impossible to breach Zion Gate, at 5:30 a.m. it was
decided to withdraw after al-Tall and the Arab Legion soldiers
"showed heavy resistance" according to a telegram sent from the
Etzioni Brigade to David Ben-Gurion.[91] According to al-Tall's
initial claims, during the attack IDF forces hit Islamic holy sites on
Temple Mount. He sent a telegram to leaders of all the Arab states
that were members of the Arab League, and to the Secretary
General of the Arab League, Abd al-Rahman Azzam, asking for the
censure and punishment of Israel for its actions, although there is
no evidence that IDF forces did indeed hit Islamic holy sites.
Interestingly, in the book he wrote later, al-Tall does not mention
these allegations.[92]

Al-Tall increased his efforts to extend control over the Old City
and also to conquer territories of the new city (West or Hebrew
Jerusalem), which were in Jewish hands. Israeli historians describe
the Legion's attempts to advance from the Old City toward the new
city, first by the failed attack on the Notre Dame Monastery area on
24 May and on 30 May, later through the Mea Shearim quarter in
mid-July and finally with the Arab Legion's heavy artillery fired on
the Jewish quarters in the new city.[93] Al-Tall never denied his intention "[my] intention is to occupy the whole city," he admitted on 24
May 1948. He decided the best way to accomplish that goal was a
siege which should give him victory in about ten days.[94] He based
his assessment partly on intelligence reports and radio monitoring
of the Israelis suggesting that they were desperate because of heavy
pressure from the Arab Legion. "The danger of death or surrender
of over a hundred thousand Jews was expected," al-Tall wrote in his
book.[95]

Al-Tall's plan to conquer the new city found concurrence with
East Jerusalem's Military Governor, Ahmad Hilmi, who had earlier
suggested that the Jordanian government should increase pressure
on the Jews in order to remove them from Jerusalem. Hilmi hoped
that if the Jews did indeed evacuate their homes, he could house
Palestinian refugees in the New City and so ease their suffering.
Hilmi thought it would be a convenient solution to the Palestinian
refugee problem in Jerusalem. However, the Jordanian government
rejected his offer. Al-Tall, who supported it, hoped that with the
help of the siege, which created optimism among the Arab Legion

officers, he could conquer Jerusalem and thereby accomplish Hilimi's plan.[96]

With the renewal of battle on 9 July, the UN Security Council strove for another truce between Israel and the Arabs. On 18 July, that second truce began and both sides met under UN mediation. The head of the UN observer teams, General William Riley, toured the front in Jerusalem accompanied by Jordanian and Israeli officers, in order to make a map of the truce area in Jerusalem. On 21 July, at a meeting between the Jordanian and the Israeli officers headed by al-Tall and David Shealtiel, in the Assyrian Convent of St. Mark near Nablus Gate, both parties signed the truce maps in the Jerusalem area along the lines of the first truce. Two days later, on 23 July, Moshe Dayan replaced Shealtiel as Jerusalem's military commander, a role which now also included supervising the truce in the area.[97]

King Abdullah had an enormous interest in ending the battle, mainly to get the financial subsidy that Britain had frozen, but also to start annexing the territories the Arab Legion had conquered. Therefore, he ordered that the truce must be observed, fearing that more shooting incidents with Israel would cause him to lose the territories he had already conquered. The announcement of the second truce symbolized the end of war in the Jordanian district and allowed the IDF to transfer its forces to other sectors where the war was still ongoing, mainly to the north against the ALA and the south against the Egyptian army.[98]

Despite the truce, gunfire continued in Jerusalem between the Arab Legion and IDF forces, partly because al-Tall and IDF commanders were not content with their leaders' decision to cease fire. On 17 August, IDF forces launched an attack on Government House in Jabel Mukaber (today the UN observer base), which was in the demilitarized area according to the maps signed by al-Tall and Shealtiel and was to be used as a barrier between the Egyptian forces south of Jerusalem and the Arab Legion forces in the north. The operation's objective was to take the building after irregular Arab fighters had settled in it. The Arab Legion forces under the command of al-Tall and with the assistance of local Arabs managed to repel the IDF attack after killing 11 soldiers, capturing five and wounding about 20. In response, IDF forces captured the Agricultural School and Arab College near Government House.[99]

The taking of both institutions by the IDF forces aroused rage among the Arab Legion forces and al-Tall promised revenge. There was fear that the battle would escalate throughout Jerusalem after it was learned that al-Tall had prepared a plan to take the two Jewish institutions on Mount Scopus: Hadassah Hospital and Hebrew University, both of which had been demilitarized since 7 July.[100] Al-Tall's decision was made independently and was not compatible with Jordanian government policy which was to avoid escalation. Despite this, according to rumors rampant amongst the Arabs, al-Tall had also prepared a wider plan for a war with the Jews far beyond the decision to attack Mount Scopus, in order to subdue them once and for all.[101]

To prevent the battle extending throughout the whole Jerusalem sector, UN observers in the city began intervening to reach a ceasefire. General Riley demanded a ceasefire from the commanders, while Bernadotte, the UN mediator, turned to the relevant governments (Israel, Jordan and Egypt) to get them to act. Bernadotte's initiative brought forward a meeting with the three commanders in Jerusalem on 3 September 1948 in the Assyrian Convent of St. Mark near Nablus Gate. The meeting included Moshe Dayan from the Israeli Army, al-Tall from the Jordanian Army, and Ahmad Abd al-Aziz from the Egyptian Army. The three commanders, who had already met during August, blamed one another for violating the truce; however they claimed that they were committed to upholding the truce. As such, the commanders agreed to maintain the demilitarized areas that had been agreed. As a result, the Israeli government ordered IDF commanders in Jerusalem to evacuate the areas captured during the last operation the following day even though al-Tall refused to leave the areas he was supposed to evacuate on Mount Zion and Dir Abu Tur. The IDF forces' evacuation from the Agricultural School and Arab College was completed that day by 2:00 p.m.[102]

Although the Jordanian government agreed to the ceasefire, it would seem that al-Tall did not. He claimed that political events among the Palestinians at that time led him to attempt to promote Palestinian interests. In the Arab League's political committee meeting from 6–15 September in Alexandria, Egypt it was decided to turn the temporary civil administration, which had been agreed to in July 1948, into an Arab government for the whole of Palestine; on 20 September an official announcement was made. The seat of the "All-Palestine Government" was to be in Gaza which was under Egyptian control at the time. The purpose behind the establishment of the Palestinian government was to minimize Jordanian political influence in Palestine after the Arab Legion had successfully conquered the West Bank, Latrun and the Old City of Jerusalem, but it inspired great hope among the Palestinians.[103]

To endow the government with legitimacy, a Palestinian National Council was convened in Gaza on 30 September 1948, under the chairmanship of the Mufti Amin al-Husayni. At the time there was a political struggle between King Abdullah, who viewed the Palestinian council as illegitimate, and the Mufti, who saw it as an opportunity to neutralize Abdullah's position in Palestine and make it harder for him to control the Arab territories which he had conquered. In an attempt to weaken King Abdullah's influence in Palestine, the Mufti offered high-ranking jobs in the government to be given to notables from the Hashemite regime in Palestine. Among those who were offered a job was Military Governor of Jerusalem Ahmad Hilmi who accepted the role of Palestinian Prime Minister in the government and therefore abandoned his alliance with King Abdullah and his role in Jerusalem, and left to serve in Gaza.[104]

With the establishment of the Palestinian government in Gaza, al-Tall sent a secret telegram to Hilmi in which he expressed his hope of establishing an Arab army to continue the struggle with Israel. If such an army were established, he would volunteer to take a part in it: "I hereby volunteer to be a soldier in that army and am putting myself at your disposal", he wrote in his book.[105] Al-Tall claimed that his relations with Hilmi and his identification with the Palestinian problem aroused suspicion about his loyalty to the Jordanian Hashemite regime, dedication as a military man, and ability to fulfill his orders as commander. Therefore, the Jordanian government decided at the end of September 1948 to dismiss him from command of the 6th Regiment in order to remove him from the military. Surprisingly, instead, the Jordanian government appointed him military governor of Jerusalem after the post was vacated by Hilmi. Muhammad al-Muaita received the command of the 6th Regiment on 1 October 1948.[106]

Al-Tall claim's that his dismissal from military service was due to his ties with the Palestinians seems peculiar: there is no evidence of al-Tall's links with the Palestinians then. On the contrary, evidence shows that he remained loyal to the Hashemite regime despite his dismissal. Moreover, his appointment as military governor of Jerusalem – the most important city in Palestine in the eyes of King Abdullah – his good relations with Abdullah, and his role as secret messenger on Abdullah's behalf in talks with the Jews (which will be described later) strengthen the opinion that he remained loyal to King Abdullah and the Hashemite regime in Jordan at that time. It would seem that his dismissal from command of the 6th Regiment was the result of both his poor relations with Glubb, whom he called a traitor (which dated back to Glubb's refusal to grant him the rank of lieutenant colonel) and also the fact that he was a strong-minded officer who did not follow orders. One example of this was the order he received from Glubb Pasha to dismantle the Mufti's military force *Jihad al-Muqaddas* in June and in September 1948 – orders which al-Tall disregarded.[107] He probably disobeyed orders not because he supported the Palestinians, but because he became friends with most of them while fighting by their side in the battle of the Old City. It can be assumed that Al-Tall had not formed a pro-Palestinian and anti-Hashemite political approach, but was merely anti-British. Jews who conversed with him at the time concurred. This anti-British stance was the real reason he was dismissed from the command of the 6th Regiment.[108]

The continuity of al-Tall's links with the Hashemite regime in Jordan on the one hand and his opposition to an All-Palestine Government and his hostility to the Mufti on the other can be seen in his actions and declarations while military governor of Jerusalem. The increase in conflict between the Jordanians and the Egyptians in the Jerusalem-Hebron-Bethlehem area on the ground, the Egyptian support of national Palestinian aspirations, and their help in establishing the Palestinian government in Gaza against King Abdullah's wishes, led him to refuse entrance for Egyptian troops into the Old City in Jerusalem, allegedly "to avoid a conflict with them", but actually to cause them harm.[109] At the Hashemite regime's initiative, al-Tall continued to harass the Egyptians, Palestinians, and Mufti's followers while cultivating good connections with Hashemite regime supporters in Palestine, as did King Abdullah. In November 1948 Anwar al-Khatib, one of King Abdullah's closest associates, was appointed mayor of East Jerusalem and a month later Sheikh Husam al-Din Jarallah was appointed Mufti of Jerusalem. Together with al-Tall they assisted King Abdullah in promoting his political ambitions in Jerusalem and preparing it for official annexation to Jordan.

To strengthen relations between Palestine and Jordan, King Abdullah increased his visits to Palestine and especially to Jerusalem where he prayed, gave sermons on the Temple Mount and met

Palestinian notables from Nablus, Hebron, Ramallah and other towns. The visits were arranged by al-Tall who accompanied King Abdullah on all his meeting and tours in the area. During a visit on 15 November 1948, King Abdullah made a speech in the Coptic Church in the Old City and declared himself "King of Palestine".[110] Other heads of the Hashemite regime also made visits, including General Glubb Pasha and the Defense Minister Fauzi al-Mulqi, who were also accompanied by al-Tall.

The political backup which the Hashemite regime gave al-Tall in Jordan helped him to continue the process of rehabilitating the city – a process he had started with Ahmad Hilmi the former Military Governor of Jerusalem during the first truce in June 1948. Al-Tall expressed his concern for the city's residents when appointed governor of Jerusalem in an announcement made to the residents on 1 October 1948: "I am not turning to you as a governor, but as a friend, who is aware of your sufferings and will try and remove that suffering from you . . . I am one of you and I work for you".[111] Thanks to al-Tall's good relationship with King Abdullah, large sums of money were transferred from Amman to Jerusalem to invest in infrastructure and improve the town's administration. Al-Tall improved the tax system, lowering taxes to ease the burden on the population, and initiated public works to minimize unemployment among the residents of East Jerusalem.[112]

When UN involvement in solving the Arab–Israeli conflict began with the establishment of the Palestine Conciliation Commission (PCC), according to the UN resolution of 11 December 1948 (Resolution 194), al-Tall opposed Palestinian participation. The PCC was supposed to further armistice agreements between Arab states and Israel and achieve an overall peace. After discussions held in Tel Aviv, Jerusalem and a number of Arab capitals, the commission, led by the French representative Claude de Boisanger decided to assemble the Arab state representatives in mid-March 1949 in Beirut to hear their opinions about negotiations with Israel. About a week before the discussions started on 13 March 1949, al-Tall announced, while still loyal to the traditional Hashemite line, that "the Mufti is not qualified to speak in the name of the Palestinians" and stated strongly that "if the Mufti or someone on his behalf participates in these kinds of discussions Jordan will not participate".[113]

The meeting started on 21 March with the participation of Jordanian and Syrian prime ministers, Lebanese and Egyptian foreign ministers and representatives from Iraq and Saudi Arabia. Despite Jordan's opposition, under pressure from the Arab states and the UN, a Palestinian delegation (consisting of five representatives of the Mufti and headed by Dr. Hussein al-Khalidi, the minister of health in the All-Palestine Government) was eventually invited to attend. Al-Tall was kept informed about the decisions, including the statement that the Arab states accepted the partition resolution of November 1947 in principle, that Palestinian refugees were to return to Palestine, and that Jerusalem needed to remain an international city. On the eve of the first meeting on 20 March, he met with King Abdullah and confirmed their position should the Arabs demand the internationalization of Jerusalem. He also met with Jordanian Prime Minister Abu al-Huda and discussed the decisions. This would seem to indicate that there was a strong link between al-Tall and the Hashemite regime in Jordan including King Abdullah, despite al-Tall's claim at the time of being anti-Hashemite and pro-Palestinian.[114]

An Officer and a Gentleman: Abdullah al-Tall, Military Governor of Jerusalem

The appointment of al-Tall as military governor of Jerusalem constitutes a turning point in his political view of Israel. If earlier, while commander of the 6th Regiment, he thought the Jews could be defeated and all Jerusalem conquered, after assuming the role of military governor of Jerusalem not only did he understand that Israel could not be defeated, but he was willing to come to a political arrangement with Israel to assure his rule of the Old City of Jerusalem. A series of friendly meetings started between him and the Israeli commander of Jerusalem, Moshe Dayan, who was impressed by al-Tall and saw him "as being far superior to the other Arab officers and political functionaries" Dayan had so far encountered.[115] It is quite possible that Israel saw al-Tall as a worthy partner because he showed little sympathy for the British and was therefore seen as independent in the eyes of the Israelis, who thus felt that local agreements could be reached with him, without British intervention.[116]

Al-Tall was immediately liked not just by Israeli military commanders, but also by senior Israeli civilian leaders and especially by Israeli journalists who accompanied Dayan in his conversations with al-Tall and described him as "handsome and gentle". They immediately recognized a different type of Arab officer. Unlike other Arab commanders, al-Tall was always ready to meet with Israeli journalists and give them private interviews, where he spoke openly about the military situation in Jerusalem. Al-Tall conveyed optimism among his listeners about a forthcoming peace between the two states and expressed his hope that "the day won't be far when we could visit your Jerusalem and you could visit ours".[117] He was seen by Israeli journalists as an officer and a gentleman with personal good-will and great human sensitivity as well as having good intentions to help the Jews solve their problems. "One time, al-Tall agreed on sending a special messenger to my house in Nahalat Shimon (near the Sheikh Jarah quarter), which had been abandoned at the beginning of the war, to go and get my private documents and bags that I had left at home," wrote Israeli journalist Yona Cohen describing the assistance he received from al-Tall during the war.[118]

The first in a series of meetings between Dayan and al-Tall was held on 28 November 1948 under the mediation of the UN representative in Jerusalem, Colonel Roger T. Carlson, and its objective was to maintain the truce in Jerusalem. During the meeting, it was apparent that they could talk directly with each other and work out their problems without the need for UN intervention. It seems there was "chemistry" between the two men as well as mutual trust and respect, so they decided to hold a meeting without a UN presence, the first in the 1948 war. At the end of the first meeting, it was decided that both would maintain the truce in Jerusalem and expand it to include the entire Jerusalem sector. On 30 November two days later, at Government House in the presence of the UN Consular Committee, the two commanders signed a "complete and sincere ceasefire" agreement which would come into effect on 1 December at 06:00. Dayan signed on behalf of Israel and al-Tall signed in the name of the Jordanian forces "and all other Arab forces in the Jerusalem area", namely, the Egyptian and irregular troops. Attached to the agreement was a map marking the ceasefire lines and the no-man's land between.[119]

The good relations between Dayan and al-Tall kept the sector peaceful. Once the "complete and sincere ceasefire" had been signed, Israeli convoys sent to the demilitarized Mount Scopus were unharmed. It was decided to expand the agreement to the Latrun sector and allow free movement for Israelis on the Tel Aviv-Jerusalem road. Other issues were to be discussed, for example the return of the Jewish Quarter in the Old City in exchange for the Qatamon quarter, which had been captured by the Haganah in April 1948.[120] Relations between the two commanders became closer and led them to waive UN mediation and set up a direct telephone line between them. This took place on 7 December, but its importance went beyond the military aspect. The two commanders also used the direct telephone line to arrange political meetings for their governments' representatives and the atmosphere remained positive.[121]

An example of the strengthening relations between al-Tall and Dayan in particular and Israelis in general can be seen in al-Tall's stand during the battle between the IDF and the Egyptian army at the end of 1948. On 15 October, IDF forces launched Operation *Yoav* against the Egyptian army in the south to repel it from Palestine. To finalize the campaign, the IDF launched another operation in December, Operation *Horev*, which led to the end of the war with the Egyptian army in January 1949. In his book, al-Tall claimed that the battles against the Egyptians were the result of a conspiracy between Israel and Jordan to assure the Arab Legion's neutrality while Israel was preparing an attack against the Egyptians. However, in conversations behind closed doors, al-Tall supported the Israelis.[122]

Undoubtedly the conspiracy claim brought by al-Tall in the 1950s after coming into conflict with King Abdullah was intended to accuse King Abdullah of conspiring in Egypt's military defeat so that Abdullah could consolidate his political influence in Palestine. This was indeed true but also because of Egyptian support of the All-Palestine Government.[123] However, the interesting point is that al-Tall was the one who was involved in a conspiracy: he secretly supported Israel. On the eve of Operation *Horev* in December 1948, Elias (Eliyahu) Sasson, the head of the Middle East Department in the Israeli Foreign Ministry, went to al-Tall and asked him what his position would be given the imminent attack on the Egyptian army. He was very clear: "Hit the Egyptians as hard as you can, our relationship would definitely be neutral".[124]

His response not only represented the Hashemite regime in Jordan (militarily and politically), but was also the result of the relationship which had developed between him and the Israelis. However, it is clear that if the Israelis had not been sure of him, they would not have asked his position on the eve of the military operation they were preparing against the Egyptian army. It seems that al-Tall feared his contact with the Jews would be exposed and damage his standing with the Arab world. He therefore requested the Israeli journalists not to praise him: "Write against me – any writing in favor of me – damages me", said al-Tall.[125] Dayan also admitted that from time to time, al-Tall would ask him to persuade the editors of the Israeli newspaper, *The Palestine Post*, to publish articles attacking him and his relations with Israel in order to preserve his good name in Jordan. One of these articles, written at al-Tall's request, appeared on 26 December 1948 under the headline "The Arabs are ready to fight for Jerusalem and clean the town of its 100,000 Jews", attacking al-Tall's allegedly radical policy.[126]

Whether it was a conspiracy or not, it is obvious that IDF operations against the Egyptians allowed the Arab Legion to advance south towards the Hebron and Bethlehem areas in order to seize Egyptian military posts which had been abandoned following earlier IDF actions. This took place on 22 October with a Legion force of up to 350 soldiers under the command of Jeffrey Lockett. Israel opposed neither the Legion forces' movement nor their establishment in those areas in return for Arab Legion neutrality when Israel fought the Egyptians.[127]

The "complete and sincere ceasefire" established throughout Jerusalem encouraged Dayan and al-Tall to continue their meetings to expand it and discuss issues arising from the second ceasefire. On 5 December, the two commanders convened along with UN overseers in the no-man's land near the Notre Dame Monastery. At the meeting, al-Tall showed a willingness to evacuate part of Latrun to allow the establishment of a mixed Jordanian and Israeli police station, in return for Israel allowing the return of the Lydda and Ramle refugees. However, Dayan's answer was negative because Ben-Gurion opposed the return of refugees to the two cities. They tried to reach an understanding on issues apart from Jerusalem, including for instance the resumption of work in the Naharayim and Dead Sea factories which had stopped when the Arab Legion captured them at the beginning of the war.[128]

A Secret Messenger: Abdullah al-Tall's Part in Talks with Israel

In February 1949, the new UN mediator Dr. Ralph Bunch officially started negotiations with the Arab states and Israel to reach an armistice agreement. Israel and the Arab states accepted the offer and sent representatives to talks in the Hotel de Roses in Rhodes. On 28 February 1949, the Jordanian delegation arrived, led by Colonel Ahmad Sidqi al-Jundi and Lieutenant Colonel Muhammad al-Muaita, the commander of the 6th Regiment which operated in Jerusalem. The Israeli delegation was led by Reuven Shiloah, the Foreign Ministry representative and Moshe Dayan, the Israeli commander of Jerusalem. Other delegates included the Arab Legion's junior officers and lawyers.[129] The fact that both the Israeli and the Jordanian commanders of Jerusalem attended demonstrated the city's importance to both sides and the possibility of political disputes over that city.

In fact, prior to Bunch's official invitation, the two governments had begun to renew contact in August 1948 through their European representatives. At the beginning of August, Sasson met in Paris with Abd al-Majid Hayder, the Jordanian ambassador to London, who was carrying a private message from King Abdullah. It is quite possible that his mission was arranged by the British who wanted an understanding between the two states to be reached. In those meetings, they discussed current issues on the agenda, including borders, the status of Jerusalem, and the Palestinian refugee problem.[130] Despite the meetings with Hayder being stopped shortly after they began because of Israeli press leaks, the two governments continued to make contact with senior Jordanian officials, including Abd al-Ghani al-Karmi, a royal court official, and King Abdullah's private physician, Dr. Shaukat Aziz al-Sati.[131] Al-Sati met with Dayan and Shiloah in no-man's land near Jaffa Gate on 25 December and discussed the possibility of achieving a permanent peace between the two states. At the same time, the two states tried to make contact through the Belgian Consul, Jean Nieuwenhuys, which was also unsuccessful because of press leaks.[132]

While it can be said that none of the meetings which took place at the end of 1948 had any significant results, apparently because of the disagreement between the two governments (over refugees, Jerusalem and more), there was opposition to talks with Israel inside Jordan from both the Jordanian government and the British. The Jordanian Prime Minister, Abu al-Huda, refused to take any part in negotiations with Israel. Although King Abdullah claimed that he did not take Jordanian government opinion into consideration because he could "replace it with the stroke of a pen", Abdullah did not negotiate because of the high regard in which Abu al-Huda was held by the Jordanian public and his influence with them. The British wanted to end the war in Palestine, but opposed Jordanian–Israeli negotiations for political reasons. According to Kirkbride, the British viewed negotiations that did not include all the Arab countries as weakening the King's position in Jordan as well as in the Arab world in general.[133]

From the beginning of January 1949, political negotiations between the two states increased and al-Tall and Dayan played a bigger part. On 1 January 1949 King Abdullah officially nominated al-Tall to negotiate with Israel, "I hereby empower you to have talks with the Israeli side on the basis that there is a will to reach a mutual understanding, in order to eliminate any difficulties which may appear in the future during the official negotiations . . . ". The next day Dayan was appointed by the Israeli government, authorizing him together with Reuven Shiloah to negotiate with the Jordanian government for the purpose of "establishing peaceful relations between the state of Israel and the Trans-Jordan Kingdom".[134]

They met for general talks on 3 January at the Mandelbaum Gate (the crossing-point between Israel and Jordan near the Sheikh Jarah quarter), where they discussed the secret authorization for negotiations, and decided to meet again on 14 January to discuss the "bones of contention" between the two states. King Abdullah wanted the Negev so that he could have an overland bridge to Egypt and also asked for Gaza as an outlet to the Mediterranean. Israel demanded the release of Israeli prisoners from the prisoner-of-war camp in Mafraq.[135] At the time, Jordan was holding 679 Israeli prisoners, only some of whom were soldiers; most were Israeli civilians captured during the Legion actions in the area of Etzion Bloc, the Jewish Quarter in the Old City in Jerusalem, and Kibbutz Gezer. More Israeli prisoners were captured by the Iraqi military in Gesher.

The talks between al-Tall and Dayan ended without any resolution and King Abdullah decided to take matters into his own hands. He ordered al-Tall to secretly invite Dayan to his winter palace in Shuna to talk with him directly about the controversial issues. Accordingly, Al-Tall drove Dayan and Elias Sasson (a Syrian native and Israeli Foreign Ministry official who spoke fluent Arabic) to the King's palace where they met on 16 January 1949. The road to the palace was dangerous, not only for the two Israelis, but also for al-Tall himself. Although the two Israelis presented themselves to the Arab Legion soldiers as Jordanians, and roadblocks would seldom stop al-Tall's car, if it were discovered that al-Tall was driving Israelis in his car, he would be assassinated immediately.[136]

Dayan and Sasson enjoyed truly royal hospitality. After a series of salutations and formulaic expressions of interest by King Abdullah in the welfare of the Israeli leaders (Prime Minister Ben-Gurion and President Chaim Weizmann), the guests played chess with the King. "It was obligatory not only to lose to the King, but also to show surprise at his unexpected moves," reported Dayan.[137] The discussion of important issues took place after dinner where the men dined at the King's table accompanied by his private adjutant, Hashem Dabasi, and his private physician, Dr. al-Sati. Although the King told the Israelis that he intended to make peace with them, he insisted that the armistice agreement be signed together with the other the Arab states under UN supervision in Rhodes.[138]

From Israel's point of view, the meeting with King Abdullah was not particularly productive and Dayan was reluctant to meet again. However, pressure on him, both from al-Tall and the Israeli government (to ensure the release of Israeli prisoners from Jordan) brought Dayan to agree to meet with King Abdullah again. The second meeting took place on 30 January and was once again arranged by al-Tall. The objective was to discuss the prisoners' exchange. According to Dayan's biography, Elias Sasson played a significant part in securing the release of Israeli prisoners from Jordan. Knowing Arab traditions well and a fluent Arabic speaker, Sasson decided to act as was customary in the Middle East. Throughout the visit, Sasson avoided raising the issue and only at the moment of departure, did he hug King Abdullah and grab his sash. Sash grabbing is a time-honored custom among Bedouin Sheikhs. When it occurs, the host must consent to any request. The King raised his hand and pleaded with Sasson to ask only for something it was possible for him to grant. Sasson then brought up the issue of the Israeli prisoners in Jordan. The King expressed surprise and asked al-Tall why he had not yet released the prisoners. "I order you to return all prisoners to them as soon as possible," said the King to al-Tall, who had earlier played a part in releasing Jewish women from the prisoner of war camp in Jordan.[139]

The arrangements for returning the Israeli prisoners were made that night, while al-Tall was taking the Israeli guests back from the palace to Jerusalem. Al-Tall decided to proceed immediately. From 3 February to 3 March, all 679 Israeli prisoners who were in the prisoner-of-war camp in Jordan were released in five groups via the

Mandelbaum Gate. In return, Israel released all Arab prisoners to Jordan, including those from other states, which King Abdullah was prepared to agree to in order to improve his political position in the Arab world.[140]

The day after all the prisoners were returned to Israel, an official negotiation on the armistice agreement was held in Rhodes as King Abdullah had demanded. Al-Jundi and al-Muaita led the Jordanian delegation and Dayan and Shiloah the Israeli delegation. Al-Tall was not included as a Jordanian delegate, despite his links with the Israelis, his proficiency in the negotiation details, and his being very close to Dayan, who was a member of the Israeli delegation. There is no doubt that the friendship between the two commanders (Dayan and al-Tall) could have contributed to the discussion's success in Rhodes and shortened the negotiations.

According to al-Tall, although many people expected him to be included in the Jordanian delegation in Rhodes, he avoided it because he assumed the negotiation would end in failure.[141] It is difficult to believe that al-Tall, who met Dayan many times, knew him well and knew how to resolve problems with him, feared that the negotiation in Rhodes would fail. There would seem to be a different reason. It is possible that King Abdullah preferred to keep al-Tall close so that he could be used as a special messenger for secret talks with Israel (which for him were more important and constructive than the ones held in Rhodes under the spotlight with UN supervision).

The first meeting at the Hotel de Roses in Rhodes was held on 4 March at 4:30 p.m. and at there was a minor diplomatic crisis on the first day. The Jordanian head of delegation, Ahmad Sidqi al-Jundi, who opposed earlier agreements, sat in his chair and refused to stand up and shake the hand of the Israeli delegation head, Reuven Shiloah. Shiloah was hurt and told Bunch that he would not continue the talks if the Jordanians behaved in that way. The Israeli Foreign Minister, Moshe Shertok (Sharett), supported Shiloah's position and sent an urgent telegram to Bunch, stating: "If the Jordanians continue to behave in this boorish manner, we shall end the negotiations and announce that they will be renewed only after we are satisfied that they have learned the elementary lessons in civilized deportment". Eventually, it transpired that there had been a misunderstanding and the Jordanians had no bad intentions. Al-Jundi apologized and explained that the handshake would be given at the end of the meeting.[142]

The beginning of the discussions was difficult. Despite preliminary contact between King Abdullah and Israeli officials, the disagreements remained and neither party was willing to compromise. Israel demanded the opening of the road leading from Tel Aviv to Jerusalem, the flow of water to Jerusalem from the Ras al-Ain pumping station which had been blown up by the Palestinian on 12 August, and the activation of the Latrun pumping station. Inside Jerusalem, Israel demanded the opening of the road to Mount Scopus, which remained demilitarized, and the renewal of the activities of the two Israeli institutions (Hadassah Hospital and the Hebrew University), as well as free access to the Wailing Wall. The Jordanians demanded the return of Arab refugees to both cities, Lydda and Ramle, the return to Arab Legion control there, the use of Haifa port, the opening of the Jerusalem-Bethlehem road which was under IDF control, and the return of some Arab quarters in Jerusalem which IDF forces had conquered during the war.

However, the main bone of contention was the issue of control of the Negev. The Jordanians demanded the area, even though according to the partition plan it was included in the territory of the Jewish state. In order to present Jordan with a *fait accompli* concerning the Negev, Israel decided to prepare a quick military operation to conquer the Negev despite the political discussions being held between both states. Ben-Gurion claimed he decided to risk a military confrontation between IDF forces and the Arab Legion because of the Negev's importance.[143]

The plan to conquer the Negev, known as Operation *Uvda (fait accompli)*, began on the morning of 5 March 1949 when the Negev Brigade's advance force set out from Beersheba to the Uja al-Hafir (Nizana) road. At the same time, the eastern column of the Golani Brigade set out towards Ein Husub escorted by an air force plane. The Negev Brigade's advance force passed Ras Al-Ruman and reached Abraham airport. There it joined with a company of Special Forces. The Golani Brigade, which had reached Ein Husub on 7 March, left for Ein al-Wiba and took control of it after the Legion platoon had abandoned it earlier. At the same time, the Alexandroni Brigade set out for Ein Husub in the north to capture Ein Gedi and the southern hilly Hebron area. The next day, on 8 March, the Golani Brigade continued to move south and by evening reached Bir Maliha where they stayed for the night. The following day, the force continued and captured Gharandal and Mount Katura. On the afternoon of 10 March, a Negev Brigade advance force arrived at the abandoned police station in Um Rashrash (Eilat), and two hours later the Golani Brigade also arrived.[144]

The operation stunned the Arabs, particularly the Jordanians. Jordan officially protested to Bunch that Israel had violated the truce and crossed the international border between the two states. However, Bunch claimed that after investigation, it was clear that all the Israeli military operations were executed inside Israeli territory and therefore he did not see it as a problem. Moreover, Bunch determined that the IDF had taken the Legion's posts in the Negev, and in Um Rashrash, not by fighting but only after Legion forces had evacuated them.[145] As a result of Operation *Uvda*, al-Tall demanded that the political process with Israel be speeded up and the armistice agreement be signed as quickly as possible. He believed that if Jordan signed such an agreement with Israel quickly, it could regain some of the areas captured by Israel during the operation. However, Israel refused to give back the conquered areas and Jordan had no option but to concede.[146]

On 11 March 1949, one day after the Um Rashrash conquest, the Israeli government was informed by intelligence sources that the Iraqi government had decided to withdraw from the Triangle (the three Arab cities: Tulkarm, Nablus and Jenin) – the area it had controlled since the Arab armies had invaded Palestine on 15 May, 1948 – and hand it over to the Arab Legion within 15 days. On 15 March, Israel sent Bunch an official protest concerning Iraqi's intention and notified him that Israel would view the handover of territory as a violation of the truce by Jordan. A message, or rather a warning, was carried the same day to King Abdullah by the director general of the Israeli Foreign Ministry, Walter Eytan, also stating that Israel would not accept the Iraqi move, but also that despite that Israel was willing to discuss the future of this area with King Abdullah. After Operation *Uvda* the full extent of Israel's power was unclear and there was no doubt that the King feared further Israeli military action. Therefore, he informed the Israeli government that he welcomed negotiations on this issue, separate from the negotiations in Rhodes.[147]

On 18 March, at 6:30 p.m., after Dayan's return from Rhodes, he met with al-Tall in Jerusalem and this time the conversation was short. Tension between the two commanders was high. Dayan made it unequivocally clear to al-Tall that if the Arab Legion took the territory when the Iraqi army withdrew, Israel wanted Wadi Ara, south of Haifa and the hills which controlled both the wadi (dry water course) and the narrow coastal plain. Al-Tall replied that this concession was not possible because of both Jordanian public opinion and the stand taken by the Iraqis. "So", said Dayan "fighting there would be renewed". That day, al-Tall went to meet Abdullah in his winter palace at Shuna to inform him, but King Abdullah wanted to hear the demand directly from the Israelis.[148]

On the evening of 19 March, Dayan and Captain Yehoshafat Harkabi went to see King Abdullah at his palace. Dayan repeated his demand for Wadi Ara in return for Israeli agreement for the Jordanians to take the Iraqi frontier. According to Glubb Pasha, Dayan threatened that if his demand was not accepted, Israel would act with force against the Arab Legion in Palestine. King Abdullah found it difficult to come to a decision and therefore the Israelis decided to let him discuss the issue with his ministers. That same night, King Abdullah sent al-Tall to the prime minister, Abu al-Huda, who was then staying in Beirut, to inform him of the talks with the Israelis and elicit his opinion. The next day, a new version of the Israeli demands was presented that made the King's decision easier. As a gesture of good will, Israel agreed to Arab Legion control of not only the Iraqi frontier, but also territories Israel held: Israel was willing to withdraw from the western and southern hills of Hebron on condition that Jordan allowed Israel control over Wadi Ara. King Abdullah accepted the Israeli terms.[149]

Discussions about the Iraqi frontier and the ramifications of the new Jordanian–Israeli border were held between the Israeli and Jordanian delegations in Jerusalem at the Mandelbaum Gate on the night of 22–23 March. The following night, a meeting was held at King Abdullah's palace where timings for the evacuation of the Arab Legion, stationed east of Wadi Ara, and the arrival of IDF soldiers in the area were discussed. It was decided that the Arab Legion evacuation would take about 15 weeks. It was also decided that the Arab Legion would control abandoned Iraqi army posts only after an armistice agreement between Jordan and Israel had been signed.[150]

It is clear that the agreement reached by the two parties, which showed considerable good will on the part of the Israelis, was mainly the result of King Abdullah's fears that Israel would renew hostilities against the Arab Legion. The Israeli threat to use military force expressed Israel's military superiority of which King Abdullah and General Glubb Pasha were well aware. Behind closed doors, Glubb Pasha confessed to Prime Minister Abu al-Huda that the Arab Legion could not hope to win against the IDF in case of an attack.[151]

Indeed, King Abdullah and Glubb Pasha's fears of an Israeli operation were well-based. From 15 March 1949, Ben-Gurion started to talk about a military action against Jordan if they did not agree to the border adjustments.[152] As a result, IDF HQ prepared a military operation to occupy parts of the Triangle (Operation *Shen Tahat Shen* "Tooth for a Tooth"), which was in fact limited. However, some Israeli generals, including Yigal Alon, commander of the southern front, aspired to take advantage of the political disagreement with Jordan and expand Israeli control to the entire West Bank. Alon held talks with Prime Minister David Ben-Gurion, Foreign Minister Moshe Shertok, Chief of Staff Yaakov Dostrovsky (Dori), and head of the operations branch, Yigael Sukenik and tried to convince them to stall the talks with Jordan to enable the IDF to occupy the West Bank. However, Ben-Gurion was opposed to this plan and cancelled it after both sides reached an agreement. His ambition was to maintain good relations with Jordan and especially with King Abdullah, which might yield a peace agreement with Israel in the future.[153]

After the agreement about exchanging territories between Israel and Jordan was reached, a few issues were still outstanding for discussion at the armistice signing in Rhodes including free access to the Wailing Wall, convoys to Mount Scopus and delineating the demilitarized territories. Discussions were held in the King's palace at Shuna on 25 March 1949 with Israeli and Jordanian officials. Under King Abdullah's guidance, the two delegations discussed these issues and did not to stop until an understanding was reached. Only by the following morning did the Jordanians and Israelis succeed in agreeing which truce lines in the Jerusalem area would be used as the borders between the two states, agreeing that the Tel Aviv-Jerusalem road would remain open, granting free access to the Wailing Wall, and permitting Israel to use the two institutions on Mount Scopus, Hadassah Hospital and the Hebrew University. It was also decided that Israel would get Wadi Ara and in return, Israel would allow the Arab Legion to control important areas in the southern hills of Hebron. In addition, Israel and Jordan decided to partition Jerusalem instead of Jerusalem becoming internationalized.

Before the two delegations parted, Walter Eytan handed King Abdullah a gift from Ben-Gurion – a silver-bound Bible. The King gave each one of the Israeli delegates a rose.[154] An armistice between the two states was signed on 3 April 1949. Ahmad Sidqi al-Jundi and Muhammad al-Muaita signed the agreement for the Jordanian side and Shiloah and Dayan signed for the Israelis.[155]

The contribution made by the Israeli and Jordanian commanders, Dayan and al-Tall, to the armistice was great. Despite the fact that both of them were military officers who had fought on opposite sides, they both had outstanding diplomatic skills, as well as the far-reaching vision and understanding needed to reach the necessary compromise. King Abdullah did not have much of a choice after he was made aware of Israel's military power. He had to demonstrate an understanding of Israel's needs, while Israel in turn acknowledged the importance of the political channel with King Abdullah – the only Arab leader who had entertained an official Israeli delegation – thereby showing great political sensitivity. However, more than that, it seems that the shared desire of both parties to bring an end to the lengthy fighting between them and the shared hope of a better future is what eventually brought about the armistice. This can be seen from King Abdullah's declaration at his meeting with the Israeli delegation on the eve of the armistice: "Tonight we have ended the war and brought peace".[156]

3

The Assassination of King Abdullah

The 1948 war brought significant changes in the Middle East and caused political shocks in Arab countries. Not only did the invasion of Palestine by Arab armies on 15 May 1948 not result in the destruction of Israel, but after the invasion Israel controlled additional territories which had been designated as part of an Arab country according to the UN Partition Plan. Amongst these were the western Galilee, Lydda, Ramle, and the cities along the coast, such as Isdud (Ashdod) and al-Majdal (Ashkelon). Thus, at the end of the war Israel found itself in control of 78% of the territory of Mandatory Palestine instead of the 56% allocated according to the UN Partition Plan. Moreover, upon Israel's signing of the armistice with Arab countries mediated by the UN (Egypt: 24 February 1949, Lebanon: 23 March 1949, Jordan: 3 April 1949 and Syria: 20 July 1949), the borders of Israel with its neighbors were recognized as the official international borders (the Green Line), which were valid until the outbreak of the Six Day War on 5 June 1967. Israel received international recognition when it joined the UN about a year after its declaration of independence on 11 May 1949.[1]

The situation in the Arab states was serious. The war left about 726,000 Palestinian refugees, scattered in several Arab countries without any property.[2] Jordan granted the refugees full rights, but the other Arab countries avoided doing so. They were not granted political status, their movements were limited solely to the refugee camp, and all rights were revoked, including the right to employment. Thus, the Palestinian refugees suffered major financial difficulties and became dependent on charity from international organizations which were set up for them and led by the UN.[3] The UN's involvement began in July 1948 while Bernadotte was trying to establish a truce and it continued with the establishment of the United Nations Relief for Palestine Refugees (UNRPR) on 9

December 1948, which a year later became the United Nations Relief and Works Agency (UNRWA), "to carry out . . . direct relief and works programs for [Palestine refugees]".[4]

However, the lack of cooperation between the leaders of the Arab countries and the heads of the UN's aid organizations prevented the success of the social-financial projects suggested by the UN and the efforts to resolve the Palestinian refugees' problem because "the Arab governments and the refugees treated the program with suspicion", claimed UNRWA manager John Blandford in the report he sent to the UN in late 1950.[5] Furthermore, the desire of the Arab states to maintain the situation "as a powerful political and propaganda tool against Israel" as well as the lack of interest on the Arab leaders' part, as Kirkbride claimed, made it difficult to find a proper solution to the refugee problem.[6]

Though militarily defeated, the importance of the army in the eyes of the Arab population grew. The military and political downfall in Palestine alerted Palestinians to the weakness of their regime in facing up to the Jews and this brought about a movement within the officers cadre to devise ways to make amends.[7] Reasoning that the army was but a mere function of Arab society, as Eliezer Be'eri claimed in his book *Army Officers in Arab Politics and Society*, the population blamed their political leaders, rather than the military, for negligence in the handling of the war. "The Syrian army was sent into the battlefield without proper equipment . . . ", wrote Dr. Adib Nassur on 27 March 1949 in the *Alif-Ba* newspaper in Damascus and continued: "I write these lines so that the officers and men may know that in these bitter days the thoughts of many Syrian citizens turn to the army".[8] Also, criticism began to spread from Egyptian officers on the actions of King Farouk and his war minister, Muhammad Hayder, who were held accountable for the defeat in the 1948 war. In his book, Gamal Abd al-Nasser wrote on the war: "[they] tricked us . . . pushed us to fight unprepared. Different ambitious plots determined our fate. We are stranded here without weapons under fire".[9]

There is no doubt that articles published in the Arab press, denouncing the Arab leaders for failing the Arab public, led to the emergence of revolutionary movements in the Arab states shortly after the end of the war. One example of this was the Free Officers movement, which carried out a coup in Egypt in July 1952 removing King Farouk from rule.

Another example was a coup in Syria in the aftermath of the 1948 war. On 30 March 1949, before Syria signed an armistice with Israel, the Syrian Chief of Staff, Husni Zaim with the assistance of several officers organized a coup, seizing power after imprisoning the President, Shukri al-Quwatli, and the Prime Minister, Khalid al-Azm, in their homes. The coup, intended "to prepare the ground for true democratic government" according to Zaim, quickly evolved into a military dictatorship and then into a Zaim-dictatorship. At the beginning of April, parliament was dispersed and all legislative and governmental authority was concentrated in Zaim's hands. Shortly after, Husni Zaim held a referendum which affirmed his candidacy for the presidency. He was the only candidate and 99% of the population voted for him. After 137 days of Zaim's rule, on 14 August 1949, another coup was led by General Sami Hilmy al-Hinnawi who took control of the country and executed Zaim.[10]

Though Zaim's regime was short, the coup he led had great significance in the Arab world at the time. He was an inspiration and a role model for those officers looking for a solution to the problems in their countries. They saw that a failing regime could be replaced by the military while enjoying the backing of the local populace and that, for them, it could be a good alternative to a civilian regime.

Abdullah al-Tall and Prince Talal: A Plot to Seize Control

Al-Tall's objection to the British in general and to the Arab Legion's commander General Glubb Pasha in particular, which developed towards the end of the 1948 war, led him to consider a coup-d'état in Jordan. Encouraged by Zaim's example, al-Tall wanted to seize power in Jordan. However, as an experienced military man al-Tall knew that he had to prepare the foundations for the coup well and plan for the aftermath. He devised his plot in great detail. He consulted with a number of Arab officers at the beginning of 1949 to receive their supporrt and convened with a number of Jordanian officers, including Ali Abu Nuwar and Mahmud al-Musa.[11] There is no evidence that these two officers took part in the coup, even though it is known that they both later conspired against the Hashemite regime, they also escaped from Jordan. If they had been part of the plot against the Hashemite regime, as al-Tall claims, it is likely that they would have been uncovered along with the other conspirators, including al-Tall himself, thanks to the quality of Jordanian intelligence at the time.[12]

But Abdullah al-Tall knew that without the assistance of an additional country he would not be able to carry out the coup. Zaim himself executed the coup in Syria only after he had received support from the USA and Britain, seeking to create a powerful regime in Syria in order to prevent a Soviet foothold in the country.[13] Being anti-British, al-Tall would not seek assistance from these two states; Syria was the only country available to him. Al-Tall agreed with Zaim's subsequent opposition to Britain and thus the relations which developed between the two seems logical, as does the assistance which Zaim gave al-Tall in carrying out the coup, for example, infiltrating Syrian agents into Jordan to disrupt the latter's stability and bring down the existing regime.[14]

On 8 April 1949 al-Tall secretly met with Prince Talal, the eldest son of King Abdullah, to update him on the details of the coup. Talal was popular among the Arab nations because he was also anti-British and opposed his father's policies. It was deemed appropriate that he should lead the coup and seize control afterwards. According to the plan, King Abdullah would be removed as the King of Jordan for his pro-British policy, but rather than being killed he would be exiled to Syria. General Glubb Pasha and the rest of the British officers would be arrested in the Arab Legion's HQ in Amman and would be expelled from the country. Talal would take control of Jordan and cooperate with the Arab officers headed by al-Tall. When Britain withdrew its support, Egypt and Syria – the coup supporters – would grant assistance instead.[15]

Delays in planning the coup in Jordan caused it to fail. On 14 August 1949 after the second coup in Syria, Zaim was executed. The new leader in Syria, General Sami al-Hinnawi, supported the Hashemite family's political ambitions to annex Syria to Iraq and was pro-British. He therefore opposed the coup against King Abdullah. The intelligence services in Jordan exposed the conspiracy and al-Tall's part in it.[16]

It is worth noting that unlike the myth that has developed since, the planned coup was not about causing the collapse of the Hashemite regime in Jordan, rather it was intended to hit the British first and foremost thereby realizing al-Tall's ambitions to take a more important role in the Arab Legion. The only connection between al-Tall, Zaim and Prince Talal was their mutual hatred of Britain. As long as King Abdullah ruled Jordan, his pro-British policy would not change. Moreover, al-Tall assumed that the fact that British officers held all the high ranking posts in the

Arab Legion, was preventing him and his fellow officers from being promoted. He felt he had to take action in order to remove British officers from command as this was the only way he would be able to take a more significant role in commanding the Arab Legion.

Indeed, al-Tall's relations with the commander of the Arab Legion, General Glubb Pasha, whom he regarded as the representative of British imperialism in Jordan, worsened during the first half of 1949. The establishment of the first branch in the West Bank of the *Ba'ath* (the resurrection) party in March 1949 generated a lot of enthusiasm among its Palestinian adherents. Its ideology of unity, liberation and socialism attracted numerous young people.[17] The party expressed the state of mind of many in the Arab world in the aftermath of the 1948 war, that is, solidarity with the Palestinian problem, Arab unity for a war against Israel, and fighting British imperialism in the Middle East.[18]

Al-Tall, like other young Jordanians, drew closer to the *Ba'ath* party because it expressed his views. As in other Arab states (mainly Syria and Iraq) the party recruited young officers, ideologists, and nationalists, hoping that many would later lead a coup in the Arab world.[19] Al-Tall used his links with the three party leaders in Jerusalem, Abdullah al-Rimawi, Abdullah Nawas and Bahjat Abu Gharbiyah, and their involvement in the city's politics, to help fortify his position. That same month (March 1949) he allowed the party members to publish the newspaper *al-Ba'ath* which criticized the old order in the Arab world and demanded unity, modernization, and social and economic reforms as vital steps toward another war against Israel.[20]

However, his links with the party members, including followers of the ex-Mufti of Jerusalem Hajj Amin al-Husayni and those who opposed the Hashemite regime, cast suspicion on his loyalty to King Abdullah. He developed an especially close relationship with Dr. Subhi Abu Ghanima, also a citizen of Irbid. He had been deported by the Jordanian authorities to Syria during the Second World War because of his support for the Axis countries. He established an underground cell in Damascus and spread Syrian propaganda against King Abdullah's "Greater Syria" plan.[21] In the eyes of the British it was wrong for al-Tall, a military officer, to be involved in politics. Glubb Pasha, having been educated in England was also opposed to this involvement in politics and tried to prevent it. Glubb Pasha ordered al-Tall to be removed from his position as governor of Jerusalem on 20 March 1949. He was replaced by Muhammad al-Muaita, commander of the 6th Regiment.[22]

Though al-Tall remained in the Arab Legion, his authority was diminished, his aura as a military commander was fading and his hostility towards Glubb increased. These could be considered grounds for al-Tall's attempted coup a few days later.

Contrary to Glubb's assumption, and apparently to that of King Abdullah as well, that al-Tall would get the hint and cease his revolutionary efforts, the result was just the opposite. Not only did al-Tall not sever his ties to the oppositionist *Ba'ath* members, he strengthened them. In March 1949, a book entitled *Ibrat Filastin* (*The Lesson of Palestine*) by Musa al-Alami, an Arab intellectual figure and the Palestinian representative in the Arab League, was published in Beirut. Not only did the book criticize the Arab regimes, as many other Arab intellectuals did, it also called for the elimination of the old social-political order and the cultivation of a new Arab generation that would rescue the Arab nations from their distress. "There must . . . be complete modernization in every aspect of Arab life . . . ", wrote al-Alami; he continued, "should the government be republican or monarchical? This is not important . . . What is important is the foundation: its effectiveness and the excellence of its ends.[23] The book was widely published and was followed by increasing criticism by *Ba'ath* members – al-Tall's friends – of the Arab regimes and also of King Abdullah. "I see that heads have grown enough and it is time to pick them", appeared in *al-Ba'ath* newspaper as a call to replace the Hashemite regime in Jordan. It was then that al-Tall decided to openly and unequivocally oppose King Abdullah and the Hashemite regime.[24] He had obviously been influenced by al-Alami's book and saw himself as the leader of the revolution to bring a new order to Jordan and perhaps to the entire Arab world. He felt that only he, because of the praise he had received from the Arabs after the conquest of the Old City of Jerusalem, could lead the Arab world into another war against Israel.

A number of factors led to the Jordanian authorities ordering Abdullah al-Tall to close down the newspaper and arresting those people who were among the opposition[25] including the publication of critical articles in *al-Ba'ath* newspaper, demonstrations against the Hashemite regime, especially after the summer of 1949, when the Little Triangle (the area around Wadi Ara) was transferred to Israel, bringing about the partition of villages and the transfer of residents from one side of the border to the other, and opposition in Jerusalem to King Abdullah from municipal factions. However, al-Tall refused to shut down the newspaper, objecting that the orders were clear provocation by the Hashemite regime. Under al-Tall's sponsorship, the newspaper stayed in print and continued to criticise the Hashemite regime in Jordan; the number of members in the *Ba'ath* grew steadily. In May and June, criticism against the Hashemite regime also grew in the press published in the West Bank, and more demonstrations took place. One major demonstration took place on 7 May in Nablus, with 10,000 participants. The Jordanian authorities felt they were about to lose control over the West Bank and therefore decided to act swiftly to repress the demonstrations and punished the organizers heavily.[26]

On 6 June, al-Tall was removed from office as governor of Jerusalem and was offered the post of military attaché in the Jordanian embassy in London to replace Kamal Hamoud.[27] Al-Tall's dismissal was intended to distance him from the center of events and to cut his ties with opposition elements in Jordan. However, al-Tall refused to accept the position and declared "I have resigned and I am not taking any other government post".[28] Al-Tall did not want to be removed from the center of events and feared that his transfer to a distant position would foil the revolution and prevent him from realizing his ambitions; therefore he insisted on a position close by from which he could influence the course of events. The position of governor of Jerusalem was appointed by the general administrative governor of Jordan in Palestine, the former Justice Minister, Falah al-Madadha, who had transferred his office from Ramallah to Jerusalem.[29] On 14 August, al-Madadha was replaced by Raghib al-Nashashibi, the Mufti's rival, after King Abdullah suspected his disloyalty.[30]

In early July while he was waiting in Irbid for the meeting with General Glubb Pasha to hear about his new appointment, al-Tall was admitted to the military hospital in al-Salt with a liver complaint.[31] After his recovery, he met with Glubb. It was a decisive meeting and al-Tall's fate hung in the balance. Glubb requested that al-Tall stay in the Arab Legion and accept the position in London. Al-Tall demanded the rank of brigadier as a condition for staying in office. Glubb could not agree. Only a year had passed since al-Tall had been promoted to the rank of colonel, against Glubb's recommendation. His military promotion was too quick for Glubb, who may have feared its effect, and he therefore refused to grant al-Tall's request. This meeting paved the way for al-Tall's resignation from the Arab Legion on 26 July 1949.[32] The formal Jordanian declaration that Abdullah al-Tall had decided to resign from the Arab Legion "only because he was not promoted to the rank of Brigadier " is not true.[33] The reason for his resignation was the disappointment he felt over his failure to establish a group of supporters amongst the Arab revolutionary officers and also because he failed to establish his position in the Arab Legion sufficiently to lead a possible coup. Therefore, he had no choice but to resign from the Arab Legion and look for other possibilities.[34] It is also probable that some of al-Tall's family, who did not support King Abdullah's regime, especially his uncle poet Mustafa Wahabi al-Tall, encouraged al-Tall to resign and withdraw his support from the King.

The Jordanian authorities took advantage of al-Tall's resignation from the Arab Legion and immediately started a purge of al-Tall's supporters among the *Ba'ath* party members, many of whom were arrested, and the party was outlawed. *Al-Ba'ath* newspaper, which was the party's main vessel against the Hashemite regime, was shut down and its editors, al-Rimawi and Nawas, were arrested and sent to the detainee camp in Bair, near the Saudi Arabian border. Also, the oppositionist weekly *al-Jil al-Jadid* (The New Generation), published in Ramallah, was shut down and its editor, Kamal Nasser, was arrested. The newspapers' editors received a pardon two months later and were permitted to return to Palestine, but they were under the scrutiny by the Jordanian security service.[35]

After Al-Tall resigned from the Arab Legion, he was also under close scrutiny by Jordanian intelligence, which suspected him of intending to carry out a coup because he was in touch with opposition elements in the Arab Legion, and politicians in Jordan and in the West Bank. Among the people closest to al-Tall, was the lawyer Shafiq Rashidat, an Irbid delegate in the Jordanian parliament known for his anti-British sentiment and objection to Dif Allah al-Hamoud, the editor of the Jordanian weekly *al-Mithaq*, who had previously gathered around him a number of members of the opposition to King Abdullah and the British officer presence in the Arab Legion, especially General Glubb Pasha These oppositionists, after al-Tall's resignation from the Arab Legion in mid-1949, sought to establish a party named *Jabah al-Shabbab* (The Young Front), but the Jordanian ministry of internal affairs, suspecting that al-Tall was behind it and that the party represented his revolutionary stance towards King Abdullah, rejected their request. The highest-ranking figure in Jordan who maintained contact with al-Tall, even though he was under observation, was Prince Talal. On 18 August, King Abdullah went on a formal visit to Spain and Britain for about three weeks and he appointed his son Talal to replace him in his absence. During Abdullah's trip, Prince Talal attempted reconciliation with al-Tall. He invited him to meet several times to "make peace", but his efforts were fruitless.[36]

After al-Tall failed to seize power for the second time and realized he was under close observation by Jordanian intelligence, he knew that he could not continue to operate freely in Jordan. He decided to continue his revolutionary activity outside the state. Egypt had acted backstage to recruit him when he resigned from the Arab Legion. He was a young and ambitious officer, loved by the Arabs, which made him a political asset. Therefore, when al-Tall secretly visited Egypt in September 1949 (probably with the authorization of Prince Talal, while King Abdullah was absent from Jordan) he heard from the Egyptian Prime Minister, Hussein Siri Pasha, that he would be willing to grant him a monthly government salary if he moved to Cairo. Al-Tall was willing to accept, convinced that only in a country such as Egypt, which was opposed to the Hashemite regime in Jordan and where he would have the status of a political refugee, could he act freely to accomplish his ambitions – overthrowing King Abdullah's regime in Jordan. However, it is possible that he also had other intentions when he chose Egypt as a destination for political exile.[37] The Egyptian national movement had started to renew its fight for Egypt's independence from the British. It is possible that Abdullah al-Tall thought that because of his popularity and power in the Arab world, he could lead the revolt against the British, and thus over time gain control of the country. It is true that shortly after his arrival in Egypt he became a popular figure opposed to the Egyptian regime and the British.

On 5 October 1949, al-Tall secretly left Jordan for Syria and five days later he arrived in Cairo. Traveling with him was his wife, his mother and his brother, Muhammad Zaki.[38] In addition to a few individuals in Syria and Egypt and a few political activists (including Abdullah al-Rimawi), Prince Talal also knew about al-Tall's intention to defect. On the eve of his decision to flee Jordan, al-Tall had secretly met with Talal. Al-Tall claims that Talal supported his decision and told him that it was indeed "best to keep acting outside the country" in order to overthrow Abdullah's regime.[39]

In early November 1949, the Egyptian newspaper *Akhbar al-Youm* reported that al-Tall had defected to Egypt. Ties between the newspaper and al-Tall had been forged when al-Tall was in Damascus. According to rumors, the newspaper purchased the exclusive rights to publish his memoirs for 20,000 Egyptian pounds.[40] About two months later, in January 1950, al-Tall appeared in public in Cairo and began to meet with Egyptian and anti-Hashemite leaders. First he met King Farouk, Abdullah's rival, and later on 19 January he had a private meeting with Hajj Amin al-Husayni, the ex-Mufti of Jerusalem, and discussed the Palestinian problem with him.[41] Al-Tall's meeting with al-Husayni, King Abdullah's greatest rival, symbolized al-Tall's clear leadership of the anti-Hashemite camp alongside King Farouk and al-Husayni, especially when he requested their help in overthrowing King Abdullah. The Mufti had returned to the Middle East after a short stay in Pakistan where he had prepared the World Islamic Conference; he then started planning to assassinate King Abdullah and cause a Palestinian revolt in the West Bank in order to bring about the fall of the Hashemite regime in Jordan. IDF research written at the time specifically pointed to al-Tall as one of the possible elements constituting a danger to the Hashemite regime's stability in Jordan.[42]

According to the new political line that al-Tall had taken and based on a clear knowledge of the Mufti's intentions, al-Tall began to declare his anti-Hashemite policy in public. About three days later, on 22 January, he claimed in an interview with an AP reporter that "the UN should force internationalization on Jerusalem and that it should not agree to divide the city between Israel and Jordan". According to his claim, the Arab Legion was not strong in Jerusalem and could not protect it from IDF forces, encouraging Israel to take advantage of this situation to conquer the city.[43]

Al-Tall voiced his claims against King Abdullah in a special press conference held on 27 January 1950 in Cairo. He presented secret documents and photos he had taken with him from Jordan to support his claims. He talked about a so-called conspiracy between the Hashemite regime in Jordan and the Jews, a description of meetings between Zionist leaders and Jordanians and claims about the deliberate absence of assistance from King Abdullah to the Arabs during the 1948 war – claims rejected by Jordan's representative in Cairo, Baha al-Din Tuqan.[44] Mostly however, al-Tall attacked the British officers in the Arab Legion, especially his arch-enemy, the

Arab Legion's commander, General Glubb Pasha, who had put a stop to his advancement in the Arab Legion.

In order to defame and question the credibility of British officers in the Arab Legion, al-Tall claimed that the British officers (General Glubb Pasha) prevented the Arab Legion's soldiers from fighting the Jews during the 1948 war out of a desire to help the Jews. He claimed that Jordan was full of British bases and that Britain had too many rights in Jordan and in the Arab Legion, far beyond the scope of the Anglo-Transjordan Treaty of March 1948. He claimed that British officers actively commanded military units while the treaty stated that the officers would only constitute a training delegation for the Arab Legion.[45]

Al-Tall's goal was clear. By making false accusations, he wanted to carry public opinion both in Jordan and the entire Arab world to pressure King Abdullah to dismiss the British officers so that he could return to Jordan as a hero and, under public pressure, be given the position of Commander of the Arab Legion after Glubb's dismissal. The presentation of copied documents and photos that he brought from Jordan, which were officially published in the Egyptian newspaper *Akhbar al-Youm* at the end of March 1950 and later on in his book, proves that al-Tall had planned this well in advance.[46]

But his claims lacked any basis in reality. Whether al-Tall did not know the content of the Anglo-Transjordan treaty or whether he deliberately forged the treaty articles, he presented false information on British officers and Britain's activity in general inside Jordan.[47]

In contrast to al-Tall's claim that "Jordan is full of British bases", the British army had only two RAF bases according to the treaty, one in Amman and one in Mafraq.[48] These bases, established in 1931, were initially for the RAF, like the other RAF bases in the Middle East (Fayid and Habbaniya), and upon the establishment of the Jordanian Air Force in July 1948, it was also to be made available to them. Thus, at the end of the 1948 war, both air forces shared the two air force bases. The British had no additional military presence beyond these two bases in Jordan.[49]

Moreover, ever since the British withdrawal from Palestine in May 1948, their military presence in Jordan, as in the rest of the Middle East, began to diminish. They only returned to the area once. Following IDF activity against the Egyptian forces in the Negev during Operation *Horev* (December 1948–January 1949) the Jordanians feared IDF aggression and turned to Britain in order to realize article 3 of the treaty which stated: "should either High Contracting Party . . . become engaged in war, the other High Contracting Party will . . . immediately come to his aid . . . ". On 5 January 1949, based on the treaty and according to the Jordanian request, the British army sent a military force to Aqaba. Several days later, the British force was reinforced with additional British soldiers and ships. It was the only occasion when Britain reinforced its presence in Jordan since withdrawing from the area, and it had done so at the request of the Jordanian government.[50]

Al-Tall's claim that the Anglo-Transjordan Treaty stated that British officers would not be engaged in any commanding role, only a consulting one, is also inaccurate. Although the treaty did not specifically state that the British officers would be in commanding roles as they had been up until then, it did say however, that "his Britannic Majesty will provide on request any British service personnel whose services are required to ensure the efficiency of the military units of the forces of the King of the Hashemite Kingdom of Transjordan".[51] Thus, it can be read that the high-ranking commanding personnel in the Arab Legion, although composed of British officers, was necessary to ensure the Arab Legion's effectiveness.

Although al-Tall was right in saying that British officers held high-ranking commanding posts in the Arab Legion, such as Commander of the Arab Legion, Head of Intelligence, Head of Operations, etc., it did not prevent the Arab Legion HQ from promoting Arab officers or assigning them to replace British officers who retired. Al-Tall himself was promoted quickly and held important command posts.[52] Officially, it was stipulated in Jordan that Arab officers could not fill these posts, but in fact there was a Jordanian agreement with British military command to prevent the intrusion of hostile elements into the Arab Legion.[53] This meant that King Abdullah knew that only the British could prevent the intrusion of hostile elements into the army, not only by filling the high-ranking commanding posts in the Arab Legion, but also by being responsible for the officer's school and officer promotion. King Abdullah preferred that the higher ranks remain in the hands of British officers to ensure his continuing rule over Jordan.[54] This political consideration explains why during the entire period after the 1948 war, King Abdullah refused to answer al-Tall and the Arab League's call to dismiss the British officers from the Arab Legion in return for financial aid from the Arab world. Money did not interest him; the fear of his regime falling did.

It is worth mentioning here that despite Glubb's position as commander of the Arab Legion, the British refused to let him or any other high-ranking British officer take part in the Anglo-Jordanian Joint Defense Board that was established by article 2 of the Anglo-Transjordan Treaty. They insisted that only Jordanian Arab officers could participate on the Board. This was almost certainly to emphasize the Jordanian-Arab identity of the Legion and the equal status of the Arab and British officers. In any case, bureaucracy caused the failure of the Joint Defense Board and it still wasn't operational in the early 1950s.[55]

The claim made by al-Tall that British officers refused to fight against the Jews is partially correct. There were only two occasions in the entire 1948 war in which Glubb preferred not to fight IDF forces. One was in Lydda and Ramle in July 1948 and the other was during the IDF's activity in the Negev. The Arab Legion HQ had ordered troops stationed in the Legion bases in the Negev to fall back in order to avoid a clash with IDF forces. The reason was not a desire to assist the Jews, as al-Tall claimed, but rather Jordanian strategic considerations based on the fear that the Legion would be defeated in the event of military conflict with Israel.

Al-Tall's presence in Cairo and his condemnation of the Hashemite regime in Jordan were a huge embarrassment to King Abdullah. Al-Tall was not one whose statements could be easily ignored. The Jordanian authorities had to face hard accusations, made by a (former) high-ranking military and government Jordanian official. Despite the fact that al-Tall was dishonest in his claims, in the eyes of the Arab public he was judged to be more reliable than King Abdullah because he apparently lacked political ambition. To minimize the damage arising from al-Tall's propaganda, the Jordanian government requested that al-Tall return to Jordan under amnesty, but he refused. The Jordanian government then officially requested the Egyptian government to hand him over, but Egypt refused, because there was no extradition agreement between the two states. Nor was there a legal basis to hand him over, because he was a political refugee, not a criminal escaping from Jordan.[56]

It seemed that al-Tall had the upper hand in the outright battle that had now started between him and King Abdullah. He had political backing from many Jordanian opposition members who had stayed in Syria and Egypt. His defection was an inspiration for the defection of additional Jordanian government and military men, including Sheikh Muhammad Fahmi, the Jordanian representative in Saudi Arabia, who defected to Cairo on 22 March, and Ahmad al-Tall, Abdullah's brother, who defected to Cairo a few days later. They joined al-Tall's propaganda and espionage campaign against King Abdullah and also published adverse comments about him in the Egyptian press.[57] Ahmad al-Tall was a junior intelligence officer in Nablus. His comments were published in April 1950 in *al-Aharam* newspaper and were given special emphasis because of his testimony on "the Arab Legion's barbaric behavior" against the resident of Nablus who opposed King Abdullah. These comments and others fanned the flames of hatred against King Abdullah in the Arab world; support to remove him grew.[58]

In a desperate attempt to refute al-Tall's claims and perhaps even encourage him to return to Jordan, the Jordanian authorities began to increase the pressure on al-Tall's family in Irbid, and on his friends and people he met outside the country. On 8 May, al-Tall's family, including his parents and brothers, were arrested and sent to prison. Although they were released a few days later, they had to report to the police station daily. Other acquaintances who were suspected of conspiring him were also arrested, including the former chairman of the Jordanian parliament, Abd al-Qadir al-Tall, who was arrested in early June 1950.[59]

On 4 May 1950 al-Tall went to Damascus for a secret visit. With the knowledge of his arrival in Damascus, a military delegation from Jordan led by the Arab Legion's Deputy Commander Ahmad Sidqi al-Jundi also departed for Damascus, demanding that the Syrian authorities turn al-Tall over to them. The Syrian government refused to comply with the Jordanian demand and allowed al-Tall to continue his visit as planned. For fear that the Jordanian author-ities would attempt to assassinate al-Tall on their soil, the Syrian security forces put him under close observation.[60] During his visit, which lasted two weeks, he met with Syrian president Hashem Atasi and many opposition leaders, including Dr. Subhi Abu Ghanima and Faisal al-Nabulsi, one of the Mufti Hajj Amin al-Husayni's followers. The purpose of al-Tall's visit was to once again examine the possibility of overthrowing King Abdullah with the help of Prince Talal and Jordanian opposition elements in Syria after rumors had grown about a possible peace between Jordan and Israel. However, on al-Nabulsi's return to Jordan in early June 1950, he was arrested by Jordanian intelligence along with other dissidents including Hasib al-Majali, one of the Legion's officers. Al-Nabulsi was released in late August after pressure was put on King Abdullah by his family in Nablus and he escaped from Jordan to Syria.[61]

The Inter-Arab and International Background for the Assassination of King Abdullah

The Lausanne Conference (Switzerland) opened on 27 April 1949 to settle outstanding issues following the signing of the armistice agreement between Egypt, Lebanon, Jordan and Israel. These issues included borders, the Jerusalem question, and the Palestinian refugee problem. Israel and the Arab states were represented by high-ranking officials from the Ministries of Foreign Affairs. The heads of the various delegations were Israeli Director General of the Foreign Ministry, Walter Eytan; Abd al-Munim Mustafa, the manager of the Arab Affairs Department in the Egyptian Foreign Ministry; Fauzi al-Mulqi, Jordanian Defense Minister; Adnan Atasi, Syrian ambassador to France; and the Director General of the Lebanese Foreign Ministry, Fuad Amon. A Palestinian refugee delegation was led by Muhammad Nimr al-Hawari, one of the Palestinian leaders during the Mandate period.[62]

The discussions started with the border issue. The conciliation commission adopted the principle of the UN partition resolution of November 1947 as the basis of discussion and convinced the Arab countries and Israel to agree. After negotiation, they agreed to accept the principle and on 12 May 1949 signed a protocol which set the partition resolution as the basis for the discussion on the permanent borders between Israel and its Arab neighbors. As an attachment to the protocol, a map of the partition from November 1947 was added.[63] Although Israel thought that signing the protocol would bring Arab recognition of a Jewish state, the Arabs later demanded that Israel not only give up the territories designated to them that it had conquered during the 1948 war, but also the Negev. Israel attempted during the discussion to negotiate directly with the Arab states' representatives separately and to reach understandings with them about the country's borders, but it was unsuccessful because of both the Arab's objection to negotiating with Israel directly and also their insistence on presenting a unified front towards Israel on all controversial issues.[64]

Nor did the parties agree on the issue of Jerusalem. The official policy of the West (including the Vatican) was to internationalize Jerusalem according to the UN partition resolution of November 1947. Israel firmly objected to this and offered at most the internalization of the holy sites alone. Jordan also had reservations about internationalizing Jerusalem, while the other Arab states, mainly Syria and Egypt, supported the idea. However, the main issue the negotiations in Lausanne had to address was the Palestinian refugee problem. Before the conference opened, the Arabs said the problem should be solved only by repatriation and claimed that this issue would be the conference's top priority. Israeli official policy was that Israel was not responsible for the fate of the Palestinian refugees, although Israel was willing to discuss the issue, and others, through direct negotiations with each Arab state.

When the conciliation commission started discussions, Israel, on its own initiative, declared as a demonstration of good will that it was willing to take back a small number of refugees and give compensation for abandoned land. The American secretary of state, Dean Acheson, put pressure on Israel to agree to the Arab demand to allow all the refugees back to their homes, but Israel refused. Eventually, with the opening of the second round of discussions on 18 July, Israel officially announced that it was willing to accept 100,000 Palestinian refugees and tried to find a solution for settling the refugees in other countries or in the Gaza Strip. However, the Arabs were not satisfied. They insisted that Israel uphold the UN Assembly's resolution of 11 December 1948 which stated that "the refugees wishing to return to their homes and lives at peace with their neighbors should be permitted to do so at the earliest practicable date". The conference ended on 12 September 1949 without any decisions having been reached.[65]

Shortly thereafter, contact between Israeli representatives and Jordan was renewed, and they persisted in trying to reach a peace agreement until April 1950. Both parties understood the enormous importance of the talks: King Abdullah reasoned that by negotiating he could get Israeli recognition for the annexation of the West Bank to Jordan; Israel thought that a peace agreement with Jordan would enable it to dismantle the Arab bloc and thereby break the Arab economic embargo.[66] The British refused to put pressure on King Abdullah and maintained a neutral stance because they feared that a separate agreement with Jordan would weaken Abdullah's position in the Arab world.[67] The talks mostly dealt with an exchange of territory in Jerusalem, a possible Jordanian outlet to the Mediterranean, and the border in the Latrun area.

An initial meeting took place on 27 November 1949 between the Israelis Eliyahu Sasson and Reuven Shiloah and Samir al-Rifai, the Royal Jordanian Court Minister. The Jordanian Prime Minister, Tawfiq Abu al-Huda, refused to take part in the meetings because of his reluctance to negotiate with Israel.[68] Al-Rifai explained that in order for the King to achieve peace with Israel he needed a "dignified settlement", meaning an outlet to the Mediterranean via Gaza and a territorial link with Gaza. His intention was clear. The Jordanians were not satisfied with Gaza alone, but requested the whole of the Negev so that they could use it to reach Gaza. Israel immediately rejected the demand to give up the Negev; however it agreed that Jordan could take Gaza as an outlet to the Mediterranean even though it was clear that the Egyptians would not give it up to the Jordanians.[69]

On 1 December, when the parties met again, when Israel refused to give up the Negev, al-Rifai suggested a corridor that would allow the Jordanians to reach Gaza from Hebron. Israel did not reject the corridor principle and said on 13 December that it would be willing to give Jordan sovereignty over a corridor conditional upon three things: 1. Israel would be given free passage at three points along the corridor; 2. the establishment of a military infrastructure and the maintenance of military units in the corridor would not be allowed; and 3. the Anglo-Jordanian Treaty would not apply to the corridor.[70]

King Abdullah attended the meeting on 13 December and the two parties agreed on the issues which were written in the "Principles of a Territorial Arrangement" which included the following points:

> 1. Israel's grant to Jordan of an outlet to the Mediterranean, with a corridor running through Israeli territory linking Jordan with the coast at Gaza.
> 2. The inclusion of the Jewish Quarter of the Old City within the Israeli sector of Jerusalem in return for the inclusion in the Jordanian sector of a road linking Bethlehem with Jerusalem.
> 3. Access for the Israelis to their enclave on Mount Scopus.[71]

Despite the many expectations created by the agreement, the talks reached a serious crisis on 23 December when it appeared that neither party had reached an agreement regarding the width of the corridor between Hebron and Gaza. The Jordanians wanted it be a kilometer wide, while the Israelis suggested that its width should only be about 50–100 meters. To try to find an alternative solution, the Israelis proposed joint control over the Gulf of Eilat and Aqaba, thus giving the Jordanians an outlet to the Red Sea. But Yadin, the Israeli Chief of Staff, objected and brought about the rejection of the proposal, despite Ben-Gurion's support.[72]

The UN resolution on 9 December 1949 to recognize again the internationalization of Jerusalem, according to the partition resolution of November 1947, aroused great anger in Israel. In response, on 13 December Ben-Gurion declared Jerusalem as the Israeli capital and decided to transfer some of the country's institutions to the city, including the Knesset building.[73] On 31 December 1950 King Abdullah appointed his close friend, Raghib Nashashibi, to be the "supervisor of the al-Aqsa Mosque and the guardian of the Islamic holy sites in Jerusalem".[74] Israel and Jordan's fear of UN involvement in the issue of Jerusalem forced the two parties to renew their efforts in finding an agreed solution. Others joined the discussions: the former Jerusalem commander, General Moshe Dayan; the Jordanian Defense Minister Fauzi al-Mulqi; and the Minister of Trade and Industry, Khalusi Khairi (of Palestinian origin). Khalusi's participation was to give Palestinian legitimization for a Jordanian solution to the Jerusalem issue.[75]

The talks started on 23 January and continued till 30 January without success. On 3 February, Israel offered to divide Jerusalem so that the north would be given entirely to Jordan and the south would be Israeli. However, the Jordanians rejected the proposal and therefore it was decided to discuss alterations to this proposed border. Israel's proposition was that the Wailing Wall, the Jewish Quarter, Mount Scopus, and the road leading to it should be under Israeli sovereignty, in return for transferring other areas to Jordan.[76]

However, the Jordanian government, led by the Prime Minister Tawfiq Abu al-Huda, who opposed the negotiations with Israel anyway, objected to any territorial concession to Israel. He managed to force his opinion on King Abdullah by making a formal statement banning Jordan from transferring territories to Israel. Abdullah had no choice but to concur and, as Kirkbride claimed, he was "endeavoring to convince everybody (including himself) that he was never prepared to agree to Israel obtaining any territory inside the city walls".[77]

Even though it was clear to everyone that the negotiations on the Jerusalem issue had failed, the two parties met again on 17 February. With pressure from King Abdullah, General Glubb Pasha and Kirkbride, Jordan agreed to discuss a proposition to sign a non-aggression pact for five years that would leave the borders as they were in the armistice agreement, and called for special committees, formed from representatives of both parties, to discuss all the issues, including Jerusalem. The proposition also called for the renewal of trade between the two countries and giving a free port to Jordan in Haifa, instead of in Gaza.[78]

On 24 February, in the winter palace at Shuna, both parties signed the draft agreement: Samir al-Rifai and Fauzi al-Mulqi for the Jordanians and Shiloah and Dayan for the Israelis. However, when the two parties met again on 28 February to sign the agreement following confirmation by the two respective governments, the Israelis found that the Jordanians had changed the agreement to suit a Jordanian government decision made two days earlier, cancelling the five-year time frame and the article regarding the renewal of trade between the states.[79] The Jordanians proved that they had no intention of signing a separate peace agreement with Israel; they merely approved the armistice agreement between the two. "We have no intention of signing a new edition of the armistice agreement, let alone an inferior one", the Israelis announced in anger. King Abdullah, who probably was not aware of the changes made by his government, was deeply embarrassed and notified the Israelis that if the need arose then he would establish a new government in Jordan that would sign the agreement.[80]

The political situation in Jordan grew worse day by day. On 2 March, Abdullah forced the government to accept the principle of renewing trade with Israel. In response, Prime Minister Abu al-Huda announced his resignation followed by the three Palestinian Ministers who held office in the Jordanian government, Rauhi Abd al-Hadi (Foreign Minister), Musa Nasser (Minister of Communication) and Khalusi Khair (Minister of Trade and Industry), who refused to be partners in a peace agreement with Israel. The King called Samir al-Rifai to form the new government; however when it became known that Abu al-Huda had resigned because he refused to sign the peace agreement with Israel, the remaining ministers were certain that al-Rifai's appointment had been made on the basis that he would sign it and they refused to join the government. King Abdullah had no choice but to return Abu al-

Huda to office on his own terms, meaning that negotiations with Israel could not continue until after the planned elections in Jordan on 11 April 1950.[81]

So King Abdullah, Fauzi al-Mulqi, and Abdullah's colleague, Sa'id al-Mufti, the Minister of the Interior, met with Shiloah and Dayan on 7 March 1950 and notified them that the negotiations would not continue because of political obstacles in Jordan. "Because of the lies . . . the right way, in our opinion, is to postpone the discussion until the election and see it as a truce and not a total break in relations", they said.[82] This was a great disappointment to the Israelis, even though not everyone was sure that Abdullah really intended to broker a peace. Many appreciated his efforts and his stance against his government, however, including Director General of the Israeli Foreign Ministry, Walter Eytan, who wrote: "King Abdullah, alone of the Arab rulers, was sincere in regarding the armistice as a step towards peace".[83]

Despite the cessation of contact, the Arab League convened in Cairo on 25 March at Egypt's request to discuss Jordan's initiative concerning the signing of a separate peace agreement with Israel. Al-Tall was one of those participating in the struggle against Jordan's leaders in the Arab League's institutions. He asked to take part in the League's discussion to make clear to the Arab world the contact Abdullah had made with the Jews during the 1948 war and to prove King Abdullah's intention of making a separate peace with Israel. The best way to foil Jordan's peace initiative, he claimed in a press conference on 19 March, was to remove King Abdullah from office. He requested that the Arab League consider asking the King to abdicate if he refused to become a constitutional monarch.[84] The Egyptian newspaper *al-Misri* exposed a secret exchange of letters between Israel and Jordan and the newspaper heavily criticized Jordan's policy: "the time has come for the Arab League to cut off relations with Trans-Jordan, a country that has betrayed Islam and Arab unity and the Arab cause".[85]

The Arab League did not allow al-Tall to participate in its discussions, but on 1 April it decided unanimously (including Jordan) to forbid any of the League's members to negotiate with Israel separately or to make any sort of peace agreement or other separate political, military or economic agreement with Israel. On 13 April, it was decided that the League's political committee, having a majority of votes (four out of seven countries), would be the deciding body over matters of violations of this decision. If the agreement was violated, decided the League, the perpetrating country would be forced to leave the League and the following measures would be taken against it: severing of diplomatic and consular relations, closing of shared borders, and cessation of economic, financial, and trade relations, as well as the prevention of any direct or indirect trade or financial contact with its civilians. When he realized that his government did not support his peace efforts, King Abdullah knew that he had to accept the League's decision.[86] Even King Abdullah's colleague, Sa'id al-Mufti, who formed the new government on 12 April after the elections, objected to signing a peace agreement with Israel and proclaimed "cut off my hand and I will still not sign on a contract with Israel".[87]

The failure of negotiations with Israel was summed up by Glubb Pasha in his book, *A Soldier with the Arabs*: "The King's attempted negotiations with Israel failed for two reasons. The first was the intense agitation raised by the other members of the Arab League, which frightened the government, though not the King. The second reason was that the Israelis, though apparently desirous of peace, wanted it only on their own terms. They were not prepared to make adequate concessions. King Abdullah realized that if he were to make peace, he would have to be able to show substantial advantages there from. With Israel unprepared to make concessions, there was little inducement to defy the other Arab countries".[88]

Danger to the Hashemite Regime? Abdullah al-Tall and the Assassination of King Abdullah

King Abdullah's actions in 1950 rocked political stability in the Middle East. In addition to the contact with Israel agreed by Abdullah and his government, the main issue concerning the Arab League was King Abdullah's stance toward the Arab territories he had conquered in the 1948 war and his pro-Western policy, which was opposed by the other of the Arab leaders.

King Abdullah's desire to officially annex the Arab territories of Palestine (West Bank) to Jordan and annul the Palestinian identity of the residents was not new and had been given British support on several occasions. In 1937, the Royal Commission recommended the partition of Palestine and the annexation of the Arab sector with Transjordan (it did not agree to establish a Palestinian country), but

Britain, which controlled Palestine, did not apply the recommendations and continued the Mandate regime for strategic reasons. In February 1948, when British Foreign Secretary Ernest Bevin met Jordanian Prime Minister Abu al-Huda, Bevin agreed to the Arab Legion taking over the Arab sector of Palestine. Eventually, in September 1948, when UN mediator Bernadotte submitted his recommendations, similar to those of the Royal Commission, to end the war, he recommended uniting the Arab territories of Palestine with Jordan. Even though Bernadotte claimed that his recommendation was generated by the military reality in Palestine and the Arab Legion's de facto occupation of the Arab territories, he also admitted that he had consulted the British before finalizing his recommendations.[89]

The activities of the Arab Legion in the Arab territories assisted King Abdullah to complete the annexation. The Arab Legion officers encouraged the population to send letters to Amman in which they authorized Abdullah to solve the Palestine problem "as he sees fit". The King increased his visits to the occupied areas and Ramallah radio, which was under Jordanian rule, described the Palestinian population as one that recognized King Abdullah as their king.[90] On 1 December 1948, the second Palestinian congress took place in Jericho with the encouragement and assistance of Arab Legion officers. The congress called for King Abdullah to annex the West Bank to Jordan and proclaimed him "king of united Palestine".[91] Since the congress had started a "Jordanization" process of the West Bank, the Jordanian government dismantled the armed Palestinian organizations in the occupied territories to prepare them for future annexation to Jordan. On 14 November 1949, limitations on movement between the two sides of Jordan were annulled as were customs on goods transferred between parts of Jordan (although they were later reinstated). On 26 December 1949, Jordanian military rule over the territories was officially annulled. In that same month, a new citizenship law came into effect stating that residents of the West Bank were now Jordanian citizens. In early January 1950, the Jordanian parliament was dispersed as the first step towards the establishment of a new united parliament consisting of 40 representatives, 20 from Jordan and 20 from the West Bank. On 11 April 1950, initial elections for the united Parliament were held, despite attempts made by the Mufti's followers to disrupt them, and the following day a new government was formed, led by Sa'id al-Mufti.[92]

In an attempt to prevent the annexation of the West Bank to Jordan, the Arab League decided on 13 April 1950, with Jordan's abstention, to adopt its earlier decision from 12 April 1948, that "the entry of the Arab armies into Palestine as a temporary measure without any suggestion of occupying or partitioning Palestine". However, King Abdullah decided to proceed with annexation and on 24 April the Jordanian government submitted a proposal of "support for complete unity between the two sides of the Jordan and their union into one state, which is the Hashemite Kingdom of Jordan, at whose head reigns King Abdullah" to the Parliament. The Parliament unanimously approved it. The next day, the Jordanian government officially announced the annexation of the West Bank to Jordan.[93]

Only Britain and Pakistan recognized the annexation of the West Bank to Jordan. A month later in May 1950, the USA, Britain and France declared that they recognized the new status quo in the Middle East and were committed to vouching for the safety and well being of all the countries of the area – which was interpreted, especially in Jordan, as recognizing the annexation, even if this was not explicitly expressed. Israel also objected to the annexation and submitted a formal protest to Jordan: "The government of Israel does not recognize the annexation and the question of the Arab areas west of the Jordan remains open."[94]

In a meeting of the Arab League which took place on 12 June 1950 in Alexandria following the annexation of the West Bank to Jordan, Egypt and Saudi Arabia demanded that Jordan should be expelled from the Arab League. However, the other Arab countries opposed such an extreme move and wanted to find a compromise. Eventually, following a suggestion from Iraq and Lebanon, a compromise was found in which it was agreed that "the Arab part of Palestine was annexed by Jordan . . . until the Palestinian case is fully solved in the interests of its inhabitants". In return for the League's approval of the compromise, King Abdullah agreed not to attempt a separate peace settlement with Israel. The compromise proposal was accepted in the Arab League and satisfied all the Arab parties: on one hand, the proposal allowed Jordan to keep the territories it wanted, but on the other hand, the League did not acknowledge the territories' official final annexation to Jordan. Moreover, Abdullah had also committed not to negotiate separately with Israel which was the main aim of the Arab countries.[95]

On King Abdullah's order, a process of assimilating the Palestinians in Jordan started. The political reason for this was the desire to remove the national identity of the Palestinians as part of a Jordanization process of the West Bank, which King Abdullah supported because he believed that he was responsible for the Palestinians' problem. The economic reason was the belief that absorbing and integrating the residents of the West Bank into the Jordanian economy would increase production because they would be an additional source of manpower to assist development.[96] Therefore, King Abdullah tried to convince the Arab countries, especially the Iraqis in late 1950, not to support the UN and the Arab League's proposals to return the Palestinian refugees to Israel, but rather to allow them to integrate into Jordan, while giving them financial assistance from the Jordanian government.[97]

In order to integrate them into the Jordanian economy and society, the Palestinians received Jordanian passports and were granted free movement. They were also recruited for governmental posts. A special office for their management was established in Jordan on 8 August 1950, headed by the Christian deputy mayor of East Jerusalem, Anastas Hanania. The Jordanian government also set aside land for the different aid organizations, the most important of which was the Arab Development Society established by Musa al-Alami, to resettle the refugees in the Jericho area. In opposition to other Arab countries, it also increased cooperation with UNRAW and allocated funds for projects, claiming that "most of the Palestinian refugees are in Jordan".[98]

Abdullah's policy of absorbing the refugees into Jordan was not acceptable to the Arab leaders who had decided in March 1949 to return the Palestinian refugees to Israel. The policy was also opposed by the majority of Jordanians, including army officers, who claimed that the Palestinian refugees were a burden on the Jordanian economy because they "do not create, they just consume". The government still fought aggressively against its opponents. For instance, in May 1950 Kamal Nasser, the editor of the weekly *al-Jil al-Jadid,* was arrested again after he wrote a article critical of King Abdullah's policy, and the following month the lawyer Munib al-Madi, editor of the *al-Nasser* newspaper, was arrested after he demanded reforms in the government. Both newspapers were shut down.[99] Political arrests in Jordan increased during 1951 and became routine as far as Israeli intelligence was concerned. From official Jordanian records it can be seen that the number of political arrests in 1951 alone was 6,887. The prisoners were held in harsh conditions in Jordanian prisons near the Saudi border.[100]

Britain and Israel also opposed the absorption of the refugees into Jordan because they feared that it would bring about the elimination of the Hashemite regime in Jordan and lead to a Palestinian takeover of the kingdom.[101] However, while Britain generally supported the Arab attitude to allow the refugees to return to Israel, the state of Israel thought that the best solution would be their absorption into Syria and Iraq, even though only a few refugees were originally from those states and both states were opposed to the idea.[102] Syria and Iraq's policy regarding the refugees was no different from that of the other Arab governments (apart from Jordan). They preferred to preserve the Palestinian refugee problem in order to use it as a political weapon against Israel, as General Glubb Pasha claimed in his book: "the excuse put forward for this failure was that the Arab governments wished to keep the refugees destitute, in order to maintain the Palestine problem as a live political issue".[103]

King Abdullah's pro-British policy, which was opposed by the other Arab leaders, found expression in the Arab Collective Security Pact (ACSP). In April 1950, through an Egyptian initiative, the Arab League decided to establish "an alliance for a mutual defense and an economic cooperation", which became known as the Arab Collective Security Pact. The idea was not new and was based on al-Alami's ideas; he wrote that the Arabs could not defeat Israel unless they united. "The Arabs are still stronger than the Jews if they unite and co-operate", al-Alami wrote.[104]

After discussions which lasted for almost a year, the Arab states eventually formulated the pact and on 2 February 1951, all Arab states members of the Arab League (except for Jordan) signed the ACSP agreement. Needless to say, without Jordan's Arab Legion – the best Arab army in the Middle East – this pact had no military value. Politically, Jordan's refusal to join the pact deeply hurt the prestige of Egypt, who had initiated the pact with Syria's support. Jordan never said why it refused to join the alliance, giving rise to claims that King Abdullah wanted to protest against the Arab League's refusal to recognize his annexation of the West Bank, as well as Egypt's demand to expel Jordan from the Arab League.[105]

Beyond political considerations in the Arab League, important as they may have been, King Abdullah's pro-western policy informed his stance towards the pact, according to which the signatories were committed to help any country engaged in a war with a third party.

Jordan feared that it would find itself dragged into a war against Britain if the Egyptians were to declare war as part of their national struggle. Confirmation of this can be found in Egyptian Foreign Minister Salah al-Din's statement in June 1951 that "Arab countries have to help Egypt, if it engages in a war with Britain".[106] Therefore, in order to avoid a war with Britain, King Abdullah preferred to refrain from joining the Arab alliance. He did not conceal his intention of joining another alliance – that of the Western countries with Britain in case of a third World War. About two weeks before he was assassinated in July 1951, Abdullah visited Turkey to discuss Jordan joining the Middle East command (MEC) that was being planned at the time by the USA, Britain, France and Turkey. He also convinced other Arab states to follow him. Abdullah's stance was a blow to the Arab League in general and in particular to Egypt, which had worked hard on the ACSP and opposed the West's defense alliance. Calls to sever connections with Jordan increased.[107]

Despite the annexation of the West Bank by Jordan and efforts to make the Palestinian population Jordanian, the Palestinians did not really become Jordanians. Not only did they keep their national identity, they also became a majority in the kingdom (400,000 Jordanians compared to 600,000 Palestinians). They dominated the Jordanians culturally and had greater political awareness; they sought to minimize King Abdullah's all-powerful regime.[108] They demanded the King sever all ties with Britain and Israel, including the Arab Legion's ties with Britain, and change the constitution to make the government responsible to Parliament and not the King. The King promised to discuss the proposals to change the constitution, but did not keep his promise. Therefore, an oppositionist majority formed in Parliament, consisting mostly of Palestinians and other opposition elements (the *Ba'ath* party and socialist delegates). On 14 August 1950, the Parliament rejected two laws submitted to it for approval. The first law was for the refugee's resettlement in Jordan which was rejected for fear that after they were resettled there would no longer be a need to demand their return to Israel. The second was a law to fight communism. They were only approved after considerable effort and the King's direct involvement.

On 29 January 1951 opposition activity in Parliament peaked when it criticized the delay in reforms and in amending the constitution regarding the government's responsibility to Parliament. They demanded the government bring it under discussion without delay. About three months later, when the government requested that Parliament approve the budget for 1951–1952, Parliament refused to approve it until constitutional reforms were introduced. In response on 14 May the King decided to order the approval of the budget without Parliament's agreement. He ordered Parliament's dispersal (even though it had just been elected) and announced new elections would take place on 29 August 1951 in a move to get rid of the opposition.[109]

Despite King Abdullah's promise, he continued to try to negotiate peace with Israel. He pressured Prime Minister al-Mufti and his Foreign Minister, Muhammad Shurayqi, to sign a peace agreement with Israel relying on the request of "a few prominent Palestinian personalities". On 22 July 1950 the Jordanian Prime Minister and Minister Foreign arrived in the West Bank to assess the Palestinians' stance regarding King Abdullah's peace initiative. In their meetings with Palestinian dignitaries in Nablus, Ramallah and Jerusalem, they found that the Palestinians opposed peace with Israel and requested that "Jordan will not make a separate peace agreement with the Jews". Three days later on 25 July King Abdullah arrived in Ramallah and convened with Palestinian dignitaries in an attempt to convince them to support a peace agreement with Israel, but they refused. As a result, the Jordanian Parliament rejected King Abdullah's peace initiative and his standing was further undermined.[110]

On the same day, the mayor of East Jerusalem, Anwar al-Khatib, was removed from office after expressing his objection to King Abdullah's peace initiative. Al-Khatib, who was close to the *Ba'ath* party, had earlier protested against Jordan's policy regarding Israel, after the IDF took a few houses in the Sheikh Jarah quarter under the terms of the armistice agreement. As a result of his criticism against the Hashemite regime al-Khatib was removed from office. The city government members resigned in protest. Al-Khatib was replaced by Arif al-Arif who was appointed mayor of East Jerusalem on 1 August 1950.[111]

The Naharayim issue led to further criticism of King Abdullah within Jordan. On 27 August 1950, Israeli farmers ploughed one kilometer of land east of Jordan in the Naharayim area. According to the international border, this territory was inside Jordanian borders and not inside (mandatory Palestine) Israeli borders. But according to the maps drawn up for the armistice agreement, it was inside Israel. Rather than raising the issue with the truce committee, in the accepted diplomatic way, the Jordanian Foreign Minister Muhammad Shurayqi sent a complaint to the UN Security Council. He also sent a request to Baghdad for Iraqi aid "to ward off aggression if necessary". When King Abdullah discovered what was happening he demanded that Prime Minister al-Mufti remove Shurayqi from office and withdraw the complaint sent to the Security Council. But the Prime Minister backed up the Foreign Minister and refused to dismiss him. In response, the King sacked the Prime Minister, but finding no other candidate, al-Mufti was reinstated.[112]

On 3 December 1950 the Arab Legion, following official orders from the Jordanian government to act against the IDF, blocked the Arava road at Kilometer 78 between Eilat and Beersheba to Israeli traffic. The IDF responded by attacking the Legion's armored cars. The UN intervened and called for a ceasefire. The King immediately ordered the Legion forces to withdraw and Prime Minister al-Mufti submitted his resignation for "health reasons". On 5 December, King Abdullah's friend, Samir al-Rifai, formed a new government in Jordan[113] and then announced his objection to peace with Israel: "Jordan will not take any step opposing the Arab countries' policy regarding a peace agreement with Israel. A separate peace pact is not part of my government's plan and we will not deal with it unless we get the Arab countries' agreement, this is the final and decisive word".[114]

Jordanian opposition exploited the Naharayim issue. Al-Tall's associate, Shafiq Rashidat, contended in a parliament meeting on 21 November that Britain had forged the border maps in the Naharayim area in order to steal Jordanian territory and to transfer it to Israel. In the same meeting other delegates attacked General Glubb Pasha, denouncing him as a traitor and calling for his prosecution or expulsion from Jordan. Others called for the Arab Legion to be cleansed of British officers and hinted at the claim which al-Tall would later be use more explicitly, that "the Arab Legion is but a mere division of the British army".[115]

During 1951 King Abdullah's position in the Arab world reached unprecedented depths for several reasons including the condition of the Palestinian refugees, hostility in the Arab world to his political moves and the anti-Hashemite propaganda encouraged by al-Tall and the Mufti Hajj Amin al-Husayni. Attempts to overthrow the Hashemite regime in Jordan and assassinate the King increased. On 26 March 1949, the first real attempt to assassinate King Abdullah since the 1948 war was exposed. Three of the Mufti's followers (Palestinians) were arrested for intending to assassinate Abdullah. They were tried and executed about a month later. Two years later, another attempt, this time by a terror organization, was discovered.[116] Palestinian groups also acted inside Jordan to disrupt political stability. They tossed hand-grenades at the Arab Legion's soldiers, tried to assassinate General Glubb Pasha, damaged infrastructures across Jordan and called for Jordanian citizens to rebel against "the losers of Palestine who chained the land with the chains of imperialism".[117]

Following Jordanian intelligence recommendations, the government increased the security budget for the years 1951–1952 to about 11 million pounds so that the Arab Legion could equip itself with additional manpower and resources and increase the personal guard for King Abdullah and heads of state. Four out of the 11 million came from the British.[118] It seems that King Abdullah was well aware of the situation and sensed that his end was coming: "I am an old man . . . I know that my power is limited", said Abdullah to an American diplomat shortly before he was assassinated and added: "I know that I am hated by my own son . . . I also know that my own people distrust me because of my peace efforts".[119]

On Friday, 20 July 1951, when King Abdullah entered the al-Aqsa Mosque in Dome of the Rock for the Friday prayer, he was shot and killed. The murderer was shot by King Abdullah's guards. In the exchange of fire, Radi Annab, the chief of police of the Jerusalem district, Muhammad Saadi, King Abdullah's adjutant, and two other officers from the Arab Legion were also injured.[120] The assassination of King Abdullah shocked the Arab and Western world and increased the fear that Jordan's Hashemite regime would fall. It also intensified the instability of the Middle East. The initial intelligence reports in Jordan, Britain and Israel suggested that the assassination had been carried out by the Mufti's followers together with Abdullah al-Tall as part of a plan to cause the collapse of the Hashemite regime in Jordan. These reports were strengthened by the fact that outbreaks of violence throughout the Old City in Jerusalem, the major cities in Jordan, and the refugee camps started immediately after the assassination. According to an Israeli intelligence report, they were intended "to raise chaos in Jordan".[121]

In order to restore order and to protect the Hashemite regime, the Jordanian security forces took a double initiative. First, they imposed a curfew on Jerusalem and other major cities in Jordan in order to prevent tension from escalating and conflict between the Palestinian population, who mostly supported Abdullah's assassination, and the Jordanians who opposed it. The curfew lasted three days and brought quiet between the two groups.[122] Second, with Jordanian police cooperation, intelligence officers arrested the Mufti's men and followers and the main Jordanian opposition activists, led by al-Rimawi, Nawas and Abu Gharbiyah, in Jerusalem and in Jordan. Thus, they foiled a possible attempt by the opposition to take advantage of the kingdom's instability in order to cause the collapse of the regime.[123]

About three hours after the assassination, the younger son of King Abdullah, Nayif, was appointed regent because Prince Talal was not in the country at the time. "As a result of King Abdullah's death and as a result of his crown-prince, his eldest son, Talal's presence in a hospital outside of the kingdom due to medical treatment for a limited time," said the government's statement, "the government has decided . . . to appoint prince Nayif as the regent with immediate effect". The Prime Minister, Samir al-Rifai, announced his resignation according to the constitution and accepted practice in Jordan. The former Prime Minister, Tawfiq Abu al-Huda was asked to form a new government.[124]

Despite the Jordanian government's swift action and ability to demonstrate governmental continuity to the public with Nayif's appointment as regent, the danger to the Hashemite regime was still present. Although the Jordanian government managed to stabilize the regime, Abdullah's two sons were not seen as influential leaders among the Jordanian public. It was doubted that they could ensure the regime's stability, enjoy British support or control the opposition. Moreover, the hostility of the Arab states around Jordan, Syria, Saudi Arabia and Egypt, also grew. Like the Palestinians and al-Tall, they tried to exploit the circumstances surrounding the assassination to achieve their own political goals at Jordan's expense.[125]

Syria, which had tried to shake the political stability of Jordan to bring down the Hashemite regime in the years prior to the assassination, aspired to take over Jordan and carry out its "Greater Syria" plan, which was centered on Damascus as in the days of the Ottoman Empire. In Syria, immediately after the assassination, a number of Syrian Parliament members called for the implementation of the plan in a special parliamentary meeting.[126] A few days after the assassination, al-Azm arrived in Riyadh for a meeting with the Saudi Arabian ruler, Ibn Saud. Ibn Saud had refused to recognize King Abdullah's regime and had also attempted to cause its collapse. According to intelligence reports, the two examined the possibility of taking over Jordan in order to eliminate it as a country. The Syrians would invade Jordan from the north, the Saudis from the south. But fear of a military clash with the Arab Legion, and possibly with the British army, whose units were stationed in Aqaba, destroyed the Syrian-Saudi plan and protected Jordan.[127]

In contrast to Syria and Saudi Arabia, Egypt's ambitions after the assassination were not only to eliminate the Hashemite Kingdom, but also to damage Britain's position in the area. Egypt assumed that with King Abdullah's death, Jordan's position had been undermined and Egypt could take upon itself the hegemony of the Arab world. It could become, as General Glubb Pasha said, "the mistress of the whole area". Egypt's goal was to weaken British influence in the Middle East and to eventually remove the British from Egypt as well.[128]

Western countries in general and Britain in particular were concerned about the effects of Abdullah's assassination. British Prime Minister Attlee claimed that "unlike certain leaders in the Middle East, King Abdullah was always capable of seeing beyond his congregation's interests", hinting at the close connection between the two states.[129] Indeed, throughout the years, Britain had maintained friendly relations with King Abdullah, and his pro-Western orientation had greatly assisted them in promoting their interests in the area. Even though King Abdullah's son, Prince Talal, declared that he would not change his father's policy, Britain was very concerned about the increase in Arab and Palestinian nationalism in the area. The fear was that Iraq would exploit the instability in Jordan in order to annex it. In Iraq the nationalist anti-British elements were dominant and had managed to thwart the Anglo-Iraqi Treaty in January 1948, so if Iraq ruled Jordan, it would ensure the removal of British officers from the Arab Legion. Britain started to intervene in Jordan to prevent nationalist elements from interfering in the kingdom until after the elections in late August 1951.[130]

Israel was also worried about the instability in Jordan. It was clear that the assassination of the King Abdullah had removed the possibility of reaching a peace agreement between the two states.[131] But what especially concerned Israel was the fear of Jordan being taken over by a hostile nation. Like the British, Israel was especially worried that the Mufti would increase hostilities against Israel from inside Jordan, as part of a fight to seize control of the country. To prevent this, in a communication to Mr. J. Chadwick, the British counsel in Tel Aviv, Reuven Shiloah maintained that Britain needed to increase its influence in Jordan and perhaps even "should take over full control of Jordan".[132]

The assassination investigation started immediately and thanks to two pieces of evidence found at the scene of the crime, the killer's body and the gun he used, the Jordanian investigators quickly managed to find all those who were involved in the assassination. The killer was Mustafa Shukri Ashu, a young man aged 21, a resident of the Old City in Jerusalem. During the 1948 war, he grew closer to the Mufti al-Husayni and joined the Mufti's military force, *Jihad al-Muqaddas*.[133] The gun he used was a Colt, which according to the Jordanian police records belonged to Abd Muhammad Aka, a butcher from the Old City. Muhammad Aka was also one of the Mufti's supporters and had been charged with the murder of two Scottish soldiers in Palestine during the 1936–1939 rebellion. The involvement of the two, both of whom were supporters of the Mufti, strengthened Jordanian intelligence's initial estimation that the Mufti was linked to the assassination. And indeed, in the summation of the investigation report, it was explicitly stated that "the Mufti al-Husayni and the King Farouk's Court joined forces with Abdullah al-Tall to commit the murder".[134]

About three weeks after the assassination, the investigators found all the culprits. Jordanian public prosecutor, Walid Salih, a Palestinian residing in Nablus who was entrusted with the investigation, decided to prosecute ten people, including al-Tall. The rest of those initially suspected were released. The ten defendants were Dr. Musa Abdullah al-Husayni, Abd Muhammad Aka and his brother Zakariya Muhammad, Abd al-Qadir Farahat, Tawfiq Salih al-Husayni, Father Ibrahim Ayyad, Dr. Daud al-Husayni, Kamil Abdullah Kaluti, Abdullah al-Tall and Musa Ahmad al-Ayubi. Three of the ten defendants belonged to the al-Husayni family – which pointed not only to the Mufti's involvement in the assassination and its planning, but also to the entire family's desire to take part in the assassination of Abdullah and the elimination of the Hashemite regime.[135]

Two defendants, Abdullah al-Tall and Musa Ahmad al-Ayubi, were tried in absentia. Al-Ayubi, like al-Tall, was originally a Jordanian (from Salt) and had also escaped from Jordan and lived in political exile in Cairo. At the time of the assassination, both were in Cairo and despite requests from the Jordanian government to hand the two over to Jordan for trial, the Egyptian government refused to do so.[136] The Egyptian government officially announced, on the eve of the trial, that it was going to request that the Jordanian government transfer documents regarding al-Tall's involvement and if it were convinced of his guilt "Egypt will ask him to leave Egypt, but will not hand him over to Jordan".[137]

On 20 August 1951, the trial of those accused of the assassination of King Abdullah opened. Because of the severity of the crime, the Jordanian Minister of Justice, Suleiman Tuqan, decided to prosecute the defendants in a military court with a special composition of judges led by the Arab Legion's Deputy Commander, Ahmad Sidqi al-Jundi. The two other judges were Ali al-Hiyari, the commander of 5th Regiment, and Habis al-Majali, the commander of the king's bodyguards. To ensure the defendants' safety (against possible kidnap by Palestinians or attack from Jordanian citizens), the government decided to fly them directly from Jerusalem to Amman for the trial.[138] During the trial, the defendants were represented by nine different lawyers, including Palestinians. At first, al-Tall requested the Egyptian government to send him Egyptian lawyers for his defense, but eventually he waived legal representation. He pleaded the same defense as the Mufti Hajj Amin al-Husayni, claiming they had had no part in the assassination of King Abdullah. "I objected [to] acts of violence and political assassinations", said al-Tall, trying to deny his involvement in the murder. He and his family claimed that not only was he not connected to the assassination, he was only accused of being involved in the assassination to prevent his return to Jordan by General Glubb Pasha and the British officers. "They want my head," said al-Tall "because I opposed the British". The Cairo police placed al-Tall under close guard in case someone tried to kill him in revenge for King Abdullah's assassination.[139]

From the investigation documents it appears that al-Tall played an important part in planning and assisting the assassintion. In early 1950, al-Tall met with the Mufti Hajj Amin al-Husayni who explained his desire to overthrow the Hashemite regime in Jordan. This struck a chord with Al-Tall who decided to ally himself with the Mufti. Shortly afterwards in Cairo he met one of the Mufti's relatives, Dr. Musa Abdullah Hajj Amin al-Husayni, a resident of Jerusalem, who had travelled to Cairo as a businessman. Al-Tall decided that the King must be killed because "we should govern ourselves by ourselves" and both of them concluded that the assassination of King Abdullah would be the opening of a series of other political assassinations, both of Hashemite and "leading Arab personalities".[140] Al-Tall also had meetings in Cairo with Musa al-Ayubi, originally from Jordan, who was another of the Mufti's followers. Al-Ayubi agreed to take part in the plot and drove to Jerusalem to meet Dr. al-Husayni to transfer money to him to finance al-Tall's mission. Dr. al-Husayni managed to recruit additional men to the conspiracy from the Mufti's military force, *Jihad al-Muqaddas*, including Abd Muhammad Aka, the owner of the gun, and Abd al-Qadir Farahat, the owner of the coffee shop in which the members met in order to prepare the assassination plans.[141]

In early May 1951, when it was known that King Abdullah was planning to visit Jerusalem and pray at the Dome of the Rock, the conspirators decided to act. However, al-Ayubi, who was supposed to return to Cairo, did not manage to catch his plane before the murder and fearing that he would be arrested, he requested them to delay the assassination. With the announcement of the King's planned visit to Jerusalem on 20 July, they decided to act swiftly. Al-Ayubi, Dr. al-Husayni and Abd Aka, found Abd Aka's neighbor, a tailor's apprentice named Mustafa Shukri Ashu, and offered him 200 dinars to carry out the mission. On the morning of the assassination, Abd Aka gave his gun to Abd al-Qadir Farahat who gave it to Ashu in his coffee shop shortly before the assassination. They also recruited Mahmud Antabli who was paid "to throw hand grenades in the mosque after the murder so that the assassin could escape in the confusion".[142] Al-Tall believed that the assassin would be killed either by King Abdullah's bodyguards or by the hand grenades, ensuring Jordanian intelligence would be unable to discover the identity of the conspirators.

During the trial, it transpired that the money transferred by al-Tall to Dr. al-Husayni for the assassination came "from a high source in Cairo", but the details remained confidential.[143] It is not clear who that source was, however it is known that al-Tall was close to King Farouk who had a strong interest in Abdullah's death. Based on the investigation's conclusions which claimed that "King Farouk's Court" was involved in Abdullah's assassination but negated the Egyptian government's involvement, it is quite likely that King Farouk was the high source.[144] In his report to Robert

Melville (the Arab Legion liaison officer), General Glubb Pasha hinted at the Egyptians' and King Farouk's involvement (without explicitly mentioning his name) and claimed that not only did the Egyptians know about the assassination, they also transferred the money for it through the Egyptian delegation in Amman. "It is unclear how much money was transferred from Egypt and Saudi Arabia for the assassination, but there is no doubt that the Egyptians knew about it and that the Egyptian Legation in Amman was co-operating in this plot", he wrote.[145]

Examples of the two men's actions against Jordan and King Abdullah were brought as part of the Jordanian prosecution's attempt to prove that the Mufti and al-Tall intended not just to assassinate King Abdullah, but to overthrow the Hashemite regime in Jordan. The Jordanian head prosecutor, Walid Salih, presented an especially negative image of al-Tall. Salih described al-Tall as "ungrateful", as one who was promoted in the Arab Legion thanks to King Abdullah's fondness of him which al-Tall eventually paid back by assassinating him. "Al-Tall is a careerist who is after mate-rialistic benefit", claimed Salih and continued that when he was asked to return to the Arab Legion he demanded a promotion he did not deserve out of "selfishness and ostentation". Salih claimed that he only defected to Egypt because he had not been promoted.[146]

On 28 August 1951, nine days after the start of the trial, the judges gave their verdict. Six out of the ten defendants were found guilty of Abdullah's assassination and were sentenced to death. The other four were acquitted. The six defendants were Abd Aka and Zakariya Aka, who were charged with hiring the killer and giving him the gun; Abd al-Qadir Farahat, the owner of the coffee shop where the assassination was planned; Dr. Musa al-Husayni, who was found guilty of knowing of the intention to assassinate King Abdullah and for transferring the money for the assassination from Cairo; Abdullah al-Tall, who planned the assassination and Musa Ahmad al-Ayubi who knew of the intention to assassinate King Abdullah and took part in the planning.[147]

When the verdict was announced, the Jordanian government submitted a request to Egypt to hand over al-Tall and Musa al-Ayubi. However, that same day (28 August) the Egyptian government officially announced that "the Egyptian government refuses to hand over Abdullah al-Tall and Musa al-Ayubi as Jordan demanded, because the two states do not have an extradition agreement". Clearly it was not the lack of an extradition agreement preventing the two from being handed over to Jordan, but rather the political tension between the two states. Israeli intelligence reports confirmed that the Egyptian government gave al-Tall full support even after the assassination and that he was still in favor with the Egyptian regime.[148] Even the wording used by the Egyptian government "the Egyptian government refuses to hand over . . . " was cold, lacking any expression of grief over King Abdullah's assassination. It is worth noting that when the Egyptian former Minister of Finance, Amin Othman, was assassinated in January 1946, and one of the killers, Hussein Tawfiq, escaped to Jordan, the Jordanian government refused to hand him over to Egypt, claiming that "there is no extradition agreement between the two states". With this background, the Egyptian government's refusal to hand al-Tall over to Jordan can be understood. Further extradition requests from Jordan during 1952 were also rejected by the Egyptians.[149]

The death penalty for the six convicted brought heavy pressure from different parts of the Arab world. The Egyptian and Syrian governments pressured the Jordanian government to commute their sentence to life in prison. The Mufti also took advantage of the situation in order to call on the Arab countries to appoint an inquiry commission to investigate "the campaign of terror, corruption and harassment being conducted by the army of Glubb Pasha". However, Jordanian Prime Minister Abu al-Huda carried out the death penalty as soon as possible in order to prevent additional pressure on Jordan. On 4 September, the four convicted men were hanged in a prison in Amman.[150]

After King Abdullah's assassination, a power struggle started between King Abdullah's two sons, Talal and Nayif. Because the elder son, Talal, was in a mental hospital in Geneva due to a nervous disease, the younger son, Nayif, was appointed regent upon King Abdullah's death, despite the Jordanian constitution specifically stating that the eldest son would take the throne. Nayif refused to give up his position and demanded to be appointed King of Jordan in place of his father, King Abdullah. Many in the political system in Jordan, including the British, preferred Talal.

In early August 1951, the Jordanian government decided to send Sa'id al-Mufti, deputy Prime Minister, to Geneva to meet Talal and see if he was capable of being appointed King. A few days later, the Jordanian Health Minister, Dr. Jamil al-Tutunji, arrived to examine him. He judged Talal to be competent and forwarded his recommendation that Talal be appointed King of Jordan. The government decided "after studying the medical reports and the constitutional results" to declare him the King of Jordan on 5 September 1951, despite Nayif's objection. Nayif attempted a coup with the help of the 10th Regiment (the Hashemite Regiment). After its failure he left Jordan and did not return until his death in 1983. On 10 September 1951, Talal's eldest son, 16-year-old Hussein, was appointed crown-prince.[151]

The Arab world congratulated Talal on his impending coronation. They perceived Talal as an anti-British Arab nationalist who had supported al-Tall's plot against King Abdullah. It was felt that a new age had started in Jordan with a King who favored Egypt and Syria, supported the Arab League, and who would join the ACSP. Therefore, Egypt and Syria were especially pleased with Talal's rise to the throne and Cairo radio announced that "his enthronement will end the intrigues of the Arab world". Al-Tall also sent a congratulatory telegram from Cairo.[152] However, because of his anti-British policy and the great sympathy he had with the Arab public, there was concern that the British would exploit his mental illness in order to prevent him becoming king. On 25 July 1951, the *al-Aharam* newspaper published a report saying "Prince Talal will not be enthroned as king". According to the report, Talal's doctors would submit a report stating that the mental illness from which he suffered was incurable and therefore he could not be King of Jordan.[153] The rumors in the Arab world that the British were intervening in order to prevent the appointment increased and many expressed distrust of British policy in the Middle East. Many leaders, led by the secretary of the Arab League, wanted an objective medical examination of Talal's condition. On 29 July, al-Tall published a message which expressed distrust in the British and called for the sending of an "unbiased" Arab team of doctors to examine Talal.[154]

Those rumors, however, had no basis in reality. The British did not support Nayif's appointment because he was perceived as "lazy" and unfit for the role. They supported Talal, despite his medical condition, in order to uphold the Jordanian constitution which maintained: "The heir to the throne must be the eldest son".[155] Talal's regime lasted a year, but he is mostly known for the new constitution approved in January 1952 in accordance with King Abdullah's promise and the demands of the opposition. The constitution stated that the Prime Minister and individual ministers would be collectively and individually responsible to Parliament for their activities and to the King, as before (Article 51), and that an absolute parliamentary majority of two-thirds against the government on a vote of no confidence must result in the government's resignation or dismissal (Article 53).[156]

4

In Exile in Egypt and Return to Jordan

After the assassination of King Abdullah and the rise to the throne of King Talal, al-Tall continued his political exile in Egypt. Despite his earlier positive relations with King Talal and his support for him, al-Tall felt that it was not yet the right moment to return to Jordan. Jordanian public opinion was still very stormy and it was doubtful whether the public would accept the return of one of those responsible for the assassination of King Abdullah. Talal was too weak and, at least initially, was under the influence of many in the previous regime, including the British. They did not want al-Tall to return to Jordan and therefore recommended that King Talal should not grant him a pardon.[1]

In any case, Egypt had become a more comfortable political arena for al-Tall's latest activity. Unlike King Abdullah's policy of promoting and cultivating connections with the British, his son Talal, together with the Prime Minister Abu al-Huda, preferred to cultivate connections with the Arab League states, especially Saudi Arabia and Egypt. Economic and commercial agreements were signed with them shortly after Talal become King.[2] Since al-Tall could no longer criticize Jordan's policy toward Britain, he focused his activities on the reawakening Egyptian national struggle against Britain.[3]

Negotiations between Egypt and Britain which took place in mid-1951 to renew the Anglo-Egyptian Treaty of 1936 for continued British presence in the Suez Canal, resulted in an impasse. Egyptian demands for the immediate evacuation of British forces from Egypt were renewed. This was a matter of principle for Egypt who was seeking to maintain its status in the Arab world and the Arab League. As long as a foreign army was stationed in their country, they felt their status was weak.[4] Therefore, under pressure from Egyptian public opinion, Prime Minister Mustafa al-Nahas submitted to Parliament on 8 October 1951 a request to cancel the treaty and the Condominium (or joint authority) in Sudan which had been in effect since 1899, claiming that in 1936 Egypt had not been free to act at will. A week later, on 15 October, Parliament decided unanimously to cancel the treaty. Egypt and Sudan were unified into one country and Farouk was crowned "the king of Egypt and Sudan" – a title that some Western countries recognized.[5]

The unilateral cancellation of the treaty caused tension between the two countries. The Egyptians, who enjoyed support and backing from Arab countries (including Jordan), hardened their position and rejected the United States' compromise proposal (in cooperation with France and Turkey) that would officially transfer the military base in the Suez Canal to Egypt in return for Egypt agreeing to join the MEC, established by the Western countries.[6] In response, the British increased their forces in the Canal Zone. At the instigation of nationalist organizations and movements, Egyptian workers and others who worked for the British army stopped work and the channel ports and Egyptian customs closed. On 14 November at one of the largest demonstrations in Egypt, about one million people, led by Prime Minister al-Nahas, marched in Cairo shouting nationalist slogans against Britain.

According to British and Israeli intelligence sources, the increase in violence in Egypt was encouraged by the Egyptian government to raise the status of the Wafd Party and its leader Mustafa al-Nahas in the eyes of the Egyptian public, and to divert attention away from the serious social-economic situation.[7] So, with the support of the government, "liberation" battalions (*fedayeen*), which were in fact terrorist groups, were set up to attack British soldiers and infrastructures in the Canal Zone. Political activists of the radical Muslim Brotherhood and the Socialist Party (formerly the Young Egypt Party) as well as retired Egyptian army officers (including the nationalist pro-German Aziz Ali al-Misri) subordinate to the Egyptian War Ministry, led by Abd al-Majid Abd al-Haq and commanded by senior Egyptian officers, joined the battalions.[8]

The main clashes between the Egyptians and the British occurred between November 1951 and February 1952 "and occasionally pitched battles were fought", as Vatikiotis described.[9] The peak of the conflict was the clash near the Suez Canal on 25 January 1952. British troops, who had arrived to reinforce the police station in Ismailia, shot Egyptian policemen after they refused to hand over their weapons. During the exchange of fire, more than 50 Egyptians were killed and hundreds surrendered. When the Egyptian people found out about the incident the following day, 26 January, they went out into the streets and attacked foreign interests, airline offices, hotels, cinemas, and set Cairo on fire. The events, known in Egyptian historiography as "Black Saturday", brought about a serious political crisis. Prime Minister al-Nahas was made to resign and Ali Maher was appointed in his place. This increased political instability in Egypt and precipitated the Free Officers revolution on 23 July 1952 which, according to the Revolutionary Council, was not supposed to take place before 1954.[10]

The events in Egypt served al-Tall well. They gave him the opportunity to return to the Arab public stage and to renew his image as a hero fighting for the independence of an Arab country from the British. He immediately enlisted as a volunteer in one of the Egyptian battalions which fought in the Canal against the British and received command of one of them.[11] Although there is no evidence of his terrorist activities against the British, al-Tall became very popular in Egypt and with the Arab public in general with his belligerent statements and criticism of the British, along with memories of his defection from the Arab Legion. He became an adored figure throughout the Arab world, more than any other Arab leader at the time, and was considered by experts on the Middle East as one who "may decide the fate of the entire Middle East in the future".[12]

He tried to exploit his public standing to undermine Arab regimes in order to carry out his plan, first published in February 1951, for the union of the Arab world into four blocks: Egypt, Sudan and Libya; Saudi Arabia and Yemen; Jordan, Iraq and Kuwait; Syria and Lebanon. They were to conduct a unified policy and "constitute a large Arab empire, which would be strong enough to overcome Israel", he said.[13] It is not inconceivable that al-Tall was influenced by Musa al-Alami but it is more likely that he derived his ideas from al-Nabhani.[14] Two months earlier, in December 1950, the Palestinian Taqi al-Din al-Nabhani published his famous book *Inqadh Filastin* (Salvation of Palestine), which proposed uniting the Arab world into six blocks, with each block having independent internal policy, but their foreign policy would be uniform.[15]

Al-Tall's proposal was in line with the entire Arab world's preoccupation with the question of Arab unity. Many of the prominent Arab leaders in those days, including Syrian Prime Minister Nizam al-Qudsi, Syrian President Adib Shishakli, and Egyptian President Muhammad Nagib, called for the unification of the Arab world. This was part of their struggle for influence and explains why al-Tall made his proposal even though it was similar to al-Nabhani's. Just stating it was sufficient to make him an influential figure and bring him renown.[16]

Al-Tall's plan, as well as that of other Arab leaders, did not materialize because of the conflicts of interest in the Arab world and hostility that existed between the countries which prevented any possibility of union between them. In addition, political developments in the Middle East at the time, including the Free Officers revolution in Egypt in July 1952 and the dismissal of King Talal after a recurrence of his mental illness a month later, were also factors.[17]

Talal's dismissal was not significant for al-Tall. Like other Arab nationalists, he suspected that the British were responsible for deposing Talal due to differences over policy. To counter these claims, Prime Minister Abu al-Huda decided to have not only Western doctors, but also doctors from Jordan, Egypt and Syria, attend the medical examination of Talal so that they could attest to his mental illness. In early August 1952 they unanimously confirmed that Talal's health was too poor for him to continue to fulfill his duties as King of Jordan. Following this recommendation and the approval of the two houses of the Parliament, Talal was removed from power on 11 August 1952, and a council of regency was appointed until Hussein, Talal's eldest son, took the throne a year later.[18]

However, Talal's removal from power was unpopular with a number of young nationalist officers, led by al-Tall's colleague, Ali Abu Nuwar. Abu Nuwar, like al-Tall, was in contact with Talal and also tried to reduce the influence of the British in the Arab Legion. With the dismissal of King Talal, Abu Nuwar argued against having either British assistance or royalty in Jordan. These statements raised allegations made by al-Tall only a few years earlier. General Glubb Pasha, who feared Abu Nuwar's statements would have influence in Jordan and endanger British interests, decided to act quickly. He recommended that the Jordanian government distance Abu Nuwar from the center of influence (as had been suggested for al-Tall). In September 1952 the Jordanian government approved Glubb's recommendation and appointed Abu Nuwar as a military attaché in Paris.[19]

On 23 July 1952, the Free Officers revolution took place in Egypt led by General Muhammad Nagib and Gamal Abd al-Nasser. King Farouk was overthrown and deported first to Monaco and later to Italy, where he stayed until his death in 1965. Political parties were dismantled and the officers set up "Liberation Rally", the only political movement allowed in Egypt. In June 1953, Egypt was declared the Arab Republic of Egypt and Muhammad Nagib was appointed President and Prime Minister, with Nasser as his deputy.[20]

Some sources claim that al-Tall's political activity against the Jordanian regime and the British inspired the Free Officers revolution,[21] whereas in fact the Free Officers movement originated many years earlier. According to Anwar Sadat the idea to form a secret revolutionary organization by Egyptian officers began in January 1939. It ripened into fruition in the summer of 1949 after Husni Zaim's attempted coup in Syria.[22] Indeed, the Free Officers tended to be anti-British and some of them, like Nasser and Sadat, had been involved in anti-British political activity even earlier. For example, in November 1935, Nasser participated in an anti-British demonstration in Cairo and was wounded in the forehead by a bullet shot by a British police officer.[23] Sadat, during his service as an officer in the Egyptian army, took part in an anti-British pro-German conspiracy together with Aziz Ali al-Misri during the Second World War. As a result, Sadat was expelled from the army, but continued to take part in political activities in anti-British organizations, including the Muslim Brotherhood.[24]

It was because al-Tall had no connection with the Free Officers that despite his many years of political exile in Egypt he had no formal role in the country. There is evidence that al-Tall and Nagib met before and, probably, after the revolution. Al-Tall even sent him a congratulatory telegram after the revolution "on behalf of the Jordanian political exiles in Egypt". Nagib was possibly influenced by al-Tall's proposal when he proposed unity in the Arab world at the end of 1952.[25] Al-Tall's brother, Ahmad, admitted that although al-Tall was present at events held by the Free Officers from time to time, he never met Nasser personally during his stay in Egypt.[26]

In Cairo al-Tall lived with his wife and children at 16 Zaytun Street in the Zamaliq Quarter, which consisted of luxurious villas on the bank of the Nile.[27] His days were spent in lectures, attending conferences on Arabs and Palestinians, visiting Arab leaders in Egypt and other Arab countries and tours.[28] His participation as one of the senior Arab officers in the 1948 war and his knowledge of the Jews following his victory on the one hand and his contacts with the

Jews on the other hand made him an expert on the war in the eyes of the Egyptians. Not only was he the leading expert in Egypt on the 1948 war, but also on Jewish affairs and Israel in general. In December 1952, al-Tall was invited to the office of Egyptian intelligence to help estimate Israeli military capabilities in the face of a possible renewal of war.[29] However, he was never recruited into the Egyptian army – perhaps because the British would not permit it. "Abdullah al-Tall's entering into the Egyptian army seems an unfriendly step", said Chief of the Imperial General Staff Field Marshal Viscount Slim to King Farouk, when he learned that al-Tall had arrived in Egypt. Attempts to recruit him into the Egyptian army later "to fight the aggressive Jews, who robbed the Arab lands" (in his words) also failed because the new regime refused to countenance the idea.[30]

In Cairo al-Tall carried a gun and was always accompanied by two bodyguards for fear that the Jordanians or other hostile elements (such as the British) would try to assassinate him. About a conversation he had with al-Tall, Khalil Totah, the author of *Dynamite in the Middle East*, wrote in April 1952, "As we talked in the hotel lobby, I was made aware of two pairs of eyes which were watching us quite closely. I asked him if they happened to be spies trailing his footsteps, but he said that they were two of his trusty relatives who constituted his bodyguard. He carried a pistol in his hip pocket and most likely he has need of it".[31]

Abdullah al-Tall and Arab Nationalism

One thing the Free Officers sought to realize immediately after the revolution was the elimination of "British imperialism" in Egypt. Relations between Egypt and Britain in general, and the British military presence in the Canal Zone in particular, was one of the most difficult aspects of Egypt's modern history. Therefore, the officers wanted to negotiate with the British government to end its military presence in Egypt quickly. An agreement signed in Cairo on 19 October 1954 between British Foreign Secretary Anthony Eden and Gamal Abd al-Nasser, the Egyptian Prime Minister at the time, stated that the British would withdraw their forces from the Canal within 20 months, but that the British could return to the Canal if Egypt was attacked by one of the Arab League countries or if there was an attack on Turkey (which already had a strategic alliance with the West as part of its membership in NATO).[32]

Nasser and his supporters described the agreement as "the biggest achievement of Egypt's national aspirations" and thought that the main contribution would be to remove the British from Egypt. However, many within the political system, especially among the Muslim Brotherhood, opposed the agreement because of the article allowing Britain to take over the Canal in the case of attack (Article 4). They believed that Nasser had given in to the demands of the British who, they felt, were looking for an excuse to take over the Canal as soon as possible.[33] Al-Tall did not make his opinion on this matter known: in light of his anti-British policy there is no doubt that he favored the position of the Muslim Brotherhood, which saw this agreement as a British ploy to allow them to return to the Canal indirectly. However, he could not criticize the new Egyptian regime which gave him protection while he was in exile. He knew that if he did, Nasser would remove his support and he would be deported from Egypt. Therefore, he forced himself to be satisfied with the actions taken.

Opposition to the agreement by the Muslim Brotherhood led them to attempt to assassinate Nasser on 26 October 1954, when he was making a speech to explain the agreement to the Egyptian people in Muhammad Ali Square in Alexandria. The assassin, Mahmud Abd al-Latif, fired eight shots, but missed. Nasser continued his speech and was not injured, while Abd al-Latif was shot and killed by Nasser's bodyguards.[34] Whether this event was staged as Jean Lacouture, the author of *Nasser: A biography* claimed, in order to raise Nasser's status with the Egyptian public, or whether this was a real assassination attempt in which he showed courage and heroism, the relationship between Nasser and the Muslim Brotherhood led to a serious crisis.[35] Two months after the assassination attempt, the Muslim Brotherhood movement was shut down, hundreds of its members were arrested, and six of their senior leaders were executed.[36]

One of the results of the assassination attempt was the dismissal of President Muhammad Nagib. As part of the investigations into the Muslim Brotherhood conducted by the security forces, the claim arose that Nagib maintained close ties with the Muslim Brotherhood and apparently knew about the attempt to assassinate Nasser. It was no secret that Nagib, and other officers, had ties with the Muslim Brotherhood, but Nasser, who sought to take over the leadership of the country, took advantage of this claim to displace Nagib.

According to Nasser, the Revolutionary Council decided on 14 November 1954 to dismiss Nagib as President and to sentence him to house arrest until the end of his life.[37]

Nasser's rise to power opened a new era in inter-Arab relations, especially between Egypt and Jordan. At the time, Jordan under the young King Hussein continued King Abdullah's policy and strengthened its ties with Britain and with the British officers in Arab Legion. Nasser, whose ambition was to achieve Arab unity under his own leadership, refused to accept Jordan's pro-West policy and was determined to stop it. Nasser's policy was similar to al-Tall's position regarding Arab unity and the elimination of British imperialism in the Middle East. Despite the similarity between the two personalities, there was no cooperation between them. The reason for this is unclear. Perhaps Nasser feared that al-Tall's popularity in the Arab world would damage his own position. Perhaps, on the other hand, Nasser suspected al-Tall of disloyalty, because he was close to the Muslim Brotherhood and the Mufti Hajj Amin al-Husayni, who opposed Nasser's regime.[38]

In any case, Nasser's activities against the British and his pan-Arab nationalism matched al-Tall's stance. One of the primary examples of this can be seen in the struggle against the Baghdad Pact – the popular name of the Central Treaty Organization (CENTO) – which Nasser led together with the Arab nationalist parties in the 1950s. Since the end of the Second World War and the development of the Cold War, the United States and Britain had developed regional defense plans to prevent the spread of communism, drawing up political and military treaties with a number of countries surrounding the Soviet Union. On 2 April 1954, encouraged by the United States, a treaty was signed between Turkey and Pakistan which became the first in a series of treaties signed between the countries which would later be called the Baghdad Pact. In February 1955, Hashemite Iraq signed the pro-Western treaty and two months later so did Iran.[39] The Western countries, led by the United States, made efforts to get additional Arab countries, primarily Egypt, to sign. But Nasser rejected the Baghdad Pact, which he claimed was a Western plot to cause a split in the Arab world and to help Israel. In addition, Nasser argued that the Soviet Union was not seen as a rival and actions should not be directed against their Soviet partner.[40]

Jordan, with its traditional military and political ties with Britain in particular, and with the West in general, was a potential ally.

Indeed, Britain had officially invited Jordan to sign the Baghdad Pact in return for the cancellation of the Anglo-Jordanian Treaty and its replacement with a new defense treaty promising significant military and economic aid to Jordan.[41] King Hussein, along with prominent Jordanian politicians such as Hazza al-Majali and Wasfi al-Tall, supported joining the Baghdad Pact because they thought that it would strengthen Jordan against extremist national elements and prevent it moving towards the Communist bloc. Moreover, they believed that the treaty would strengthen the Arab Legion and give them the opportunity to deal more effectively with Israeli raids into Jordan at the time (Kibya in October 1953, Na'alin in March 1954). However, other politicians, such as Naim Abd al-Hadi and Azmi al-Nashashibi, opposed the treaty and thought that Jordan would not benefit from signing it, feeling it was aimed primarily at defending Western interests in the Middle East.[42]

Meanwhile, Nasser's position in the Arab world had been consolidated with his non-aligned policy introduced following the Asian–African Conference in Bandung (Indonesia) in April 1955, and more especially as a result of an arms deal with Czechoslovakia, announced in September 1955. This strengthened the confidence of the Arabs and encouraged them to believe that under Nasser's leadership they could win the next war against Israel.[43] Therefore, in November 1955, when King Hussein announced his intention of joining the Baghdad Pact, Nasser began a propaganda campaign against him on Radio Cairo. Nasser managed to destabilize the Jordanian regime by bribing opposition politicians and government ministers to resign in an attempt to create anarchy. His agents in Jordan sent the opposition on to the streets to demonstrate.[44]

Consequently, Sa'id al-Mufti's government, which opposed the Pact, resigned at the beginning of the crisis on 13 December and King Hussein was unable to form a new government. After the visit of the British Chief of the Imperial General Staff, Field Marshal Sir Gerald Templar, to Amman for talks with King Hussein, and amidst the growing fear that Jordan would join the Baghdad Pact, the Jordanian opposition, encouraged by the Egyptian government, protested on 17 December in the largest demonstration ever known in Jordan. Pressure from Jordanian public opinion and opposition in the Arab world forced King Hussein, after 26 days and three different governments (al-Mufti, al-Majali, Hashem), to appoint Samir al-Rifai as Prime Minister on 8 January 1956. The new government immediately declared its intention to cooperate with the

Arab world and the possibility of Jordan joining the Baghdad Pact was lost.[45]

To restore his position and to demonstrate leadership, King Hussein decided to take the initiative. On 1 March 1956, he dismissed General Glubb Pasha and the rest of the British officers in the Arab Legion and ordered them to leave the country within 48 hours.[46] He tried to portray the dismissal as merely a professional decision without political considerations caused by a disagreement with Glubb Pasha about the defense of the West Bank in a future war with Israel, and his desire to promote Arab officers in opposition to General Glubb Pasha. However, it seems that King Hussein could no longer resist the pressure exerted by Jordanian national factions, who called for the dismissal of the British officers in the Arab Legion.[47]

In addition to political movements in Jordan which opposed British imperialism and King Hussein's connections with the West,[48] in the mid-1950s a group of young nationalist officers began to form, led by Ali Abu Nuwar. It was supported by Nasser and was called the "Free Officers", inspired by the Free Officers who brought about the revolution in Egypt. Following the Israeli raid into Kibya in October 1953, these officers began to declare themselves in opposition to Hussein's regime. They won wide popular support: they claimed that Glubb Pasha and the British officers did not help the Palestinians, that they had allowed a massacre by the Israelis in Kibya and that they wanted to make the Arab Legion into a Jordanian national army.[49]

Despite Radio Cairo's claim that the dismissal of Glubb Pasha "had been King Hussein's wish for a long time", and despite the news that King Hussein had planned Glubb's dismissal in advance, it would appear that Britain was not expecting it. The injury to Glubb Pasha's status and prestige symbolized the injured status of Britain in the Middle East and its plans in the area, including the Baghdad pact[50] because General Glubb Pasha was a symbol of British imperialism in the Middle East and expressed Britain's unlimited influence in Jordan. Therefore, the joy felt by the Arabs at the news of Glubb Pasha's dismissal was understandable. Al-Tall, who had tried to bring about his dismissal a few years earlier, expressed this feeling writing: "Thank God for eliminating one of the bases of imperialism in the Middle East. Today the Jordanian people is liberated from enslavement and exploitation . . . ".[51]

Beyond the decline in Britain's position in the Middle East,

Glubb's dismissal affected the capability of the Arab Legion. The appointment of unskilled Arab officers instead of the British officers weakened the Legion's operational capacity.[52] Command of the Arab Legion went to Radi Annab, Glubb's deputy, who had earlier been the Chief of Police of the Jerusalem district. Habis al-Majali was appointed deputy commander; Ali al-Hiyari was appointed Chief of General Staff, and Hikmat Mahyer was appointed Director of General Investigations. Following the dismissal of Glubb Pasha the name was changed from the Arab Legion to the Jordanian army.[53]

On 24 May 1956, Ali Abu Nuwar was appointed commander of the Jordanian army when Radi Annab retired. Abu Nuwar, who had led the campaign for the dismissal of Glubb Pasha, was a close friend of al-Tall and was known for his pro-Nasser tendencies and loyalty to the *Ba'ath* party. In the summer of 1954, when King Hussein visited Paris, he met Abu Nuwar who was then military attaché there. He was impressed with him and ordered him to return to Amman as his adjutant.[54] It seems that the close ties between al-Tall and Ali Abu Nuwar were based on their similarity. Both were officers originally from cities (al-Tall from Irbid and Abu Nuwar from Salt), young and ambitious, they were promoted rapidly in the army thanks to the support of the King (King Abdullah supported al-Tall, King Hussein supported Abu Nuwar). While al-Tall participated in the secret talks with Israel during the 1948 war, Abu Nuwar participated openly and publicly in negotiations with Israel in Rhodes.[55]

Therefore, the appointment of Abu Nuwar as commander of the Jordanian army fulfilled not only his own ambitions, but also those of al-Tall. Together with extreme nationalist parties within and outside Jordan, he tried to influence King Hussein's policy to become close to Egypt and Syria and abandon the strategic alliance with pro-British Iraq.[56] At the end of May 1956, there was a closening of relations between Syria and Jordan after Syrian president Shukri al-Quwatli's visit to Jordan. During his visit, King Hussein declared cooperation between the countries. Two months later, on 26 July, Jordan praised Egypt when it nationalized the Suez Canal and challenged the West. At the end of October 1956, Jordan joined the military alliance with Egypt and Syria, which had been signed a year earlier, and allowed the subordination of the Jordanian army to the Egyptian army commanded by Abd al-Hakim Amer. Despite the Suez war of 1956 with the attack of Israel, Britain and France on Egypt, Jordan did not give substantial aid to the Egyptian army. However, Jordan did show solidarity with the Arabs by allowing their armies to enter its territory to threaten Israel.[57]

Real expression of Nasser's growing influence in Jordan, together with that of the radical left parties, can be seen in the first free elections held in Jordan on 21 October 1956. The Socialist National Party, led by Suleiman al-Nabulsi, won 11 seats (out of 40) in the parliament. On 29 October King Hussein asked him to form a new government together with the Communist Party, called the National Front, who had won three seats and the *Ba'ath* party (two seats), in addition to independent candidates from the established al-Nabulsi Socialist bloc.[58] Al-Nabulsi, a lawyer by profession, served in the Jordanian government in the early 1950s as Minister of Finance and in 1953 was appointed Jordan's ambassador to London, but he was deposed from office due to anti-British activity. He was arrested for his activity against the Jordanian government during the events opposing the Baghdad Pact at the end of 1955.[59] There were other prominent Jordanians in the new government, some of whom were in contact with al-Tall and supported his political position, such as Anwar al-Khatib (Minister of Labor), Shafiq Rashidat (Minister of Justice and Education) and Abdullah al-Rimawi (Ministry of Foreign Affairs).[60]

Al-Nabulsi's government policy was generally anti-Western. Following the Suez war, Jordan severed diplomatic relations with France. Later, it unilaterally canceled the Anglo-Jordanian Treaty of 1948 and established diplomatic relations with the Soviet Union and China. On 20 January 1957, Jordan signed a solidarity agreement with Egypt, Syria and Saudi Arabia and was granted 36 million dollars in aid instead of the financial aid from Britain.[61] Internally, the government re-organized the army and replaced those who were identified as supporters of the old regime. Among the prominent Jordanians forcibly retired were Bahjat Tabbara, the head of general security, Muhammad Amin al-Shanqiti, a long time government member and personal friend of King Abdullah, and Abd al-Munim al-Rifai, the Jordanian representative of the United Nations and former Prime Minister Samir al-Rifai's brother. Officers identified as socialists close to *Ba'ath* party were promoted with the encouragement of Abu Nuwar, the commander of the Jordanian army.[62]

From February 1957 King Hussein began to act openly against the government, fearing the collapse of the Hashemite regime.

Senior figures in government, or close to the government, began to speak openly about the possibility of making Jordan a republic and removing the King from the power. The commander of the army, Abu Nuwar, also talked about this possibility and claimed that he kept a new flag of the "Republic of Jordan" in his office.[63] Indeed, the danger of the regime's collapse was real, as Amnon Cohen claimed, because members of the National Socialist Party began to prepare for a coup; they began to collect weapons which were smuggled through the Gaza Strip and forged links with those outside Jordan, mainly from Egypt, who wished King Hussein's regime to fall.[64]

Initially, King Hussein sent a message to Prime Minister al-Nabulsi saying that he was opposed to communist ideas and wanted to protect Arab nationalism in Jordan. He also ordered the press to stop attacks against the Eisenhower Doctrine, which ensured American military and economic aid to countries if threatened by aggression. Later he banned the publication of *Tass* in Jordan and restrictions were placed on mail coming from Syria and Lebanon.[65] On 10 April, after an attempted revolt by military officers, King Hussein forced Prime Minister al-Nabulsi to submit his resignation.[66] However, Hussein was not satisfied. On 25 April 1957 a law was enacted dispersing other parties, including the Communist Party which was also declared illegal. In the following month, dozens of orders for the arrest of Communist activists were issued. Parliamentary immunity was abolished and those arrested were sentenced to long prison terms.[67]

In addition to the turbulent demonstrations organized by left-wing parties in Jordan in protest against the dismissal of al-Nabulsi, on 13 April there was an attempted military coup. In the evening, Ma'an Abu Nuwar, a cousin of Ali, the commander of the army, planned to leave Zarqa for Amman with an artillery regiment. However, when the Bedouin 3rd Regiment soldiers loyal to King Hussein heard about it, they surrounded the camp and prevented the soldiers, whose loyalty was with Abu Nuwar, from going to Amman. In an attempt to break the siege, battles broke out between loyalists and the opposition killing three officers. Meanwhile, King Hussein received an update on events unfolding in the Zarqa camp and asked the commander, Ali Abu Nuwar, to accompany him on a visit to the camp. On their way to Zarqa, they met Bedouin soldiers who cheered the King, but wanted to kill Abu Nuwar. King Hussein defended the commander of the army and told him to return to

Amman, while he continued on to the camp in Zarqa. There, he met Bedouin soldiers and was given an enthusiastic welcome.[68]

The next morning, the commander of the army, Ali Abu Nuwar, who was behind the conspiracy, was dismissed and asked King Hussein to allow him to leave Jordan. Hussein gave his permission and he went to Syria and from there he continued on to Egypt. Later, it was discovered that Mahmud al-Musa, Abu Nuwar's deputy, was part of the conspiracy together with 20 other Jordanian officers, only some of whom were captured and put on trial because the rest had escaped to Syria. Ali al-Hiyari replaced Abu Nuwar as the commander of the army, but three days later he defected from Jordan and sought political asylum in Syria.[69]

Hussein's courage in going to the camp and the loyalty of the Bedouin soldiers saved the Hashemite regime from collapse. On 16 April, about 200 Bedouin tribal heads went to Amman to meet with King Hussein, indicating their loyalty to the Hashemite kingdom. Following the attempted coup, King Hussein cleansed the army of nationalist officers. Officers sacked by Abu Nuwar were returned to service and Palestinian units in the army were dismantled. The command of the army was given to the officer most loyal to the Hashemite regime, Habis al-Majali, who served in that position until 1965.[70]

The political developments in Jordan led to an increase in the number of political exiles from the army and government who were concentrated in two cities – Cairo and Damascus. Among the various exiles, the desire to bring about the collapse the Hashemite regime in Jordan was a unifying factor. Al-Tall, who knew some of them from his military service in the Arab Legion (for example Mahmud al-Musa who served with him in 6th Regiment during the 1948 war) and some from his opposition activity (for example Abdullah al-Rimawi who knew him from Jerusalem) met with them in October 1957 after escaping from Jordan to plan the collapse of the Hashemite regime. They discussed the need to join all forces and increase cooperation between the Jordanian exiles from different political parties (*Ba'ath* party, Socialist National Party, military officers, etc.). A year later, with the assistance of Syrian intelligence officer Abd al-Hamid Saraj, and on al-Tall's initiative, the exiled Jordanians established a Revolutionary Council. Al-Tall, together with Mahmud al-Musa and Ali al-Hiyari were among its most prominent members. They were elected in June 1960 to represent all Jordanian exiles to the Egyptian and Syrian authorities.[71]

The most significant activity of the political exiles was to foster the collapse of the Hashemite regime in Jordan during the union between Egypt and Syria (the United Arab Republic, UAR) from 1958 to 1961. The establishment of the UAR, led by Nasser, was greeted enthusiastically by the Arab world and gave rise to renewed hopes for a larger Arab union and the renewal of the war against Israel. "The UAR is the first step in saving Palestine and establishing a comprehensive union as it existed during the time of Saladin who drove the Crusaders from Palestine," declared al-Tall upon hearing the news.[72] However, despite the wishes of Jordanian nationalists, Hussein refused to join the UAR, preferring to initiate an alternative union with Hashemite Iraq (Arab Union) to weaken and neutralize the influence of Nasser in the Arab world.

Nasser and his followers in Jordan refused to recognize this. "Collaborating with imperialism is more dangerous than imperialism itself," stated Nasser when he heard about the Arab Union.[73] The UAR increased its efforts to bring about the collapse of the Hashemite regime in Jordan, using Jordanian officers who were Nasser's followers who had tried to overthrow Hussein's regime in cooperation with the Jordanian Revolutionary Council. Despite conflicts among its members, mainly between al-Tall and Ali Abu Nuwar over the question of leadership,[74] the Revolutionary Council dealt with the collection of military and political information on Jordan, recruited and trained local citizens for terror operations, and was involved in smuggling weapons to the West Bank and to refugee camps near Amman. Those arrested because of their terrorist operations received financial assistance from the Revolutionary Council. The UAR also tried to recruit a revolutionary vanguard among Jordanian students at universities in Syria and Egypt and tried to assassinate prominent political personalities in Jordan such as Samir al-Rifai, Hazza al-Majali and Bahjat Talhouni.[75]

In July 1958, the first conspiracy to bring about the collapse of the Hashemite regime in Jordan during the time of the UAR was uncovered. The Jordanian ambassador to the United States, Mahmud al-Rusan, together with 11 officers tried to assassinate King Hussein by throwing grenades. The conspiracy was planned in Damascus at the initiative of former Arab Legion officer, Mahmud al-Musa. King Hussein would be murdered in his palace and the conspirators would declare Jordan a republic and join the UAR. The plot was uncovered thanks to intelligence received in Jordan from the United States and Israel simultaneously.[76] Al-

Rusan was known for his anti-British policy and support for Nasser but despite his closeness to Abu Nuwar he deeply resented the fact that he had not been promoted when the latter took command of the army. After al-Rusan shot at Abu Nuwar's loyalists, he was arrested and sentenced to three years in prison. He was not in jail for long but was released and appointed ambassador to the United States. Following further activities against the regime, he was sentenced in February 1959 to 15 years in prison.[77]

Al-Rusan's conspiracy occurred simultaneously with the military revolution in Iraq, led by Abd al-Karim Qasim, which led to the collapse of the Iraqi Hashemite regime on 14 July. Although there is no known connection between the two events, King Hussein, who feared a general conspiracy against his regime, turned to the West two days later and formally requested direct military involvement in his country. He argued that with the elimination of the Hashemite regime in Iraq, Jordan remained the only anti-communist state in the Middle East and it needed help to prevent an increase in the Soviet Union's influence. Two days later, British paratroops arrived in Amman from Cyprus, while the United States sent troops to Lebanon, which was also in rebellion supported by the UAR. British forces stayed to support the regime in Amman and American aeroplanes sent military supplies to Jordan, with the approval of the Israeli government, which allowed the passage of foreign aircraft over its territory because of its expressed commitment to keeping the Hashemite regime in power.[78]

British forces remained in Amman until the beginning of November 1958, only leaving when it was decided that the Hashemite regime was stable. However, several months later in March 1959 another anti-Hashemite conspiracy was discovered, led by Deputy Commander of the army Sadiq al-Shara'a. Al–Shara'a was originally from Irbid like al-Tall, but he had no known contact with al-Tall or Ali Abu Nuwar. In July 1959, he was tried and sentenced to death but was pardoned in the summer of 1963 and allowed to leave Jordan. He went to Kuwait where he took up a position as a military advisor.[79]

The most prominent action of the Revolutionary Council was the planning and assassination of Jordanian Prime Minister Hazza al-Majali on 29 August 1960. Al-Majali was murdered in his office after two bombs exploded within the space of 30 minutes; a further ten people were killed and 24 injured. The Revolutionary Council planned the assassination in Syria with Syrian intelligence officer

Saraj and Jordanians who had infiltrated Jordan from Syria, escaping back there after the assassination. Eleven of the accused men were found guilty and sentenced to death. Seven of them were outside Jordan during the trial and were sentenced in absentia. The four condemned men actually present at the trial were publicly hanged in Amman on 31 December 1960. One of them was a junior Arab Legion officer, Hisham al-Dabbas, who was a relative of one of the conspiracy leaders, Shaker al–Dabbas.[80]

Rather than Bedouin officers who had proved their loyalty to the regime, the conspirators against the Hashemite regime in Jordan were officers who came from the cities of Irbid and Salt. These two cities had become centers of radical nationalism because of their proximity to Jordan's opponents: Irbid to Syria and Salt to the West Bank. Al-Tall, Mahmud al-Musa, Mahmud al-Rusan and Sadiq al–Shara'a came from Irbid and Ali Abu Nuwar, Ali al-Hiyari and Hisham al-Dabbas came from Salt.[81]

While al-Tall maintained contact with the Jordanian political exiles in Cairo and in Damascus to further his efforts to cause the collapse of the Hashemite regime in Jordan, he also had contact with Algerian national movement leaders who had fought to liberate Algeria from French occupation. The French had controlled Algeria since its occupation by the Allies during the Second World War. They had viewed it as an integral part of France ever since it was first conquered in 1830. The first nationalist riots began on 8 May 1945 in the city of Setif, east of Algeria, and were brutally repressed by the French army, which increased the tension between the Algerians and the French.[82]

However, with the failure of the French in Vietnam (in the battle of Dien Bien Phu) in the summer of 1954, the nationalist movement was resurrected. One of the nationalist leaders, Ahmad Ben Bella, created the Revolutionary Committee of Unity and Action (CRUA), the purpose of which was to unify the Algerian militia forces as a first step toward a general revolt against France. Meanwhile, nationalist Arab activists led by Nasser, who tried to benefit from the crisis in Algeria, began to intervene and encouraged the CRUA to declare a revolt against the French. They promised support and demanded that the entire Arab world support their struggle.[83]

In September 1954 in Cairo al-Tall met the two leaders of the CRUA, Muhammad Khayder and Sa'id Farhi. He gave them the value of his military experience and advised them how to act against the French military by pointing out locations of strategic importance in Algeria. He promised to help them in Egypt by collecting weapons and ammunition for the revolt and gave them his own gun as a symbol of his solidarity. "Never had I felt so great a joy in anything I did, as when I handed my gun to assist to rebellion in Algeria", said al-Tall at the end of the meeting with the Algerians.[84]

Based on the promises of assistance, on 1 November 1954 the CRUA announced a revolt against the French. In the proclamation from Cairo they called on all Muslims in Algeria to join the national struggle for the "restoration of the Algerian state, sovereign, democratic, and social, within the framework of the principles of Islam". The CRUA became the National Liberation Front (FLN), based in Cairo. The revolt began in Kabylia, north of Algeria, and spread rapidly throughout the country; the rebels attacked military installations, police bases, communication facilities and public buildings, and assassinated those who collaborated with the French.[85]

The French government believed that the insurgency would be easy to repress, but soon found Algerian resistance stronger than they had initially estimated.[86] France increased the number of troops stationed in Algeria to half a million and began to take a stronger stand against the Muslim civilian population. In October 1956, the French captured an aeroplane on which were some of the FLN leaders, led by Ben Bella; they were arrested and imprisoned in Paris.[87] The appointment of the new French President, Charles De Gaulle in November 1958, together with his moderate statements regarding Algeria, led to the opening of negotiations between the French and the Algerians, which resulted in a ceasefire agreement signed on 18 March 1962. About four months later, after a referendum held in Algeria, the French government officially recognized Algerian independence and released the FLN leaders from prison. After his release, Ben Bella was appointed president of an independent Algeria.[88]

Nasser had helped the rebels, as promised, by providing weapons, propaganda, intelligence and Arab political support for their cause. For example, when the Asian–African Conference opened in Bandung in April 1955 a delegation of the FLN attended at Nasser's request, and at the end of the conference he called on the members to support Algerian independence. Egypt had supported the Algerian revolt from the outset and countries located near Algeria, such as Morocco and Tunisia, also gave assistance to the rebels. They were joined by other Arab and non-aligned countries. On 19 September 1958, FLN leaders, supported by Nasser, established a government in exile in Cairo. Abbas Farhat was Prime Minister and his deputies were Karim Ben Qasim and Ahmad Ben Bella. The government was recognized by 15 countries, including the Soviet Union and China.[89]

Al-Tall had contact with the Algerian rebels from the beginning of the revolt which was supported by the Arab world, who considered it a model for the struggle against Western imperialism. It also inspired militant revolutionary movements among the Palestinians, who were close to the rebels and continued to maintain links with them.[90] Despite this, there is no evidence that al-Tall fought in the revolt, despite his earlier promises to do so. His brother, Ahmad, did not mention it in his book. There is, however, evidence that in 1959 the rebels asked him to train them in return for payment, but he refused to do so.[91] A year later, it became known that al-Tall had been increasingly involved in Algerian affairs. In April 1960, he laid the foundations for the Arab Brigade to be sent to Algeria to commit terrorist attacks. He began to train the Algerian rebels and, according to his brother, Ahmad, also joined the Arab Brigade for military operations in Algeria. His activities were written about extensively in the Egyptian newspaper *al-Musawar*, which described al-Tall as a "pioneer military volunteer in the Arab Brigade which was established to help the Algerian fighters".[92]

It is unclear why al-Tall only assisted the revolt years after its outbreak. Perhaps Arab solidarity and the desire to renew nationalistic activities in the 1960s propelled him to join the fight against the French as other Arab leaders had. On the other hand, perhaps it was the result of al-Tall's difficult economic situation at the time. Since going to Egypt, under pressure from the Mufti Hajj Amin al-Husayni, al-Tall had received a monthly salary from the Arab League of 270 Egyptian pounds, but this stopped in 1957. When his economic situation worsened, he may have felt that he had no choice but to help the rebels in return for payment in order to survive the many years of exile in Egypt.[93]

Whatever the reason, to Algerian leaders, al-Tall was considered a hero who contributed to their independence. Proof of this can be seen in al-Tall's invitation, one of the first, to an official visit to the country after it received its independence. The visit was held in November 1962, just four months after independence, during which al-Tall talked with President Ben Bella and other heads of the country, who thanked him for his assistance in the struggle for independence. They also asked him to stay in the country and take a political role so that they could continue to work with him, but al-Tall refused. As a gesture of appreciation, they gave him an Algerian diplomatic passport.[94]

Supporting the Algerian revolt and his other activities in early 1960 was a turning point in al-Tall's life in Egypt. He had been forgotten by the Arab public after the British left Egypt and Jordan and General Glubb Pasha was dismissed. An Israeli newspaper described him as "bald and fat from idleness". At this point, he returned to the public stage.[95] After the publication of his book, *Karithat Filastin* (The Catastrophe of Palestine), a year earlier, the Palestinian question resurfaced engaging the attention of Arab leaders and those who competed to support the Palestinians. In March 1959, Nasser raised the idea of the "Palestinian entity", in order to organize Palestinians scattered throughout the Arab world into one political framework. At the end of that year, Iraqi President Abd al-Karim Qasim called for the establishment of a Palestinian republic including the West Bank and Gaza and joining Israel to the Palestinian republic after the envisioned Arab occupation,.[96]

In order to weaken the position of Qasim and neutralize his initiative which had won Palestinian support, particularly by the Mufti, in early 1960 Nasser called for the establishment of a Palestinian government in Cairo led by al-Tall. Although al-Tall was not of Palestinian origin, he was considered the best man to head the government for several reasons. He continued to maintain contact with Palestinian officials, participated in conferences dealing with the Palestinian question, wrote and lectured about the Palestinian question, and his book had given him much publicity. The government, which previously comprised a committee to organize the Palestinians to examine how they could attain their "legal rights",[97] was established in early 1960. Apart from the Palestinian government, Nasser also called for the establishment of a Palestinian army under the command of Ali Abu Nuwar.[98]

The Palestinian government collapsed shortly afterwards because of "differences of opinion, envy and jealousy" among the Palestinians, according to Ahmad al-Tall, who opposed the appointment of al-Tall as Prime Minister. He felt that because al-Tall was not Palestinian he could not represent them effectively. Despite this, al-Tall's status suffered no harm. In April 1962, when the proposal to establish a Palestinian government in Gaza, led by Naim Abd al-Hadi, was raised again, al-Tall was asked to serve as defense minister. This government was never established but al-Tall continued to be a symbol of the struggle against Israel, a role model, and a source of admiration among groups of young nationalist Palestinians. The founders of the *Fatah* movement, established in October 1959 in Kuwait, Kamal Adwan and Khalil al-Wazir (Abu Jihad), met him in Cairo (separately) during the years 1960 to 1961, to hear his views on the struggle against Israel. Al-Tall had also met *Fatah* leader Yasser Arafat while he was a student at Cairo University in the 1950s. He maintained contact with other Palestinian activists and as long as he was in Cairo updated them on activities against Israel.[99]

From Anti-Israel to Anti-Semitism: Abdullah al-Tall and his Islamic Perspective

From the mid-1960s, while he was in Egypt, al-Tall began to publish anti-Semitic books. It is unclear when al-Tall became anti-Semitic and from where he absorbed those ideas, but there are two main possible sources of inspiration. One may have been his relationship with British officers in the Arab Legion and in Palestine during the period of the Mandate and the second may have been his drawing closer to Islam. During the period of the British Mandate in Palestine, many British officers were suspected of being pro-Arab and anti-Semitic. Many of these officers came from the Arab Bureau in Cairo, which was a kind of British intelligence office, part of the Foreign Office in London. The officers spoke Arabic and maintained political ties with Arab leaders. Thus, during the British Mandate, especially in its early years, British officers were ambivalent about violent attacks on Jews and sometimes even encouraged them.[100]

This anti-Semitic outlook was not only true of British officers in Palestine, but also among British officers in the Arab Legion. According to research by historian Benny Morris, the commander of the Arab Legion, General Glubb Pasha was suspected of anti-Semitic tendencies. He referred to Jews as Nazis and saw Israel as a Nazi state. Moreover, he claimed that Hitler's racial theory was identical to the Jewish belief that God had chosen them. Therefore, he concluded that "Hitler was not original in his conception of a 'master race.'"[101]

Israelis who met al-Tall during 1940s did not feel that he was anti-Semitic. Neither did British or Israeli documents suggest it. Therefore, it would seem that he had not yet consolidated his anti-Semitic outlook although, as noted, it was common among British officers. It is more likely that he adopted this attitude later when he was living in Cairo and became closer to Islam. His close relationship with the Mufti Hajj Amin al-Husayni, the Muslim Brotherhood in Egypt, and scholars from al-Azhar University were probably the crucial factors that shaped his anti-Semitic views in the 1960s.[102]

Indeed, anti-Semitism had existed to a degree in Egypt from the middle of the 19th century (the first publication accusing Jews of ritual slaughter was published in Cairo in 1844), but with the formation of the Muslim Brotherhood movement in April 1929 by Sheikh Hassan al-Banna, anti-Semitism became commonplace in Egypt. The rise of Nazi and fascist parties in Europe made a significant contribution to the spread of anti-Semitic ideas in the Arab world in general and Egypt in particular. A party in the spirit of fascism called *Misr al-Fatat* (Young Egypt), similar to the Nazi party in Germany, was established in 1933 in Egypt by Ahmad Hussein. It copied the Hitler salute, military parades and ceremonies, and personality cult of the leader. Egyptian delegations participated in the annual Nazi Party conference in Nuremberg in 1936.[103]

The Muslim Brotherhood in Egypt also had close ties to the Nazi party before the Second World War, was subsidized by the Nazi party, and spearheaded the distribution of Hitler's infamous book, *Mein Kampf,* and the "*Protocols of the Elders of Zion*" in Cairo. The relationship between the Mufti Amin al-Husayni and Hitler was well known. The mufti organized the Muslim S.S. division in Bosnia-Herzegovina, tried to prevent the Jews from escaping Nazi authorities, and daily broadcast pro-Nazi, anti-Semitic harangues in Arabic. In one of his radio broadcasts, he called to his Arab followers to murder their Jewish neighbors: "Kill the Jews wherever you find them. This pleases God, history and religion".[104]

Abdullah al-Tall published his anti-Semitic teachings in three books. The first was *Khatar al-Yahudiya al-Alamiya Ala al-Islam wal-Masihiya* (The Danger of World Jewry to Islam and to Christianity) which was published in Cairo in 1964. The second was *Judhur al-Bila* (Roots of Evil) published in Amman in 1970. The third was published in Amman a year later and called *al-Af'a al-Yahudiya fi Ma'aqil al-Islam* (The Jewish Viper in the Islam Mentality). Most of the anti-Semitic ideas that he presented in his books were not new, but were taken from Christian anti-Semitism which had reached the Arab world via Christian missionaries in the mid-19th century.

Al-Tall claimed that Jewish settlement in Palestine was based on God's false promise to the Jews. This promise first appears in Genesis, when God said to Abraham, "to your seed I will give this land" (Genesis, 12: 7) and is repeated again and again throughout the Torah (Hebrew Bible). According to al-Tall, these promises, which God also gave to Isaac and Moses, were just "nonsense spread by the Jewish sages in their historical-religious books".[105] Al-Tall's argument and that of other Arab intellectuals that the Jews distorted the Torah was not new. It is written in the Qur'an, intending to repeal the historic right of the Jews to Palestine.

In the early days of Islam, when the Prophet Muhammad tried to befriend the Jews, he treated the Torah and Jewish traditions with respect. He ordered Muslims to consult with Jews when in doubt about religious commandments because the Jews knew better: "So if you are in doubt, about that which we have revealed to you then ask those who have been reading the scripture before you [i.e. the Jews]. The truth has certainly come to you from your God, so never be among the doubters" (Qur'an, 10: 94). Moreover, at the time Muhammad did not deny the fact that Palestine belonged to the Jews and said: "O my people enter the Holy Land which God has assigned to you and do not turn back [because] you become losers" (Qur'an, 5: 21). Only after the Jews refused to accept his new religion did Muhammad begin to claim that the Jews had turned a blind eye to biblical prophecies announcing the future arrival of the Prophet Muhammad. "Those to whom we gave the scripture know him as they know their own sons. But indeed, a party of them conceals the truth, while they know" (Qur'an, 2: 146). Following the Qur'an, writers of classical Islamic history wrote specifically about the distortion of the Torah by the Jews.[106]

Al-Tall claimed that Palestine (the land of Canaan), from which the Jews came to Egypt, was inhabited by "brave Arabs who defended their land".[107] This argument was very similar to the Palestinian claim of the early 1920s with the emergence of the Palestinian national movement. In an attempt to deny the right of the Jews to Palestine, the Palestinians claimed to be descendants of the Canaanites, who were in Palestine before Jewish settlement. In an open letter to Winston Churchill on 16 March 1921, the Palestinian newspaper clearly stated: "The first to settle in Palestine in the earliest antiquity were none other the Amalekite Arabs, our early ancestors". However, in official reports, the Palestinians admitted that Arabs had only settled in Palestine since the Muslim conquest in 634.[108]

According to al-Tall, the Jews not only distorted God's promise of Jewish settlement in Palestine, but extended that promise to include other areas.[109] "Every place where on the sole of your foot shall tread shall be yours: from the wilderness, and Lebanon, from the river, the river Euphrates, even unto the hinder sea shall be your border" (Deuteronomy, 11: 24). The desire to spread "Greater Israel" is rooted in what he termed the Jewish nature or Jewish race. "Aspiration for expansion is a fact rooted in the rotten minds and hearts of stone that will not rest until they have conquered Iraq, Syria, Jordan, Palestine, Lebanon, Sinai . . ."[110] According to Prof. Harkabi (who was Chief of Israeli Military Intelligence, 1955–59) this was based on the alleged intentions of the Jews to expand which was widespread in the Arab world in the 1960s. Its aim was to give legitimacy to the destruction of Israel. In other words, al-Tall claimed that because the Jews wanted to take over neighboring Arab countries and drive the Arab residents to the "Arabian Peninsula, their first homeland", Israel had no legitimacy or right to exist among civilized nations.[111]

In all three of his books, al-Tall focused on what he considered common traits of the Jewish people, displaying them as the most dangerous threat to Christianity and Islam. He claimed his "theory" was based on the Torah, which "frankly describes the characteristics of the Jewish people"[112] and stories in the Qur'an which refer to Jews. He confirms the authenticity of these traits from his own experience and familiarity with the Jewish people during the 1948 war. Among the main features that he claims were inherently Jewish were:[113]

Cowardice: "This is the basic nature of the Jews even if they try to behave differently", said al-Tall. He claimed that the Jews tried to present themselves as brave heroes, but were actually cowards, afraid of death and cling to life. Their fear is mentioned many times in the Torah, for example when they escaped from Egypt: "the children of Israel lifted up their eyes and Egyptians marched after them and they were sore afraid; and . . . cried out into the God" (Exodus, 14: 10), or when the spies returned from Israel and claimed "the land, through which we have passed to spy it out, is a land that eats up the inhabitants thereof; and all the people that we saw in it are men of great stature" (Numbers, 13: 32). The Qur'an also mentioned their fear: "They (Jews) do not fight you, but in cities secrete themselves behind the fence" (Qur'an, 59: 14); after Moses told the Jews to enter the Holy Land as God commanded, "said to Moses we did not go ever to the country, as long as they are in, go you and your Lord to fight and we will sit here" (Qur'an, 5: 24). The Jews' fear, said al-Tall, was evident during the 1948 war, when he claimed they were afraid to fight face to face against the Arabs and preferred to fight in the dark of night.[114]

Cruelty and injustice: According to al-Tall, history knows no cruelty greater than that of the Jews. He wrote that the Torah itself described the God of Israel as warlike with titles such as "The God of the armies of Israel" to encourage the Jews to be like him. He claimed that God's commandments in the Torah were cruel, and became part of Jewish nature. In al-Tall's harangue, one of the most prominent examples of cruelty, also mentioned in the Qur'an, was the story of Joseph, whose brothers plotted against him and persuaded their father to send him to them "so that they can carry out their schemes" (Qur'an, 12: 12). Relying on other Arab historians' claims, al-Tall insisted that the cruelty of the Jews was infamous throughout world history, from the ancient Greeks to modern times, the most recent event demonstrating their cruelty being a massacre in the village of Deir Yassin (west of Jerusalem) in April 1948.[115]

Al-Tall also claimed that the Jews were unjust. He maintained that the Torah is the only religious book to allow the killing of innocent people. For example, he claimed that Judaism allows children to be killed for their parents' acts of as well as allowing collective punishments.[116] Among the examples he found in the Torah on which to base his claim was the story of Dathan and Abiram, the sons of Eliab, who together with their families, a total of 250 people, were killed because they had sinned (Numbers, 16: 35). He also mentioned the story of the taking of spoils by Achan, the son of Carmi, during the Battle of Ai, for which he died, "his sons, and his daughters . . . and all that he had" (Joshua, 7:24).

Prostitution: "Prostitution and lawlessness had never been legitimate in any religion of the world, but the Jewish Torah gave it legitimacy", said al-Tall. To support his invective, he described examples from Genesis about forbidden relationships between family members to justify the claim that indecent acts were permitted by the Jews. An example he used was the story of Lot, whose two daughters lay with him and bore his children, Moab and

Ben-ammi (Genesis, 19: 31–38) and the story of Judah and Tamar, when Judah, the son of Jacob, lay with his dead son's wife (Genesis, 38: 14–30).[117] For these reasons, according to al-Tall, the Jews were despised among other nations, as mentioned in the Qur'an: "Cursed are those who disbelieved among the Children of Israel by the tongue of David and of Jesus, the son of Mary. That was because they disobeyed their sin" (Qur'an, 5:78). Al-Tall argued that the Jews were the world's brothel owners, using their money to purvey sexual permissiveness to destroy human values.[118]

Cheating: Abdullah al-Tall wrote that the Torah allowed Jews to cheat and steal to achieve their goals including, surprisingly, some of the Jewish prophets. He further claimed that Judaism was the only religion that gave legitimacy to cheating and that the Torah was full of such stories. The first story on which he relied for his diatribe was the story of Jacob and Esau. Rebecca, Isaac's wife, encouraged Jacob to impersonate Esau in order to receive the blessing intended for Esau (Genesis, 27: 1–7). Another example al-Tall used was the story of Shechem, the son of Hamor, who lay with Dinah, and then wanted to marry her. Jacob's sons agreed on condition that all males were circumcised. But on the third day after the circumcision "when they were in pain, that two of the sons of Jacob, Simeon and Levi, Dinah's brethren, took each man his sword, and came upon the city unawares, and slew all the males . . . " (Genesis, 34: 25).[119]

In addition to these and other alleged negative traits of the Jewish people[120] Abdullah al-Tall tried in his books to portray the Jewish religion as dangerous to Christianity and Islam and to argue that there would always be animosity between them. In al-Tall's view, the origin of this conflict between Judaism and Christianity was, of course, Jewish opposition to Jesus. According to al-Tall, Jesus wanted the Jews to return to the original Torah of Moses, which had been distorted over time. Al-Tall claims that Jesus called for goodness and tried to undo the bad qualities of the Jews (racism, exploitation, discrimination, etc.). According to al-Tall the Jews, fearing that Jesus would succeed, decided to kill him. Al-Tall wrote that the Qur'an taught that although Jesus had not been murdered, because God had reincarnated him, the Jews were still responsible for killing him because of their intention to do so.

Al-Tall continued that after killing Jesus, the Jews tried to prevent the spread of the Christian faith. He claimed they said that Mary, the mother of Jesus, was a prostitute and encouraged writings against Christians. He contended that the Jews took advantage of any opportunity they had to slaughter Christians. The first time was in 610 when the Persians invaded Syria to destroy the Byzantine Empire. Jews joined the Persian forces against the Byzantine Christians and massacred the prisoners.[121]

When Jesus failed to return the Jews to the correct path, according to al-Tall, God sent the Prophet Muhammad to all nations with a message of peace and brotherhood. Al-Tall repeated the idea found in Islamic tradition that Jewish sages knew that Muhammad's coming was predicted, but they deliberately distorted the Torah to hide this from the Jews.[122] Despite their efforts to deny the Prophet Muhammad, the religion spread and many converted to Islam. In al-Tall's view, this was very troubling to Jews, who felt that it endangered their religion and so began a campaign of hatred against Islam, despite the Prophet Muhammad urging patience and allowing them to remain as Jews living under Islam. He claimed the first Muslims suffered from Jewish deception as written in the Qur'an: "They [disbelievers] wove plots and God wove plots, but God is the best plotter" (Qur'an, 3:54). According to al-Tall, Jewish conspiracies to harm Islam continued throughout the years and, through various schemes and plots, they were able to recruit converts to Islam to take over key positions and promulgate infor- mation to harm Islam.

In conclusion, Abdullah al-Tall stated that the conflict between the Jews and Islam was obligatory, because they were diametrically opposed. "Naturally, there would be a conflict between Jews and Muslims after it became clear that Islam calls for lofty values which contradict what the Jews call for". He concluded, "Islam forbids unjustified bloodshed, theft and prostitution. Jews allow the shed- ding of the blood of non-Jews, stealing from non-Jews and causing them harm. It is true that the Ten Commandments of the Jews prohibit murder, stealing and prostitution, but the Jews explained it for themselves; 'do not murder' means do not murder Jews, 'do not steal' means do not steal from Jews and 'do not commit adultery' means do not commit adultery with a Jewish woman".[123]

Al-Tall came to two conclusions regarding Judaism. First, that the Arab–Israeli conflict was in fact a religious conflict between Islam and Judaism (he meant between good and evil), and therefore the solution should be a religious solution, that is, *Jihad*. "Any solu- tion that is not based on religion", said al-Tall, "will fail".[124] Second, he did not differentiate between Judaism and Zionism. "Many think that Zionism is very different from Judaism, but in fact they are the same thing, since Zionism is a mechanism of world Jewry, acting to destroy the world and control it".[125]

Thus, al-Tall adopted the Christian anti-Semitic view, seeing the *Protocols of the Elders of Zion* as the protocol of the first Zionist Congress in 1897 "proving" a Zionist conspiracy to control the whole world. Since being translated into Arabic for the first time in 1927, the *Protocols* have become an integral part of Arab anti-Semitism, imitating Christian anti-Semitism. Abdullah al-Tall attached so much importance to the *Protocols* that he put them on a par with Jewish religious books such as the Torah and the Talmud, which together he claimed "shaped the Jewish character". "*Protocols of the Elders of Zion*", said al-Tall, "are the third fundamental foundation of Jewish faith" and therefore "no Jews opposed Zionism".[126]

Even today, the *Protocols of the Elders of Zion* are very popular in the Arab world. Inspired by this late 19th-century Russian forgery, in 2002 a television series of 41 episodes called "*Horseman without a Horse*" was produced and broadcast on Egyptian television.[127] Some Arab intellectuals admitted recently that the *Protocols* were forged. The deputy rector of the Islamic University in Qatar said that "it seems that we [the Arab nations] are the only ones who believe that the *Protocols of the Elders of Zion* are real".[128]

Another anti-Semitic idea adapted by al-Tall from the Christians is that of the libelous accusation of ritual killing by the Jews which was very common in Europe during the Middle Ages. It claimed that Jews used the blood of Christians for Jewish religious ceremonies, including baking matzos for Passover. The origin accusations were made in the earliest days of Antiochus Epiphanes (2nd century BCE), but they were resurrected in England in 1144, after the body of a boy named William was found near Norwich. The Jews were charged with ritual murder. The libel spread from England to the rest of the West, and then to the Arab countries. Al-Tall explained that the Jews use the blood of Christian children because "the God of the Jews was not satisfied with animal sacrifices, but there is a need to please him with human sacrifices".[129]

In light of his anti-Semitism, it is easy to see why al-Tall justified Nazi crimes. "It was clear to the Germans," said al-Tall "that the Jews are to blame for Germany's defeat in the First World War and therefore they were afraid that they would cause defeat in the Second World War, as indeed happened". To al-Tall, Hitler did no more harm to the Jews than previous leaders such as Pharaoh, Titus, and Nebuchadnezzar, or the Romans, the Byzantines and others in

139

Europe who butchered Jews long before him. Al-Tall thought that Hitler had decided to do to the Jews what had been done throughout the preceding generations: to kill, burn and expel Jews from countries whose people had been cheated by them.[130]

Closure: Abdullah al-Tall's Return to Jordan

Aspirations for Arab unity under Nasser's leadership vanished with the dissolution of the UAR in September 1961, and the failure of the union between Egypt, Syria and Iraq in 1963 which Nasser had sought to establish. Nasser's position as the leader of the Arab world also began to disintegrate because of the differences over the question of support for *fedayeen* (guerilla) organizations operating against Israel.[131] While Syria supported the struggle and sponsored activities along the border with Israel, Nasser feared *fedayeen* activities would lead to war with Israel before the Arabs were ready. The military coup in Yemen on 26 September 1962, led by Colonel Abdullah al-Sallal, caused a split in the Arab world. Nasser supported al-Sallal as part of his policy to establish new pro-Egyptian regimes, but Saudi Arabia and Jordan supported Imam Muhammad al-Badr fearing that the revolution would inspire similar movements in their own countries.[132]

There was an opportunity to achieve Arab unity and create political cooperation in the mid-1960s when Israel decided to continue its National Water Carrier project. This project had begun in the early 1950s and was designed to bring water from the Jordan River to Israeli settlements in the Negev, but was stopped because of Arab opposition and international involvement. Israel's decision to resume the project caused great anger in the Arab states which declared that this was a *casus belli*.[133] In light of this, in December 1963 Nasser called a summit meeting of heads of Arab states to find a solution to the problem. In fact Nasser, who wanted to take the praise for spearheading a new diplomatic initiative, emphasized the special status of Egypt in the Arab–Israeli conflict.

On 13 January 1964, the first Arab Summit Conference convened in Cairo attended by all the heads of the Arab states except Libya and Lebanon. Policy meetings between Arab leaders created an atmosphere of brotherhood and they agreed to "put an end to disagreements, clear the Arab atmosphere of all discord, suspend all campaigns by information media . . . ". Regarding Israel

– the main subject of discussion – it was decided to urgently divert the water sources of the Jordan and take all military steps necessary for its defense. A joint command was established with the Egyptian chief of staff, General Ali Amer, as Supreme Commander and financial aid from the Arab League was assigned to the three countries concerned: Syria, Lebanon and Jordan. In addition, Arab leaders decided to adopt Nasser's initiative of setting up a political organization with its own military force to represent the Palestinians.[134]

Following the Arab Summit Conference on 28 May 1964, the first Palestinian Congress convened in the Intercontinental Hotel in East Jerusalem and announced the establishment of the Palestine Liberation Organization (PLO). Ahmad al-Shuqairi, was appointed to lead the organization, at Nasser's recommendation, as a representative of the Palestinians in the Arab League.[135] The appointment of his associate al-Shuqairi was a great success for Nasser because it enabled him to take a significant part in the PLO activities and to determine its political path. Moreover, it was the end of an important stage in the development of the Palestinian National Movement, bringing to an end the traditional Palestinian leadership of the Mufti Hajj Amin al-Husayni and his followers. The conference decided to establish a Palestinian military force and adopted the Palestinian National Covenant as the PLO's founding document. At the second Arab Summit Conference, held in September 1964 in Alexandria, the Arab states officially recognized the PLO as representing the Palestinians and sought help from Arab states for its operations.[136]

From the beginning, King Hussein opposed the establishment of the PLO, fearing that the organization would engender feelings of solidarity among the Palestinians living in Jordan with those outside it and politically destabilize the kingdom. Hussein could not speak openly against Nasser's initiative which had won the support of all Arab states. It is quite likely that he supported it, thinking that it would give him the legitimacy which he lacked. This was probably the reason why Hussein allowed Palestinians to convene a congress in East Jerusalem and also why he agreed to al-Shuqairi's request to establish there the office of the PLO.[137]

Al-Tall believed that the rapprochement between Jordan and Egypt following the Arab Summit, with its renewed diplomatic relations and Hussein's gestures toward Nasser (such as removing support for Imam al-Badr and his proposal to mediate between

Egypt and Saudi Arabia on the issue of Yemen) created optimism for future cooperation between the states regarding Israel. In a congratulatory telegram he sent to King Hussein a week after the first Arab Summit he wrote that "against the Zionist danger, which threatens Jordan in particular and the Arab nation in general . . . I support you and call on God to give success to Jordan's way through the next campaign along with other Arab countries' strength, faith and confidence".[138]

PLO activities in Jordan soon increased. Al-Shuqairi claimed to be recruiting Palestinians to the Palestinian Army, giving them weapons training and allowing them to take part in elections for the Palestinian National Council. King Hussein opposed this because he felt that it undermined the Hashemite regime in Jordan. To prevent Palestinians from sweeping the PLO to victory and to counteract the PLO's propaganda against Jordan, King Hussein decided to appoint Wasfi al-Tall Prime Minister in February 1965. Wasfi al-Tall, Abdullah al-Tall's cousin and a close friend of King Hussein, had already served as Prime Minister (January 1962–March 1963) and before that he had been responsible for political propaganda against Egypt. During his first term as Prime Minister in July 1962, Wasfi al-Tall issued "the White Paper", Jordanian policy on the Palestinian question. The main thrust was that Jordan alone was responsible for the Palestinian problem because most of the Palestinians were in its territory and thus Jordan should bear responsibility for the struggle against Israel. Al-Tall asked Egypt and other Arab states to stop tackling the Palestinian problem.[139]

As Prime Minister, Wasfi al-Tall took a number of actions against the PLO, culminating in July 1966 with the closing of the PLO office in East Jerusalem and denying recognition of the PLO as the sole representative of Palestinians in Jordan. King Hussein also made a number of gestures to pacify Jordanian opposition. In March 1965, he ordered the burning of 20,000 files of General Intelligence, which was responsible for internal security in Jordan, and a month later he issued a general amnesty in Jordan.[140] The amnesty was approved by the two houses of Parliament on 4 April and was the most comprehensive law for 15 years. It included amnesty for all offenses except for spying for or contact with Israel. "We will remove the residue of the past and return to being a family filled with love one for another", said King Hussein when the general amnesty law was published. The names of prisoners to be released were announced and the prisoners themselves were released three days later.[141]

The amnesty allowed the return of Jordanian political exiles, estimated at more than 100, most of whom lived in Cairo, but some in Damascus, Beirut, Baghdad and Kuwait.[142] This had been made possible by the new atmosphere created among the Arabs and the renewed calm on the Jordanian front. King Hussein did not fear that the exiles would be a threat to the Hashemite regime of Jordan. Asher Susser claimed Hussein believed that by making a gesture towards the opposition, he could gain legitimacy for activities against the PLO which was a far greater threat. Al-Tall, who was among the exiles allowed by the amnesty to return to Jordan, announced that "the amnesty ended the political exile of the 'Free Jordanians' and there is no impediment to the return of all them to Jordan".[143]

Since his defection to Egypt in October 1949, al-Tall had made several attempts to return to Jordan, but without success. He had based his attempts on his acquaintanceship with King Hussein whom he had met in Cairo in February 1955 and had tried to persuade him to agree to his return to Jordan, but the King had refused to pardon him. Al-Tall's friend, Naim Qal'aji, tried to mediate between him and the Jordanian regime, but his mediation efforts failed. Another initiative came in July 1959, when al-Tall's relatives, Wasfi and Idris, initiated a plan for a letter to be sent to the Prime Minister of Jordan, Hazza al-Majali, stating that al-Tall had had nothing to do with the assassination of King Abdullah. They hoped that the government would then approve his pardon and King Hussein would grant amnesty to al-Tall, sending a special aeroplane to return him to Jordan. Al-Majali did not trust the plan and ensured that it did not materialize.[144]

Following the publication of the general amnesty, some of al-Tall's family went to Cairo on 9 April to meet him and finalize the date of his return to Jordan. On 13 April, al-Tall arrived in Amman and met the Director of General Intelligence, Muhammad Rasul al-Kilani, who greeted him at the airport. From there, he went to Irbid, his hometown where he met with his cousin, Prime Minister Wasfi al-Tall, at his home. A week later, on 21 April, the al-Tall family published a notice in the *Filastin* newspaper, thanking King Hussein for granting the amnesty which had enabled al-Tall's return to Jordan.[145]

Although Ahmad al-Tall claimed in his book that "there was

great excitement and the enthusiasm of the masses was immense for the return of Abdullah al-Tall to Jordan", this was probably not the case. The Jordanian press did not even mention his return. No ceremonies, parties or special events were held in his honor. Moreover, there was no meeting between al-Tall and King Hussein. Even his brother Ahmad stated in his book that while al-Tall went to the King's Palace on 17 April, signed his name in a book of notables and met with the Royal Court Minister, Sharif Ben Nasser, there was no meeting with the King.[146] It seems that King Hussein deliberately avoided meeting al-Tall. He refused to grant him a political position in contrast to Ali Abu Nuwar who was appointed Jordanian ambassador to France or Dr. Subhi Abu Ghanima, who was appointed Jordanian ambassador to Syria (both of whom had returned to Jordan together with al-Tall). This indicates strongly that King Hussein did not trust al-Tall. The Jordanian government had probably avoided advocating al-Tall's return to Jordan before in an attempt to minimize his standing in the eyes of the Jordanian population.

After his return to Jordan, al-Tall's situation was precarious; he had to prove his loyalty to the Hashemite regime which was a problem for him. Since his return to Jordan, along with activities spreading Islam and participation at the World Islamic Conference, he was busy countering the criticism of elements hostile to the Jordanian government.[147] For example, on 25 January 1967, he wrote a protest letter, incorporated in his book *Karithat Filastin* (The Catastrophe of Palestine), to Nasser about the editor of the *al-Aharam* newspaper, Muhammad Hassanein Haykal, Nasser's friend and confidant. Al-Tall argued that it was wrong to assert that the Jordanian government was inimical to Arab interests. In his letter, he claimed that he was convinced that King Abdullah's policy had been "far-sighted" and that he had promised the Arabs control of Old Jerusalem.[148]

Although written in light of the elections held in Jordan and his desire to run for Parliament as the representative of Irbid, it seems that the letter was sent with the encouragement of, or even at the order of, the Jordanian government. However, from July 1966 al-Tall attacked everyone who used his book (such as al-Shuqairi) on the one hand and protected the Hashemite regime on the other.[149] Thus, in 1971, al-Tall retracted all his arguments against the Hashemite regime during the reign of King Abdullah. For example, he argued that King Abdullah's agreement to transfer the Little

Triangle to Israel in 1949 was caused by Israeli threats in the war against Jordan "if its claims were not met". The annexation of Arab territories to Jordan, explained al-Tall in October 1967, was because "most Palestinians wanted to be annexed to Jordan because they saw the Hashemite regime as their saviour", that they preferred to live under Jordanian rather than Israeli rule.[150]

After the Six Day War in June 1967 when the Arabs were defeated, the influence of the *fedayeen* in both Jordan and the whole the Arab world increased. The *Fatah* movement, led by Yasser Arafat, led the struggle against Israel from its bases in Jordan while it received financial and moral support from Arab countries, especially the Gulf States. In March 1968, IDF forces attacked one of the largest *Fatah* bases in Jordan at Karamah village about 20 kilometers north of the Dead Sea. During the operation, in contrast to earlier intelligence estimates, the Jordanian army intervened on the side of the *Fatah* fighters against the IDF forces, who were forced to retreat having lost their numerical superiority. Despite the many *fedayeen* and Jordanian army casualties (more than 150), the Palestinians interpreted the operation as a victory after IDF forces were forced to abandon their weapons during the withdrawal from the battlefield.[151]

Enthusiasm for the Palestinian stance against the IDF, especially after the Arab armies had been defeated six months earlier, overcame many in the Arab world who then saw *Fatah* under Arafat's leadership as the only Arab force capable of defeating Israel. Recruitment to *Fatah* and other *fedayeen* organizations grew. They were very popular inside and outside Jordan for having restored Arab honor. "In the forty-eight hours after the battle," wrote Shlaim "5000 new recruits applied to join *Fatah*". Consequently, the *fedayeen* were given special status in Jordan and were allowed to go about armed.[152]

King Hussein, fearing that he would lose control over Jordan, reached an agreement with Arafat in November 1968 to prevent the *fedayeen* from walking around the streets armed, but they violated the agreement. Moreover, the *fedayeen* increased their terrorist attacks against Israel in order to bring IDF forces into Jordan, trying to sabotage the peace initiative initiated by the Nixon administration. For the first time, in February 1970, the Jordanian army acted against the *fedayeen* and killed 300. However, because of pressure from Nasser, Hussein was forced to order the cessation of the operation and sacked the Internal Minister, Muhammad Rasul al-Kilani, who was responsible for the action, in accordance with PLO demands.[153]

The activities of American Secretary of State William Rogers in the Middle East in the mid-1970s and King Hussein's agreement to join the Egyptian–Israeli ceasefire caused controversy within the PLO. It led radical Palestinian movements to increase resistance to the Hashemite regime. While PLO Chairman Yasser Arafat believed that the PLO did not need to intervene in Jordanian politics, other radical Palestinian leaders such as George Habash, the leader of the Popular Front for the Liberation of Palestine (PFLP), and Nayif Hawatmeh, the leader of the Democratic Front for the Liberation of Palestine (DFLP), clearly stated that it was time to replace the Jordanian regime and called on Palestinians to revolt. "All power to the resistance," they said. At the Palestinian National Congress held on 27 August 1970 in the al-Wahdat refugee camp in Amman, the two leaders publicly suggested dispersing the Jordanian parliament and establishing a Palestinian government in Jordan.[154]

Open defiance against the Jordanian government received substantial expression a few days later. On 1 September 1970, the PFLP fighters tried to assassinate King Hussein on his way to the airport in Amman. Six days later, they hijacked three international aeroplanes. Two planes, Swissair and TWA, landed at Zarqa airport, while the third, PanAm, landed in Cairo. Three days later, another aeroplane, British Overseas Airways Corporation (BOAC), was hijacked and also landed in Zarqa airport. The passengers were taken hostage. In return for their release, the *fedayeen* demanded the release of their comrades from prisons in Switzerland, Britain and West Germany. After the three countries agreed to free the Palestinian prisoners, the *fedayeen* released the hostages and blew up the empty aeroplanes.[155]

The situation in Jordan was serious. King Hussein was criticized by military officers and his own family (especially his younger brother, Prince Hassan). He debated taking decisive action against the *fedayeen*. On 15 September, after a dramatic meeting between King Hussein and the loyalists among the military officers and his close friend, Wasfi al-Tall, King Hussein decided to act. The next day, he set up a temporary military government led by Muhammad Dawud (of Palestinian origin) with the participation of 12 military officers, replaced the Chief of Staff who had showed leniency toward the *fedayeen* and appointed Habis al-Majali, who was loyal to the Hashemite regime, in his place. Al-Majali was also appointed Military General Governor of Jordan. His deputy was Mazen Ajluni, known for his opposition to the *fedayeen*. In response, the *fedayeen* called for a general revolt against the Hashemite regime, declared northern Jordan to be liberated and Mahmud al-Rusan, one of the conspirators against the Hashemite regime in 1958, was appointed as Palestinian military commander in the north.[156]

On 17 September, Jordanian forces attacked the *fedayeen* positions in the main cities (Zarqa, Salt and Irbid) and the refugee camps in Amman. There was house to house fighting, resulting in many casualties on both sides. While Arab countries were beginning to intervene in what amounted to a civil war in Jordan, Syrian armored forces invaded Jordan, ostensibly to help conquer the north of Jordan, which was under Palestinians control. They hoped to separate it from the central regime in Amman. Because he could not fight on two fronts simultaneously, and concerned that the Syrian invasion threatened the Hashemite regime, King Hussein turned to Unites States for assistance. However, with no military base in the area, the United States could not give Jordan assistance quickly enough and turned instead to Israel to help Jordan. Israel reinforced its forces in the north and used its air force to threaten the Syrians. Fearing that Israel would indeed intervene in Jordan, Syria began to retreat. A ceasefire was signed in Cairo on 27 September following the involvement of other Arab states, which recognized the right of the *fedayeen* to continue to live in Jordan.[157]

One day after the ceasefire agreement and fearful of renewed fighting with the Jordanian army on 13 October, Arafat, who knew that his position had been weakened after Nasser's death, signed another agreement – which was in fact a surrender agreement. It recognized the absolute rule of King Hussein in Jordan and restricted the *fedayeen*. As a gesture of goodwill, the King granted amnesty to all *fedayeen* who had been arrested and allowed the return of Palestinians who had fled Jordan, including the two leaders, Habash and Hawatmeh. However, both refused to fulfill the agreement which Arafat signed and called for continuing the war against King Hussein. Under the new government of Wasfi al-Tall, one of their prominent opponents, the campaign to eliminate the *fedayeen* continued in Jordan.[158] In November 1970, the Jordanian army took control of Jerash and in March 1971 it also took the city of Irbid. The *fedayeen* were then concentrated in the area of Ajlun. There, they continued to attack Jordanian army vehicles. On 13 July

1971, the Jordanian army began a final attack on the 2,500 *fedayeen* remaining in the mountains of Ajlun and the Jordan Valley. Within five days, the Jordanian army took control of the area; many *fedayeen* were killed while others fled to Israel and Syria or surrendered to the Jordanian army. On 19 July 1971, the PLO ceased to exist in Jordan. King Hussein stated that Jordan was "completely quiet".[159]

King Hussein's actions saved the Hashemite regime from collapse and stabilized its position in Jordan and abroad. Nonetheless, Prime Minister Wasfi al-Tall who personally commanded the operations against the *fedayeen*, paid the price. On 28 November 1971, he was assassinated by four gunmen outside the Sheraton Hotel as he was returning from routine Arab defense talks. His stance in the session had been very moderate and would have enabled *Fatah* to continue to operate in Jordan within a political framework as Arafat had wanted.[160] The assassination was carried out by a new organization known as "Black September". Their aims were to highlight the Palestinian problem in the international and regional arena and also to avenge the deaths of the *fedayeen* during the confrontations with the Jordanian army in 1970–1971, especially the death of a *Fatah* commander, Walid Ahmad Nimr (Abu Ali Iyad), a personal friend of Arafat and one of the men with the potential to eventually replace him. According to his men he was arrested and killed by Wasfi al-Tall during the fighting in Ajlun and they sought to avenge his death by assassinating Wasfi al-Tall.[161]

From its foundation in September 1971 in Damascus by *Fatah* leaders Salah Khalaf (Abu Iyad) and Ali Hassan Salameh (Abu Hassan), son of one of the Palestinian leaders who fought in the 1948 war, "Black September" became the most popular of the Palestinian terrorist organizations operating in the 1970s and many Palestinians sought to join.[162] It was responsible for many operations against targets in Jordan, Israel and the West in general, including an assassination attempt on the Jordanian ambassador to London, Zayid al-Rifai, on 30 November 1971, the Belgian Sabena aeroplane hijacking in May 1972 and the massacre of Israeli athletes at the Munich Olympics in September 1972.[163]

The assassination of Wasfi al-Tall, a close friend of King Hussein, did not affect the Hashemite regime in Jordan. On the contrary, to symbolize the continuation of Jordanian policy and at the same time to express appreciation of Wasfi al-Tall, the Jordanian government formed by him continued to serve even after his death

– unusual in Jordanian politics. Abdullah al-Tall, Wasfi's cousin, who was then governor of the Interior Ministry, was appointed by special order of King Hussein issued on 9 December 1971, to replace Wasfi in the upper house of the parliament (the Senate) and Sai'da, Wasfi's wife, was appointed as a member in Executive Committee of National Union.[164] Al-Tall's service in the Senate continued until his death. On Monday, 13 August, 1973, when he was only 55 years old, al-Tall died as a result of illness and was buried in the family cemetery in the city of Irbid.[165]

Epilogue

Abdullah al-Tall pioneered revolutionary activities against the Hashemite regime from the end of the 1948 war onwards, which laid the groundwork for such activities in the Arab world. But he did so for personal reasons. Although he was influenced by political developments in the Arab world, he made a personal dispute between him and General Glubb Pasha into an ideological fight against the Hashemite regime in general. Abdullah al-Tall lived at a time of revolution – the desire to influence, to take the diplomatic initiative and decide their own fate was as essential to al-Tall as it was to other Arab officers after the 1948 war. However, unlike Husni Zaim, Gamal Abd al-Nasser or Abd al-Karim Qasim, who succeeded in leading military coups in their countries and taking power into their hands, Abdullah al-Tall failed to instigate revolution successfully.

Perhaps he was not a true revolutionary. His naivety and lack of understanding of the political reality in Jordan and the degree of British control of the Arab Legion foiled his attempted coup. He did not understand that as long as the British controlled the Arab Legion, his efforts were doomed to failure. He was just an enthusiastic young officer who tried to change the situation in which he lived in many ways, especially with regard to Israel, relations with the British, and the French. He talked a lot, but did little. Put to the test, he failed to change anything after his defection from the Arab Legion. This is why, despite all his political and military activities, he is known today in Arab history in general, and in Jordanian history in particular, only for his actions during the war in 1948 to occupy the Old City of Jerusalem. The rest of the activities in which he took part (the struggle against the British at the Suez Canal, contributions to the Algerian rebellion, etc.) have been forgotten and erased from Arab public consciousness.

A prominent expression of this is his nickname "Hero of Jerusalem" and the fact that his name is usually coupled with that of Salah al-Din (Saladin) and other Muslim heroes who conquered Jerusalem in earlier periods. The Jordanian poet Sadin al-Samuah published a hymn in his honor in the Jordanian newspaper *Al-Liwaa* in 1982 describing the battle to occupy Jerusalem. "The lands of Jerusalem were watered with his blood", wrote al-Samuah, when he described al-Tall's heroism in the 1948 war.

Abdullah al-Tall is commemorated today in the mosque bearing his name in his hometown of Irbid. The mosque, located north of Yarmouk University, on Abdullah al-Tall Street, covers 1,000 square meters which were donated by Abdullah al-Tall himself. The mosque was inaugurated in 1978, five years after his death.

Notes

1 The First Years in the Arab Legion

1 Marc Ferro, *The Great War, 1914–1918* (London: Frank Cass, 1973), p. 241; John D. Grainger, *The Battle for Palestine 1917* (Woodbridge: The Boydell Press, 2006), p. 235.

2 Among the Arab officers who served in the Arab Army were Iraqi Othman officers such as Ja'far al-Askari and Nuri al-Sa'id who would later be Prime Ministers in Iraq. For the movements of the Arab Revolt in Tran-Jordan see: Tariq Tell, "Guns, Gold and Grain: War and Food Supply in the Making of Transjordan", in Steven Heydemann (ed.), *War, Institutions, and Social Change in the Middle East* (California: University of California Press, 200), pp. 44–48; Frederick G. Peake, *A History of Jordan and its Tribes* (Coral Gables, Florida: University of Miami Press, 1958), pp. 99–103; George Antonius, *The Arab Awakening: The Story of the Arab National Movement* (Philadelphia: J.B. Lippincott, 1939), pp. 230–237.

3 Mary C. Wilson, *King Abdullah, Britain, and the making of Jordan* (Cambridge: Cambridge University Press, 1990), p. 48.

4 On Abdullah's motives for coming from Hijaz to Ma'an see: Panayiotis J. Vatikiotis, *Politics and the Military in Jordan: A Study of the Arab Legion* (London: Frank Cass, 1967), p. 42.

5 Uriel Dann, "The Beginnings of the Arab Legion", *MES*, 5/3 (October 1969), pp. 181–182; Ma'an Abu Nowar, *The History of the Hashemite Kingdom of Jordan* (Oxford: St. Antony's College, 1989), p. 24.

6 Actually, there were seven British officers in Transjordan: Lt. Colonel F.G. Peake, Major I.N. Camp, Major H.F.R. Somerset, Captain C. D. Brunton, Captain Alan L. Kirbride and his brother Captain Alec L. Kirbride and Captain R.F.P. Monckton. Dann, "The Beginnings of the Arab Legion", p. 183.

7 Abu Nowar, *The History of the Hashemite Kingdom*, pp. 25–26; Vatikiotis, *Politics and the Military*, p. 40.

8 Dann, "The Beginnings of the Arab Legion", pp. 183–187; Vatikiotis, *Politics and the Military*, pp. 60–61. Colonel Peake attributed the establishment of the Reserve Force to himself and claimed it consisted of 150 soldiers. Frederick G. Peak, "Trans-Jordan", *Journal of the Royal Central Asian Society*, 26 (1939), p. 382.

9   Among the tribe leaders who had contact with the Hashemite family during the Arab revolt were: Nuri al-Sha'alan from the Rawalah tribe and Talal Fayiz from the Bani Sakhr tribe. Wilson, *King Abdullah*, p. 48; Tell, "Guns, Gold and Grain", p. 4; Benjamin Shwadran, *Jordan: A State of Tension* (New York: Council for Middle Eastern Affairs Press, 1959), p. 129; Suleiman Musa and Munib al-Madi, *Ta'arikh al-Urdun fi al-Qarn al-Ishrin* (The History of Jordan in the 20th Century, Arabic), Amman, 1997, I, p. 133.

10   Abdullah ibn Hussein, *Muzakarat al-Malik Abdallah* (Memoirs of the King Abdullah, Arabic), Amman, 1947, pp. 168–170.

11   Among those welcoming, there were also relatives of al-Tall from Irbid Khalaf and Ahmad al-Tall. They will play an important role in the Arab Legion. Wilson, *King Abdullah*, p. 226, note 38.

12   Abdullah, *Muzakarat al-Malik Abdallah*, p. 173.

13   Shwadran, *Jordan*, p. 130.

14   Peak, "Trans-Jordan", p. 383; Joseph Nevo, *King Abdallah and Palestine: A Territorial Ambition* (Basingstoke: Macmillan, 1996), p. 6; Antonius, *The Arab Awakening*, pp. 316–317.

15   Abdullah, *Muzakarat al-Malik Abdallah*, pp. 180–182; Vatikiotis, *Politics and the Military*, pp. 43–44; Peak, "Trans-Jordan", p. 383

16   Colonel Peake wrote in his memoirs: "We must not forget the assistance given to us by Hussein, King of the Hijaz, and his sons . . . for service against the Turks . . . ", Peak, "Trans-Jordan", p. 376.

17   Of these eight ministers, only one was Transjordanian. Of the rest, three were Syrian, two were Hijazi, one was Palestinian and one was from Lebanon. Kamal Salibi, *The Modern History of Jordan* (London: I.B. Tauris, 1998), pp. 93, 96; Wilson, *King Abdullah*, p. 62; Shwadran, *Jordan*, p. 138.

18   Nevo, *King Abdallah*, p. 8.

19   Abdullah, *Muzakarat al-Malik Abdallah*, p. 191.

20   See below.

21   Shwadran, *Jordan*, p. 146.

22   Tell, "Guns, Gold and Grain", p. 4; Salibi, *The Modern History of Jordan*, p. 102.

23   Peak, "Trans-Jordan", p. 384; Vatikiotis, *Politics and the Military*, pp. 60–61; Musa and al-Madi, *Ta'arikh*, I, pp. 160–162; Shwadran, *Jordan*, p. 146; Guide to Arab armies, Israel Defence Forces Archive (IDFA) 1286/922/1975.

24   Musa and al-Madi, *Ta'arikh*, I, p. 162.

25   Vatikiotis, *Politics and the Military*, p. 61; Report on the Arab Legion, 30 May 1945, Haganah Archives (HA) 105/138.

26   In 1929, the name of the company was changed to Iraq Petroleum Company (IPC). On the agreement see: "Oil Agreement: Great Britain and France, 24 April 1920", J.C. Hurewitz, *Diplomacy in Near*

and Middle East: A Documentary Record (New York: Octagon Books, 1972), II, pp. 75–77.

27 Guide to Arab armies, IDFA 1286/922/1975; Know your Enemy – Jordan, IDFA 131/535/2004. The Reserve Force consisted of in 1922–1921: 3 Cavalry companies, 2 Infantry Companies, 1 Battery of mountain artillery, 1 Machine-gun Company, 1 Signal squadron. Vatikiotis, *Politics and the Military*, p. 62.

28 Wilson, *King Abdullah*, p. 56; Musa and al-Madi, *Ta'arikh*, I, p. 311.

29 Wilson, *King Abdullah*, pp. 61–62.

30 Ibid., p. 226, note 38.

31 Salibi, *The Modern History of Jordan*, p. 105.

32 Tell, "Guns, Gold and Grain", p. 51.

33 Vatikiotis, *Politics and the Military*, p. 63. Because of Adwan's call to deport foreign residents, most of whom were usually anti-British, a claim was made in Jordan that the British were behind the rebellion. Musa and al-Madi, *Ta'arikh*, I, p. 233.

34 Shwadran, *Jordan*, p. 148.

35 Vatikiotis, *Politics and the Military*, p. 64; Wilson, *King Abdullah*, pp. 77–78; Report on the Arab Legion, 30 May 1945, HA 105/138.

36 Wilson, *King Abdullah*, p. 234, note 69; Peak, "Trans-Jordan", pp. 388–389; Salibi, *The Modern History of Jordan*, pp. 106–107.

37 Vatikiotis, *Politics and the Military*, p. 64; Shwadran, *Jordan*, p. 148.

38 Shwadran, *Jordan*, p. 149.

39 Peak, "Trans-Jordan", p. 387 Musa and al-Madi, *Ta'arikh*, I, p. 184; Abu Nowar, *The History of the Hashemite Kingdom*, p. 77.

40 Wilson, *King Abdullah*, p. 84; Peak, "Trans-Jordan", p. 387.

41 Ibid., p. 389.

42 Wilson, *King Abdullah*, p. 84.

43 Wilson, *King Abdullah*, p. 87; Shwadran, *Jordan*, p. 154; Antonius, *The Arab Awakening*, pp. 336–337; Musa and al-Madi, *Ta'arikh*, I, pp. 251–252.

44 It should be noted that Ibn Saud recognized officially the annexation of the two districts to Transjordan only in 1965.

45 On the debate about Aqaba and Ma'an districts see: Shwadran, *Jordan*, pp. 154–158; Musa and al-Madi, *Ta'arikh*, I, p. 248.

46 The Agreement was signed on November, 1925 and was known as the Hadda Agreement.

47 Vatikiotis, *Politics and the Military*, p. 70; Eliezer Galili, *Tzvaot Ha'aravim Bedoreno* (Arab armies in our generation, Hebrew), Tel Aviv: Ma'archot, 1948, p. 150.

48 Jeffery A. Rudd, "Origins of the Transjordan Frontier Force", *MES*, 26: 2 (1990), p. 172; Know your Enemy – Jordan, IDFA 131/535/2004; Shwadran, *Jordan*, p. 148; Galili, *Tzvaot Ha'aravim Bedoreno*, p. 151.

49 The full text of the agreement see: "Agreement: The United Kingdom and Tranjordan", Hurewitz, *Diplomacy in Near and Middle East*, pp. 156–159.

50 Abu Jaber S. Kamel, "The Legislature of the Hashemite Kingdom of Jordan: A Study in Political Development", *The Muslim Word*, LIX (July–October 1968), p. 223. Only in 1974 did women in Jordan receive the right to vote and run in general elections.

51 Gianluca P. Parolin, *Citizenship in the Arab World: Kin, Religion and Nation-State* (Amsterdam: Amsterdam University Press, 2009), p. 86.

52 John B. Glubb, *The Story of the Arab Legion* (London: Hodder and Stoughton, 1948), p. 77; Peter Young, *The Arab Legion* (London: Osprey Publishing, 1972), p. 17; Report on the Arab Legion, 30 May 1945, HA 105/138; Benny Morris, *The Road to Jerusalem: Glubb Pasha, Palestine and the Jews* (London: I.B. Tauris, 2003), pp. 2–3.

53 Vatikiotis, *Politics and the Military*, p. 69; Young, *The Arab Legion*, p. 5.

54 Report on the Arab Legion, 30 May 1945, HA 105/138.

55 Know your Enemy – Jordan, IDFA 131/535/2004; Young, *The Arab Legion*, p. 6.

56 Earl Peel, "The Report of the Palestine Commission", *International Affairs*, 16/5 (1937), pp. 761–779.

57 Antonius, *The Arab Awakening*, pp. 268, 282–283; Nevo, *King Abdallah*, pp. 8, 16; Wilson, *King Abdullah*, p. 89. The full text of the Faysal–Weizmann agreement of 1919 see: Antonius, *The Arab Awakening*, pp. 437–439.

58 Anita Shapira "The Option on Ghaur al-Kibd: Contacts between Emir Abdallah and the Zionist Executive, 1932–1935", *Journal of Israeli History*, 1/2 (1980), pp. 244–245; Avi Shlaim, *Collusion across the Jordan: King Abdullah, the Zionist Movement, and the Partition of Palestine* (Oxford: Clarendon, 1988), pp. 50–52.

59 William W. Haddad and Mary M. Hardy, "Jordan's Alliance with Israel and its Effects on Jordanian-Arab Relations", in Efraim Karsh and P.R. Kumaraswamy (eds.), *Israel, the Hashemites, and the Palestinians: The Fateful Triangle* (London: Frank Cass, 2003), p. 35; Ronen Yitzhak, "A Short History of the Secret Hashemite-Zionist Talks: 1921–1951", *Midstream*, LIII (May–June 2007), p. 9; Nevo, *King Abdallah*, p. 13.

60 Report on the situation in Transjordan, 30 May 1945, HA 105/138.

61 Memorandum which Glubb wrote on the future of Transjordan, December 1947, National Archives, London (NA), CO 537/3994; Glubb, *The Story of the Arab Legion*, p. 252; Young, *The Arab Legion*, p. 6.

62 The Golden Square was the nickname of the four dominant officers in Iraq during the war: Salih al-Din Sabbagh, Fahami Sa'id, Mahmud Salman and Kamil Shabib. Eliezer Be'eri, *Army Officers in Arab Politics and society* (Jerusalem: Israel Universities Press, 1969), p. 30.

63 Robert Lyman, *Iraq 1941: The Battles for Basra, Habbaniya, Fallujah and Baghdad* (London: Osprey Publishing, 2006), p. 12; Be'eri, *Army Officers in Arab Politics*, p. 35.

64 The situation in Transjordan during Rashid Ali al-Kilani rebellion, 30 May 1945, HA 105/138.

65 The full text of the Anglo-Iraqi Treaty of 1930 see: Hurewitz, *Diplomacy in Near and Middle East*, I, pp. 178–181.

66 Be'eri, *Army Officers in Arab Politics*, p. 39.

67 Glubb, *The Story of the Arab Legion*, p. 252.

68 The task was given to the platoon of TJFF commanded by Shukri Omri, but he recruited his soldiers against the British and spoke in Ali al-Kilani's favor and eventually they rebelled against Abdullah. The rebellion was suppressed, Omri and his soldiers were arrested and his platoon was disbanded. "Behavior of the TJFF during Ali al-Kilani rebellion", 12 January 1945, HA 105/138. Lyman, *Iraq 1941*, p. 57.

69 Report on the Arab Legion, 30 May 1945, HA 105/138; Glubb, *The Story of the Arab Legion*, p. 265; Lyman, *Iraq 1941*, p. 61.

70 The British force was named "Habforce", an abbreviation of "Habbaniya Force" and it was under command of Major-General Clark. Glubb, *The Story of the Arab Legion*, p. 259.

71 Lyman, *Iraq 1941*, pp. 76–77.

72 Report on the Arab Legion, 30 May 1945, HA 105/138; Young, *The Arab Legion*, p. 7.

73 Guide to Arab armies, IDFA 1286/922/1975; Glubb, *The Story of the Arab Legion*, p. 313.

74 "The Arab Legion", p. 14, IDFA 178/1046/1970; Young, *The Arab Legion*, p. 8.

75 Israel Gershoni, "King Abdallah's concept of a 'Greater Syria'", in Anne Sinai and Allen Pollack (eds.), *The Hashemite Kingdom of Jordan and the West Bank* (New York: American Academic Association for Peace in the Middle East, 1977), p. 141.

76 Yehoshua Porath, "Abdallah's Greater Syria Programme", *MES*, 20/2 (1984), pp. 181–182; Nevo, *King Abdallah*, p. 45. Yoav Gelber, *Jewish–Transjordanian Relations 1921–1948* (London: Frank Cass, 1996), p. 175.

77 Memorandum which Glubb wrote on the future of Transjordan, December 1947, NA, CO 537/3994.

78 Vatikiotis, *Politics and the Military*, p. 72; Guide to Arab Armies, IDFA 1286/922/1975.

79 Memorandum which Glubb wrote on the future of Transjordan, December 1947, NA, CO 537/3994; Ronen Yitzhak, "Jordanian Intelligence under the Rule of King Abdullah I (1921–1951)", *International Journal of Intelligence and Counterintelligence*, 23/4 (2010), pp. 649–650.

80 One of the examples of Britain's government concessions to the USA's demand was in November, 1945 when British Foreign Secretary Ernest Bevin agreed to participate in the Anglo-American committee about the issue of Palestine.

81 Wilson, *King Abdullah*, pp. 148–149.

82 Kamel, "The Legislature of the Hashemite Kingdom", p. 227.

83 Zayid was the grandson of Hussein ibn Ali, the grandson of the Prophet Muhammad.

84 The others less popular versions claim that the family came from the village of al-Tall 12 km north Damascus or the village of al-Tall north of Acre. One of the prominent family members was Daher al-Omar, who was the ruler of the Galilee in 18th century. Peake, *A History of Jordan*, p. 149; http://ezabadani.com/vb/showthread.php?t=83.

85 Eugene Rogan, *Frontiers of the State in the Late Ottoman Empire: Transjordan, 1850–1921* (Cambridge: Cambridge University Press, 2002), pp. 59, 120; *Arab al-Yawm*, 18 July 2009.

86 Wilson, *King Abdullah*, p. 56; Musa and ak-Madi, *Ta'arikh*, I, p. 311.

87 According to Ali Khalki's memoirs, the al-Tall family was the last family who came to Irbid. http://ezabadani.com/vb/showthread. php?t=83.

88 *Al-Ghad*, 13 March 2009.

89 Wilson, *King Abdullah*, p. 226, note 38; *al-Liwaa*, 23 March 2010.

90 Ibid., 12 February 2006.

91 Ibid., 23 March 2010.

92 Ibid., 12 February 2006; Musa and al-Madi, *Ta'arikh*, I, p. 160.

93 Ahmad Y. al-Tall, *Abdallah al-Tall Batal Ma'arakat al-Qauds* (Abdullah al-Tall: The Hero of the Battle of Jerusalem, Arabic), Amman 1999, I, p. 30.

94 *Al-Liwaa*, 6 April 2010.

95 *Arab al-Yawm*, 18 July 2009.

96 *Al-Liwaa*, 20 April 2010.

97 Among his famous slogans were: "Transjordan was for the Transjordanians" and "foreigners must go". Salibi, *The Modern History of Jordan*, p. 117.

98 The average salary in the Arab Legion for the year 1948 was about 4.5 pounds. *Davar*, 29 May 1959; Intelligence Report, April 1948, HA 105/129.

99 Vatikiotis, *Politics and the Military*, p. 99; *al-Dustour*, 31 August 2008. http://www.addustour.com/ViewarchiveTopic.aspx?ac=\opin-

ionandnotes\2008\08\opinionandnotes_issue331_day31_id78044.ht m.

100 Al-Tall, *Abdallah al-Tall*, I, p. 31; John B. Glubb, *A Soldier with the Arabs* (London: Hodder and Stoughton, 1957), p. 255.

101 Al-Tall, *Abdallah al-Tall*, I, p. 34.

102 Arab sources on the Arab Legion, no date, HA 105/69.

103 Details on the military training see Abdullah Y. al-Tall, *Rihla ila Britaniya* (Journey to Britain, Arabic), Jerusalem, 1947. The training was from 18 December, 1946 until 25 February, 1947.

104 Al-Tall, *Abdallah al-Tall*, II, p. 691.

105 "Equipment Requirements of Foreign and Allied Government", March 1948; NA, WO 261/19; War Office to MELF, 19 March 1948, NA, CO 537/3938; Intelligence Report, 5 March 1948, HA 105/138.

106 Foreign Office to Secretary of chiefs of staff, 30 November 1947, NA, DEFE 5/10; Glubb to War Office, 2 April 1948, NA, WO 216/677; "Hiram" to "Tene", 29 February 1948, HA 105/138; "The British Factor in Independence War", p. 102, IDFA 174/1046/1970.

107 The 1st Brigade consisted of the 1st and 3th Regiments and the 3th Brigade consisted of the 2nd and the 4th Regiments. Glubb, *A Soldier with the Arabs*, p. 92; War Office to Foreign Office, 13 September 1948, NA, FO 371/68832; "Transjordan's Army: The Arab Legion", *Palestine Affairs*, 3 (1948), p. 44

108 Intelligence Report, 25 July 1948, HA 105/129.

109 The list of the senior officers is found in two sources: Abdullah Y. al-Tall, *Karithat Filastin, Muthakart Abdullah al-Tall Qai'd Ma'arakat al-Qauds* (The Catastrophe of Palestine: Memoirs of Abdullah al-Tall Commander of the Battle of Jerusalem, Arabic), Amman, 1959, pp. 81–83; Suleiman Musa, *Ayam la Tunsa: Al-Urdun fi Harb 1948* (Unforgettable Days: Jordan in 1948 War, Arabic), Amman, 1997, pp. 200–205.

110 *Al-Dustour*, 31 August 2008.

111 The Arab League in the 1948 war consisted of seven members: Egypt, Iraq, Syria, Lebanon, Transjordan, Saudi Arabia and Yemen.

112 "In the Arab Camp", 14 December 1947, Israel State Archives (ISA), S25/9046.

113 Cairo (Clyton) to Foreign Office, 23 November 1947, NA, FO 816/115; "Notes on Proceedings of the Meeting of the Arab Premiers in Cairo, December 8th to 17th 1947", NA, FO 371/68364; *Taqrir Lajnat at-Tahqiq al-Niyabiyya fi Qadiyyat Filastin* (Report of the Parliamentary Committee of Enquiry into the Palestine Question, Arabic), Baghdad, 1950, pp. 187–189.

114 Al-Tall, *Karithat Filastin*, p. 2.

115 Ibid., p. 16.

116 Ibid., p. 17.

117 Quoted in Yona Bendman, "Haligion Ha'aravi Likrat Milhemet Ha'atzmaut" (The Arab Legion toward the War of Independence, Hebrew), *Ma'archot*, 294–295 (1984), p. 42.

118 "The Arab Legion", p. 27, IDFA 178/1046/1970. Arab sources state that the Arab Legion did not intervene in the attack on the Jews. "Tene" Report, 11 December 1947, HA 105/69; Mahmud al-Rusan, *Ma'arik Bab al-Wad* (The Battles of Bab al-Wad, Arabic), Amman, 1950, p. 37.

119 "The Arab Legion", p. 28, IDFA 178/1046/1970.

120 *Al-Dustour*, 14 May 1948.

121 Al-Tall, *Karithat Filastin*, p. 4.

122 On the Arab Legion activities in Haifa see: *Filastin*, 24 September 1955; Reports from Haifa, 28 December 1947, 4 January 1948, 4 February 1948, IDFA 799/100001/1957; complaints about The TJFF and the Arab Legion 1944–1948, ISA, S25/6293; Review Report and Activities on the Arab Legion, 2 April 1948, HA 115/32.

123 The two Jordanian historians Musa and al-Madi claim that about 200 Arab Legion soldiers resigned from the Legion in order to assist the Arabs in Palestine. Musa and al-Madi, *Ta'arikh*, I, p. 467.

124 "The Arab Liberation Army in 1948: Catalogue of Documents", p. 9, HA 69/78; Review Report and Activities on the Arab Legion, 2 April 1948, HA 115/32.

125 Among the Arab Legion officers who resigned were: Dayif Allah al-Rusan, Mashur Hassan and Muhsein Yaish. Al-Rusan, *Ma'arik Bab al-Wad*, pp. 37–38.

126 The British's officer claims were quoted in Intelligence Report, 3 December 1947, HA 105/69. Also see report on some Arab Legion soldiers who defected from their bases with their weapons. "Tene" Report, 4 December 1947, HA 105/69.

127 Review Report and Activities on the Arab Legion, 2 April 1948, HA 115/32; letter from soldier who participated in the attack, 28 March 1948, "The Arab Legion", p. 185, IDFA 182/1046/1970.

128 Al-Tall, *Karithat Filastin*, p. 17.

129 Ibid., p. 31.

130 Ibid.

131 Ibid., p. 32; Intelligence Report, no date, HA 105/133.

132 Al-Tall, *Karithat Filastin*, pp. 32–33.

133 Report on the Etzion Bloc, 16 May 1948, IDFA 75/5254/1949.

134 Intelligence Report, 14 May 1948, IDFA 799/10000/1957.

135 Intelligence Report, 15 May 1948, IDFA 660/922/1975; Intelligence Report, 14 May 1948, IDFA 799/10000/1957; Report on fall the Etzion Bloc, 29 May 1948, IDFA 660/922/1975.

136 Glubb, *A Soldier with the Arabs*, p. 78; *al-Nasr*, 13 May 1948.

137 "Tene" Report, 24 April 1948, IDFA 353/2644/1949; Intelligence

Report, 30 April 1948, IDFA 353/2644/1949; M.E.L.F. to War Office, 30 April 1948, NA, WO 32/15037.

138 Report on the fall of the Etzion Bloc, 29 May 1948, IDFA 660/922/1975.

139 Intelligence Report, 29 May 1948, IDFA 660/922/1975; Musa, *Ayam la Tunsa*, pp. 107–109.

140 Al-Tall, *Abdallah al-Tall*, I, p. 34.

141 Etzioni to Yadin, 14 May 1948, IDFA 1/464/1954; Al-Tall, *Karithat Filastin*, pp. 404–405.

142 *Filastin*, 27 April 1948.

143 *Taqrir Lajnat at-Tahqiq*, pp. 191–192.

144 Gelber, *Jewish–Transjordanian Relations*, p. 211; Joshua Landis, "Syria and the Palestine War: Fighting King Abdullah's 'Greater Syria Plan'", in Eugene Rogan and Avi Shlaim (eds.), *Rewriting the Palestine War: 1948 and the History of the Arab–Israeli Conflict* (Cambridge: Cambridge University Press, 2001), pp. 179, 185

145 Protocol of Meeting between Golda Meyerson and Amir Abdullah, 17 November 1947, HA 105/138.

146 Golda Meir, *My Life* (Jerusalem: Steimatzky, 1975), p. 218.

147 Al-Tall, *Karithat Filastin*, p. 67.

148 *Yedioth Aharonoth*, 28 February 1975.

149 Bevin to Kirkbride, "Conversation with the Transjordan Prime Minister", 9 February 1948, NA, FO 371/68366; Glubb, *A Soldier with the Arabs*, pp. 63–66.

150 The report is quoted in "The Arab Legion", p. 24 ,IDFA 178/1046/1970; Foreign Office to Amman, 10 February 1948, NA, CO 537/3993.

151 Haddad and Hardy, "Jordan's Alliance with Israel", p. 36.

152 "The Arab Legion", p. 23, IDFA 178/1046/1970.

153 Haddad and Hardy, "Jordan's Alliance with Israel", p. 38; Landis, "Syria and the Palestine War", p. 179.

2 Conqueror of Jerusalem

1 Intelligence report, "in the Arab camp", 26 April 1948, HA 105/142.

2 Morris, *The Road to Jerusalem*, p. 153; "The Arab Legion", p. 46, IDFA 178/1046/1970.

3 *Taqrir Lajnat at-Tahqiq*, p. 194; Avraham Sela, "Transjordan, Israel and the 1948 War: Myth, Historiography and reality", *MES*, 28/4 (October 1992), p. 647.

4 Report was written by Ismail Safawat, the Commander of Military committee of the Arab League, "The Establishment of the Arab forces and the sector of them activities", 1 January 1948, HA, 230/General/8; "The Arab Liberation Army in 1948: Catalogue of Documents", p. 5, HA, 69/78.

5   Amman to Foreign Office, 14 May 1948, NA, FO 371/68372.
6   "The Arab Legion" p. 38, IDFA, 178/1046/70; Muhammad Abd al-Munim, *Asrar 1948* (Secret 1948 War, Arabic), Cairo, 1968, pp. 316–317.
7   "Meeting with representatives of the Arab Legion", 3 May 1948, ISA, 130.02/2513/2; Glubb, *A Soldier with the Arabs*, p. 109; Sela, "Transjordan", pp. 639–642.
8   Nevo, *King Abdallah*, p. 135.
9   Amman to Foreign Office, 23 April 1948, NA, FO 816/170; Glubb, *A Soldier with the Arabs*, p. 108.
10 Operation *Kilshon* was part of the Plan D, which planned in Haganah HQ during March 1948; was to be carried with the British withdrawal from Palestine. "Plan D", 10 March 1948, IDFA 93/6127/1949; Yoav Gelber, *Palestine 1948: War, Escape and the Emergence of the Palestine Refugee Problem* (Brighton, Portland, Toronto: Sussex Academic Press, 2001), p. 98.
11 David Shealtiel, *Yerushalyim Tashah* (Jerusalem in 1948, Hebrew), Tel Aviv: Misrad Habitahon, 1981, p. 145; Sela, "Transjordan", p. 645.
12 Jerusalem to Foreign Office, 17 May 1948, NA, FO 371/68505; al-Tall, *Karithat Filastin*, p. 100.
13 Glubb, *A Soldier with the Arabs*, p. 111; "The Arab Legion", p. 74, IDFA 178/1046/1970.
14 John Phillips, *A Will to Survive* (New York: Dial Press, 1977), p. 8.
15 Amman to Foreign Office, 19 May 1948, NA, FO 371/68505; Musa, *Ayam la Tunsa*, pp. 150–151; *al-Misri*, 31 March 1950.
16 Hazza al-Majali, *Muzakarati* (My Memoirs, Arabic), Amman, 1960, p. 67; Arif al-Arif, *Nakbat Filastin* (Palestine Disaster, Arabic), Amman, 1956, II, p. 451.
17 Abdullah to Kirkbride, 16 May 1948, NA, FO 371/68829; Morris, *The Road to Jerusalem,* p. 157.
18 Ali S. El-Edroos, *The Hashemite Arab Army 1908–1979: An Appreciation and Analysis of Military Operation* (Amman: The Publishing Committee, 1980), p. 253.
19 Glubb, *A Soldier with the Arabs*, p. 111
20 Al-Tall, *Karithat Filastin*, p. 101; Dominique Lapierre and Larry Collins, *O Jerusalem* (London: Simon and Schuster, 1972), p. 436.
21 From Etzioni to Yadin, 17 May 1948, IDFA 1/464/1954.
22 Glubb, *A Soldier with the Arabs*, p. 113.
23 Sela, "Transjordan", p. 653.
24 Glubb, *A Soldier with the Arabs*, p. 113.
25 The official Jordanian claim written in the MELF report. MELF to Foreign Office, 28 May 1948, NA, WO 275/119; Glubb, *A Soldier with the Arabs*, p. 113; Ma'an Abu Nowar, *The Jordanian–Israeli War*

1948–1951: A History of the Hashemite Kingdom of Jordan (Reading: Ithaca Press, 2002), p. 92.

26 Foreign Office to United States Embassy, London, 22 May 1948, NA, FO 371/68830; A. Cunningham, "Palestine – The last days of the Mandate", *International affairs*, 24/4 (October 1948) pp. 489–490; Uri Bar-Yoseph, *The Best of Enemies – Israel and Trans-Jordan in the War of 1948* (London: Frank Cass, 1987), p. 68; David Tal, *War in Palestine, 1948: Strategy and Diplomacy* (London: Routledge, 2004), p. 213; Sela, "Transjordan", p. 645.

27 Etzioni to Yadin, 17 May 1948, IDFA 1/464/1954; Fauzi al-Qawuqji, "Memoirs, 1948" – Part 2, *Journal of Palestine studies*, 2/1 (Autumn 1972), p. 14.

28 Diary military operation of Hasmonay, 15 May 1948, IDFA 116/525/1949; al-Arif, *Nakbat Filastin*, II, p. 456.

29 Phillips, *A Will to Survive*, p. 8.

30 For more on the reasons which brought King Abdullah to conquer Jerusalem, see Ronen Yitzhak, "A Small Consolation for a Big Loss: King Abdallah and Jerusalem during the 1948 War'" *Israel Affairs*, 14/3 (July 2008), pp. 408–410.

31 Bar-Yoseph, *The Best of Enemies*, pp. 70–1; Jerusalem to Foreign Office, 18 May 1948, NA, FO 371/68505.

32 It should be noted that Abdullah al-Tall changed his story in his book and wrote this version: "To prevent bloodshed, I call on the Jews of Jerusalem to surrender". Al-Tall, *Karithat Filastin*, p. 106; Jerusalem to Foreign Office, 17 May 1948, NA, FO 371/68505; Information report on Etzioni Brigade, 20 May 1948, IDFA 617/4944/1949.

33 Telegrams from the Old City in Jerusalem, 16 May 1948, 9:50 a.m. and 4:22 p.m., IDFA 39/500/1948.

34 Shealtiel, *Yerushalyim Tashah*, p. 173; Telegram from the Old City in Jerusalem, 17 May 1948, 11:30 a.m., IDFA 39/500/1948; Etzioni to Yadin, 18 May 1948, 2 a.m., IDFA 1/464/1948.

35 Etzioni to Yadin, 18 May 1948, 11:40 a.m., IDFA 1/464/1948

36 Jerusalem to Foreign Office, 25 May 1948, NA, FO 371/68505; Etzioni to Yadin, 18 May 1948, IDFA 1/464/1948.

37 Jerusalem to Foreign Office, 20 May 1948, NA, FO 371/68506; "Hiram" to "Tene", 20 May 1948, HA 105/147.

38 Jerusalem to Foreign Office, 20 May 1948, NA, FO 371/68506; Al-Arif, *Nakbat Filastin*, II, p. 456.

39 MELF to War Office, 21 May 1948, NA, CO 537/38672; David Ben-Gurion, *Yuman Hamilhamh* (Ben-Gurion's War Diary, Hebrew), Tel Aviv, 1982, II, pp. 448, 451.

40 Etzioni to Yadin, 25 May 1948, 05:10 a.m., IDFA 1/464/1948; Musa, *Ayam*, pp. 281–282.

41 Jerusalem to Foreign Office, 17 June, 1948, NA, FO 371/68508;

Jerusalem to Foreign Office, 2 August 1948, NA, FO 371/68508; "Yeruham" to "Tene", 25 May 1948, HA 105/129; Ben-Gurion, *Yuman Hamilhamh*, II, pp. 448, 451.

42 Etzioni to Yadin, 27 May 1948, 6:50 a.m., IDFA 1/464/1948; Etzioni to Yadin, 27 May 1948, 6 p.m., IDFA 1175/922/1975; Etzioni to Yadin, 27 May 1948, 6:50 a.m., IDFA 1/464/1948; Jerusalem to Foreign Office, 30 May, 1948, FO 816/124.

43 Jerusalem to Foreign Office, 28 May, 1948, FO 371/68374.

44 Report on the Old City fall – Intelligence Jerusalem district, 4 June 1948, IDFA 279/7249/1949; The Jewish quarter surrender, 28 May 1948, IDFA 39/500/1948.

45 List of Jewish prisoners, IDFA 67/109/1951.

46 Meeting with Abdullah al-Tall, 12 July 1948, IDFA 39/500/1948; Yitzhak Levi, *Tish'a Kabin: Yerushalyim Bekravot Milhemet Ha'hatzmaot* (Jerusalem in independence war, Hebrew), Tel Aviv, 1986, p. 69.

47 Conversion with Arab deserter, no date, IDFA 39/500/1948; Jerusalem to Foreign Office, 28 May 1948, NA, FO 371/68508.

48 Al-Tall, *Karithat Filastin*, p. 103.

49 News from the Arab world, 12 July 1948, HA 105/147.

50 Investigation of Arab Captured, 2 August 1948, HA 105/130; Weekly intelligence report, 21 August 1948, IDFA 74/5254/1948.

51 Al-Tall, *Karithat Filastin*, p. 103.

52 Report on the Old City fall – Intelligence Jerusalem district, 4 June 1948, IDFA 279/7249/1949.

53 Nevo, *King Abdallah*, p. 140.

54 Musa, *Ayam*, pp. 287–288.

55 Glubb, *A Soldier with the Arabs*, p. 255; Al-Tall, *Karithat Filastin*, p. 210.

56 Al-Tall, *Karithat Filastin*, p. 158.

57 Amman to Foreign Office, 22 May 1948, NA, FO 371/68507; Foreign Office to New York (to United Kingdom Delegation to the United Nations), 26 May 1948, NA, FO 371/68508.

58 Mount Scopus Agreement, ISA, 130.16/19; Israeli Attorney General to Israeli Foreign Minister, 2 September 1948, ISA, 130.16/19; Moshe Dayan, *Story of My Life* (Jerusalem: Steimatzky, 1976), p. 95.

59 Folke Bernadotte, *To Jerusalem* (London: Hodder and Stoughton, 1951), pp. 30–31.

60 Anis Sayigh, *Al-Hashemion Waqadiyat Filastin* (The Hashemite and Palestine Question, Arabic), Beirut, 1966, p. 357.

61 Bernadotte, *To Jerusalem*, p. 99; al-Arif, *Nakbat Filastin*, III, p. 547.

62 Intelligence report, 11 June 1948, HA, 105/147; al-Arif, *Nakbat Filastin*, III, p. 547.

63 Lapierre and L. Collins, *O Jerusalem*, p. 536; al-Tall, *Karithat Filastin*, 203.

64 Ben-Gurion, *Yuman Hamilhamh*, II, p. 489; Amman to Foreign Office, 6 June 1948, NA, FO 816/122; MELF to Foreign Office, 12 July 1948, NA, FO 371/68830.

65 Amman to Foreign Office, 3 July 1948, 9 July 1948, NA, FO 371/68830.

66 Bernadotte, *To Jerusalem*, pp. 63–68.

67 Ibid., p. 106; al-Tall, *Karithat Filastin*, 203.

68 Ibid,. p. 216.

69 Intelligence report, 25 June 1948, IDFA 308/959/1949; Intelligence report, "in the Arab camp", 27 June 1948, HA 105/147.

70 Amman to Foreign Office, 9 June 1948, NA, FO 371/68570; Intelligence report, "in the Arab camp", 11 June 1948, HA 105/147.

71 Amman to Foreign Office, 26 June 1948, NA, FO 371/68857; al-Majali, *Muzakarati*, pp. 74–75

72 Intelligence report, "in the Arab camp", 27 June 1948, HA 105/147.

73 Intelligence reports, "in the Arab camp", 11 June 1948, 27 June, 1948, HA 105/147; "Report on the Arab enemy", 7 July 1948, IDFA 284/7249/1949.

74 A general review on the Arab Legion, p. 2, IDFA 660/922/1975.

75 The company was named Manko, who financed the company activities in Palestine. Musa, *Ayam*, p. 51; Intelligence report, 25 June 1948, IDFA 308/500/1948.

76 Meeting with Abdullah al-Tall, 12 July 1948, IDFA 39/500/1948.

77 News from the Arab world, 12 May 1948, HA 105/142; Intelligence report, "in the Arab camp", 11 June 1948, HA 105/147.

78 Intelligence report, 25 June 1948, IDFA, 308/959/1949; Intelligence report, "in the Arab camp", 27 June 1948, HA 105/147.

79 Intelligence report, "in the Arab camp", 27 June 1948, HA 105/147; News from the Arab world, 12 July 1948, HA 105/147; Nevo, *King Abdallah*, p. 139.

80 Intelligence report, 15 July 1948, IDFA, 284/7249/1949.

81 The goal of operation, IDF HQ/ Southern front to operation *Larlar*, 26 June 1948, IDFA 93/6127/1949.

82 Telegrams from Dani HQ to Yadin, 11 July 1948, 12 July 1948, IDFA 1/464/1954.

83 Amman to Foreign Office, 25 July 1948, 6 August 1948, NA, FO 816/127.

84 Al-Tall, *Karithat Filastin*, 247.

85 Ibid., p. 248.

86 Amman to Foreign Office, 25 July 1948, NA, FO 816/127; Glubb, *A Soldier with the Arabs*, pp. 142–3, 161; El-Edroos, *The Hashemite Arab Army*, p.261.

87 Intelligence report, 11 June 1948, HA 105/147; Intelligence report, 25 June 1948, IDFA, 308/959/1949.

88 6th Brigade to Yadin, 16 May 1948, IDFA 1176/922/1975; Levi, *Tish'a Kabin*, p. 311, Tal, *War in Palestine*, p. 327.

89 Sela, "Transjordan", p. 662; al-Tall, *Karithat Filastin*, p. 270.

90 Yadin to Etzioni Brigade, 16 July 1948, IDFA 1182/922/1975.

91 Shealtiel, *Yerushalyim Tashah*, p. 173; Ben-Gurion, *Yuman Hamilhamh*, II, pp. 596–597.

92 Copy of the telegram from 17 July 1948, HA 92/105.

93 Jerusalem to Foreign Office, 30 May 1948, NA, FO 371/68509; Nevo, *King Abdallah*, pp. 136–137.

94 Conversation with Abdullah al-Tall, 24 May 1948, NA, FO 371/6864.

95 Al-Tall, *Karithat Filastin*, p. 197.

96 Intelligence report, "in the Arab camp", 11 June 1948, HA 105/147; Gelber, *Palestine 1948*, p. 175.

97 Dayan, *Story of My Life*, p. 97.

98 Amman to Foreign Office, 25 July 1948, NA, FO 371/68822; Amman to Foreign Office, 6 August 1948, NA, FO 371/68845; Nevo, *King Abdallah*, pp. 151–153.

99 Jerusalem to Foreign Office, 18 August 1948, NA, FO 816/127; al-Tall, *Karithat Filastin*, p. 325; Levi, *Tish'a Kabin*, p. 311; Ben-Gurion, *Yuman Hamilhamh*, II, p. 655.

100 Jerusalem to Foreign Office, 18 August 1948, 228 August 1948, NA, FO 816/127.

101 Gelber, *Palestine 1948*, p. 175.

102 Report on commanders meeting, 4 September 1948, IDFA 394/721/1972.

103 Amman to Foreign Office, 24 September 1948, NA, FO 371/68641; Tal, *War in Palestine*, p. 352.

104 Amman to Foreign Office, 25 September 1948, 29 September 1948, NA, FO 816/129.

105 al-Tall, *Karithat Filastin*, p. 342

106 Ibid., p. 359; Amman and Palestine: Military intelligence report, 11 October 1948, NA, FO 371/6869.

107 al-Tall, *Karithat Filastin*, pp. 359–60.

108 Meeting with Abdullah al-Tall, 12 July 1948, IDFA 39/500/1948.

109 *Davar*, 6 October 1948.

110 Ibid., 13 March 1949.

111 al-Tall, *Karithat Filastin*, p. 358.

112 *Davar*, 6 October 1948.

113 Ibid., 13 March 1949.

114 Ibid., 22 March 1949.

115 Dayan, *Story of My Life*, p. 101.

116 Meeting with Abdullah al-Tall, 12 July 1948, IDFA 39/500/1948.

117 Interview with Abdullah al-Tall, Davar, 16 March 1949.

118 Yona Cohen, *Yerushalyim Bematzur* (Jerusalem under siege, Hebrew), Tel Aviv, 1976, p. 159.

119 The full text of the agreement in ISA 13.15/2; Jerusalem to Foreign Office, 30 November 1948, NA, FO 371/68690; Dayan, *Story of My Life*, pp. 100–101; Levi, *Tish'a Kabin*, p. 422.

120 Jerusalem to Cairo, 1 December 1948, NA, FO 141/1247; Ben-Gurion, *Yuman Hamilhamh*, III, p. 854

121 Dayan, *Story of My Life*, p. 101; Levi, *Tish'a Kabin*, p. 422; Tal, *War in Palestine*, p. 412.

122 Amman to Foreign Office, 18 October 1948, NA, FO 816/131; al-Tall, *Karithat Filastin*, p. 407.

123 Gelber, *Palestine 1948*, p. 180.

124 Telephone conversion between Sasson to al-Tall, 14 December 1948, ISA 130.15/68; al-Tall, *Karithat Filastin*, p. 407.

125 Cohen, *Yerushalyim Bematzur*, p. 159.

126 *Palestine Post*, 26 December 1948, p. 4; Dayan, *Story of My Life*, p. 103. Al-Tall repeated this headline in his book, but for him this was an expression of his negative opinion toward the Jews. Al-Tall, *Karithat Filastin*, p. 457.

127 Amman to Foreign Office, 22 October 1948, NA, FO 816/131; "The Part Played by the Arab Legion in the Arab–Jewish hostilities in Palestine 1948–1949", Research Department, Foreign Office, 1950, FO 816/170.

128 Conversion between Dayan and al-Tall, Etzioni report, 5 December 1948, IDFA 394/721/1972.

129 Al-Tall, *Karithat Filastin*, p. 469; al-Arif, *Nakbat Filastin*, IIII, p. 775.

130 Sasson to Eytan, 8 August 1948, ISA 130.16/3

131 Al-Tall, *Karithat Filastin*, p. 470.

132 Bar-Yoseph, *The Best of Enemies*, p. 106.

133 Amman to Foreign Office, 8 November 1948, NA, FO 816/132; Amman to Foreign Office, 13 December 1948, NA, FO 371/68512; al-Tall, *Karithat Filastin*, p. 457; Morris, *The Road to Jerusalem*, p. 197.

134 al-Tall, *Karithat Filastin*, pp. 449–51.

135 Sasson to Eytan, 5 January 1949, ISA 130.16/3; Bar-Yoseph, *The Best of Enemies*, p. 173.

136 Dayan, *Story of My Life*, p. 106.

137 Ibid., p. 109; Bar-Yoseph, *The Best of Enemies*, p. 183.

138 Al-Tall, *Karithat Filastin*, p. 472; Dayan, *Story of My Life*, p. 107.

139 Speech by Glubb to the Anglo-Arab Association, 6 May 1949, NA, FO 371/75295; Dayan, *Story of My Life*, p. 113.

140 Al-Tall, *Karithat Filastin*, pp. 404–405; Bar-Yoseph, *The Best of Enemies*, p. 180.

141 Al-Tall, *Karithat Filastin*, p. 468.

142 Shiloah to Shetok, 4 March 1949, ISA 130.02/243/1; Dayan, *Story of My Life*, p. 110.
143 Ben-Gurion, *Yuman Hamilhamh*, III, p. 972.
144 Shiloah to Shetok, 11 March 1949, ISA 130.02/4373/12; Tal, *War in Palestine*, p. 460.
145 Speech by Glubb to the Anglo-Arab Association, 6 May 1949, NA, FO 371/75295; Shiloah to Eytan, 22 March 1949, ISA 130.16/3.
146 Gelber, *Palestine 1948*, p. 251.
147 Sasson to Eytan, 21 March 1949, ISA 130.16/3.
148 Dayan, *Story of My Life*, p. 112; Gelber, *Palestine 1948*, p. 252.
149 Speech by Glubb to the Anglo-Arab Association, 6 May 1949, NA, FO 371/75295; Dayan, *Story of My Life*, p. 113.
150 Eytan to Shertok, 23 March 1949, ISA 130.12/4373/12; Bar-Yoseph, *The Best of Enemies*, pp. 220–222.
151 Glubb, *A Soldier with the Arabs*, pp. 234–235.
152 Ben-Gurion, *Yuman Hamilhamh*, III, p. 976; Gelber, *Palestine 1948*, p. 252.
153 Moshe Carmel, The commander of the northern front, also supported Alon's plane.
154 Dayan, *Story of My Life*, pp. 113–114.
155 The full text of the agreement see: Hashemite Jordan Kingdom-Israel General Armistic Agrement, 3 April 1949, ISA, 102.0/13.
156 Dayan, *Story of My Life*, p. 114.

3 The Assasination of King Abdullah

1 On the armistice agreements see: Ilan Pappe, *The Making of the Arab–Israeli Conflict, 1947–51* (London: Tauris, 1992), pp. 176–194.
2 Benny Morris, *The Birth of Palestinian Refugee Problem, 1947–1949* (Cambridge: Cambridge University Press, 1987), p. 602.
3 Among the national organizations were: The British Red Cross and the Church Missionary Society's Refugee Relief Centre. Winifred A. Coate, "The Condition of Arab Refuges in Jordan", *International Affairs*, 29/4 (October 1953), p. 451; Elizabeth Monroe, "The Arab–Israel Frontier", *International Affairs*, 29/4 (October 1953), pp. 445–446.
4 Robert Bowker, Palestinian Refugees: Mythology, Identity, and the Search for Peace *(London: Lynne Rienner Publishers, 2003)*, p. 124.
5 Monroe, "The Arab–Israel Frontier", p. 445; Coate, "The Condition of Arab Refuges in Jordan", p. 454; D. Alexander, "Ezrat Ha'um Laplitim Ha'aravim" (U.N. Aid to Arab Refugees, Hebrew), *Hamizrah Hehadash: Quarterly of the Israel Oriental Society*, 5/1 (1953), p. 8.
6 Morris, *The Birth of Palestinian Refugee*, p. 600.
7 A number of Arab books dealt with the question of repairing societies

and the Arab regimes as a result of the Arab defeat in 1948 war. The major ones are: Constantin Zureiq, *Ma'na al-Nakba* (The Meaning of the Disaster, Arabic), Beirut 1948; Muhammad N. al-Khatib, *Min Athar al-Nakba* (Consequences of the Disaster, Arabic), Damascus, 1951; Musa al-Alami, *Ibrat Filastin* (The Lesson of Palestine, Arabic), Beirut 1949.

8 Be'eri, *Army Officers in Arab Politics*, pp. 55–56.

9 Gamal Abd al-Nasser, *Falsafa al-Tawra* (The Philosophy of the Revolution, Arabic), Cairo, 1953, p. 13.

10 Be'eri, *Army Officers in Arab Politics*, pp. 57–58.

11 Salibi, *The Modern History of Jordan*, p. 188.

12 On Jordanian Intelligence see: Yitzhak, "Jordanian Intelligence", pp. 647–662.

13 Shlaim, *Collusion across the Jordan*, p. 425.

14 Al-Tall, *Karithat Filastin*, p. 588; Zvi Ne'eman, *Mamlekhet Abdallah Leahar Hasipoh* (The Kingdom of Abdullah after the Annexation, Hebrew), Tel Aviv, 1950, p. 32.

15 Al-Tall, *Karithat Filastin*, p. 588; Intelligence Report, 31 July 1951, IDFA 232/1559/1952; Vatikiotis, *Politics and the Military in Jordan*, p. 106.

16 Al-Tall, *Karithat Filastin*, p. 592.

17 The Ba'ath party was founded in Syria in 1943 by Salah al-Din al-Bitar and Michel Aflaq.

18 Amnon Cohen, *Political parties in the West Bank under the Jordanian Regime, 1949–1967* (Ithaca: Cornell University Press, 1982), p. 233.

19 The first coup by the Ba'ath party was in Iraq in February 1963 and a month later there was the second in Syria.

20 Avraham Sela, *Haba'ath Hafalastini* (The Palestinian Ba'ath, Hebrew), Jerusalem, 1984, p. 10; C. Bailey, *Jordan's Palestinian Challenge 1948–1983: A Political History* (Jerusalem: Studies in International Politics, The Hebrew University of Jerusalem, 1984), p. 8; Betty S. Anderson, *Nationalist voices in Jordan: The Street and the State* (Texas: University of Texas Press, 2005), p. 136.

21 There were rumors that King Abdullah offered Abu Ghanima the chance to be Prime Minister if he ceased his hostile activity. Ne'eman, *Mamlekhet Abdallah Leahar Hasipoh*, p. 31.

22 Glubb, *A Soldier with the Arabs*, p. 256; Salibi, *The Modern History of Jordan*, p. 188.

23 Al-Alami, *Ibrat Filastin*, pp. 59–60.

24 Vatikiotis, *Politics and the Military in Jordan*, p. 105.

25 Pappe, *The Making of the Arab–Israeli Conflict*, p. 189.

26 Sela, *Haba'ath Hafalastini*, p. 11; *al-Ahram*, 8 April 1950; *Hamizrah Hehadash*, 1/1 (1949), p. 61.

27 *Ha'aretz*, 9 June 1949.

28 *The Palestine Post*, 13 June 1949.

29 *Hamizrah Hehadash*, 1/1 (1949), p. 60.

30 Benjamin Shwadran, "Jordan Annexes Arab Palestine", *Middle Eastern Affairs*, 1/4 (April 1950), p. 105.

31 *The Palestine Post*, 7 July 1949.

32 Shwadran, *Jordan: A State of Tension*, p. 305; Vatikiotis, *Politics and the Military in Jordan*, p. 107; *Hamizrah Hehadash*, 1/1 (1949), p. 61.

33 *Al-Ahram*, 9 February 1950.

34 Vatikiotis, *Politics and the Military in Jordan*, p. 105; Ne'eman, *Mamlekhet Abdallah Leahar Hasipoh*, p. 18; al-Tall, *Abdallah al-Tall*, II, p. 882.

35 Sela, *Haba'ath Hafalastini*, p, 11; *Hamizrah Hehadash*, 1/1 (1949), p. 60.

36 *Hamizrah Hehadash*, 1/3 (1950), p. 216, Ne'eman, *Mamlekhet Abdallah Leahar Hasipoh*, p. 33. According to Ahmad al-Tall the meeting took place in 28 August and 3 September. Al-Tall, *Abdallah al-Tall*, II, p. 685.

37 Glubb, *A Soldier with the Arabs*, p. 256; Vatikiotis, *Politics and the Military in Jordan*, p. 104.

38 Al-Tall, *Karithat Filastin*, p. 598.

39 Ibid., p. 597.

40 *Davar*, 29 May 1959; *Akhbar al-Youm*, 10 November 1949.

41 *Al-Ahram*, 14 January 1950.

42 Glubb to Melville, 6 August1951, NA, FO 371/91838; Intelligence on the Middle East, 7 March 1950, IDFA 235/535/2004; Ne'eman, *Mamlekhet Abdallah Leahar Hasipoh*, p. 61.

43 Arab Press review, 25 January 1950, IDFA 289/535/2004; *Hamizrah Hehadash*, 1/3 (1950), p. 217.

44 Tuqan claims are quoted in *al-Ahram*, 9 January 1950.

45 *Al-Misri*, 28 January 1950. Al-Tall repeated these claims in April 1950 when Bevin arrived in Cairo. Intelligence on the Middle East, 30 April 1950, IDFA 235/535/2004.

46 The documents were published officially on 18 March, 1950 in *Akhbar al-Youm*.

47 On the treaty see: "Treaty of Alliance between His Majesty in Respect of the United Kingdom of Great Britain and Northern Ireland and His Majesty the King of the Hashemite Kingdom of Transjordan, 15th March, 1948, A. S. Kirkbride, Tewfiq Abul Huda and Fauzi El Mulki," *MEJ*, 2/4 (October, 1948), pp. 469–473.

48 "The Hashemite Kingdom of Transjordan invites His Britannic Majesty to maintain units of Royal Air Force at Amman and Mafrak airfields". Annex, Article 1 (d).

49 On the military airport in the middle east see: IDFA 115/5/2004.

50 Minutes of cabinet meeting from 8 March1949, NA, PREM 8/1251; Wilson, *King Abdullah*, p. 185.

51 Annex Article 6 (4).

52 *Al-Misri*, 28 January 1950.

53 "The Political Developments in the Arab World in 1948 War", IDFA 631/922/1975, p, 42.

54 Mark Heller, "Politics and the military in Iraq and Jordan, 1920–1958: The British influence", *Armed forces and society*, 4/1 (November, 1977), pp. 90–91.

55 Foreign Office to Amman, 9 March 1948, NA, CO 537/3993. Reports on the meetings see: NA, DEFE 6/5; Intelligence Review, November 1950, IDFA 38/43/1953.

56 *Hamizrah Hehadash*, 1/3 (1950), p. 218.

57 Ne'eman, *Mamlekhet Abdallah Leahar Hasipoh*, p. 32; *Hamizrah Hehadash*, 1/4 (1950), p. 304.

58 *Al-Ahram*, 8 April 1950; Intelligence on the Middle East, 14 April 1950, IDFA 235/535/2004.

59 Abdullah al-Tall loyalists were mostly junior government and public service officials, junior military officers, disgruntled and various unemployed people. Foreign Office: Research Department, 22 March 1950, ISA, 130.02/1/787; *Hamizrah Hehadash*, 1/4 (1950), p. 304.

60 *Hamizrah Hehadash*, 1/4 (1950), p. 304; Intelligence on the Middle East, 18 May 1950, IDFA 235/535/2004.

61 *Hamizrah Hehadash*, 1/4 (1950), p. 304.

62 The Jordanian delegation, 28 April 1949, ISA, 130.02/2447/6; Pappe, *The Making of the Arab–Israeli Conflict*, p 203.

63 Protocol of Lausanne Conference, 15 May 1949, ISA, 130.02/2447/6.

64 Walter Eytan, *The First Ten Years: A Diplomatic History of Israel* (New York: Simon and Schuster, 1958), p. 52.

65 Morris, *The Birth of Palestinian Refugee*, pp. 549, 574; Bowker, *Palestinian Refugees*, p. 126. Criticism of the Arabs' stand and their insistence on the problem of Palestinian refugees was expressed by the *Filastin* newspaper about a year later. In one of the newspaper's articles, it was claimed that "while Israel was willing to compensate the refugees, there's no guarantee that it will agree to do so in the future" and therefore it was claimed that there was a need to accelerate the signing of a peace agreement with Israel. *Filastin*, 22 July 1950.

66 Itamar Rabinovich, *The Road not Taken: Early Arab–Israeli Negotiations* (New York: Oxford University Press, 1991), pp. 118–119.

67 Amman to Foreign Office, 15 November 1949, NA, FO 371/75344;

Foreign Office to Amman, 17 November 1949, NA, FO 371/75344; Foreign Office: Research Department 16 January 1951, ISA, 130.02/1/787.

68 Amman to Foreign Office, 23 November 1949, NA, FO 371/75344.

69 Rabinovich, *The Road not Taken*, p. 125; Foreign Office to Ministry of Defence, 8 December 1949, NA, FO 371/75344.

70 Rabinovich, *The Road not Taken*, p. 127.

71 Amman to Foreign Office, 13 December 1949, NA, FO 371/75345; Dayan, *Story of My Life*, p. 144.

72 Rabinovich, *The Road not Taken*, p. 129.

73 Eytan, *The First Ten Years*, p. 73.

74 In the letter of appointment it was written that "the supervisor over the al-Aqsa Mosque will deploy his custody on all congregations and pilgrims from all nations, will persevere on keeping their safety and ensuring their freedom, their holiness, rituals and temples, return everything into its' place, will give every right its' place according to the known status quo – as the rights of the congregations, mosques, churches and synagogues". *Filastin*, 14 February 1951; "Israel and Jordan", 10 January 1951, ISA, 130.02/1/787.

75 Rabinovich, *The Road not Taken*, pp. 131–132; "Israel and Jordan", 10 January 1951, ISA, 130.02/1/787.

76 Amman to Foreign Office, 20 February 1950, NA, FO 371/82177; Meeting Dayan and Shiloah with al-Mulqi, 24 January 1950, ISA, 130.02/1.

77 Rabinovich, *The Road not Taken*, p. 133.

78 Glubb said in his book: "King Abdullah's approach was more practical. Israel is stronger than Jordan, therefore we cannot fight them. Israel wants peace. Why not see what they have to say? Perhaps we shall get better terms that way" Glubb, *A Soldier with the Arabs*, p. 259. Meeting with the King Abdullah and al-Rifai, 17 February 1950, ISA, 130.02/1/787; Mordechai Gazit, "The Israel–Jordan Peace Negotiations (1949–51): King Abdallah's Lonely Effort", *Journal of Contemporary History*, 23/3 (1988), p. 421.

79 Meeting with the King Abdullah, al-Rifai and Mulqi, 24 February 1950, ISA, 130.02/1/787.

80 Rabinovich, *The Road not Taken*, pp. 138–139.

81 Ibid., p. 139.

82 Meeting Dayan and Shiloah with the King Abdullah, 7 March 1950, ISA, 130.02/1.

83 Eytan, *The First Ten Years*, p. 42.

84 *MEJ*, 4/3 (1950), p. 339; *The New York Times*, 20 March 1950.

85 Quoted in Shwadran, "Jordan Annexes Arab Palestine", p. 107.

86 The severing of ties with Jordan was a Syrian initiative in which the Syrian Prime Minister Khalid al-Azm declared on 6 March that he

would close the border with Jordan if Jordan decided to renew trade with Israel. Arab Press review, 9 April 1950, IDFA 289/535/2004.

87 *Filastin*, 14 April 1950.

88 Glubb, *A Soldier with the Arabs*, p. 258.

89 Bevin to Kirkbride, "Conversation with the Transjordan Prime Minister", 9 February 1948, NA, FO 371/68366; Chiefs of Staff Committee Joint Planning Staff, 29 September 1948, NA, DEFE 6/7; Shwadran, "Jordan Annexes Arab Palestine", p. 102; Bernadotte, *To Jerusalem*, pp. 235–344.

90 Nevo, *King Abdallah*, p. 193.

91 Gelber, *Palestine 1948*, p. 180; Wilson, *King Abdullah*, pp. 185–186.

92 Arab Press review,25 January 1950, IDFA 289/535/2004; Shwadran, "Jordan Annexes Arab Palestine", p. 106; Zvi Elpeleg, *The Grand Mufti: Haj Amin al-Hussaini, Founder of the Palestinian National Movement* (London: Frank Cass, 1993), p. 121.

93 Shwadran, "Jordan Annexes Arab Palestine", pp. 110–111; Gazit, "The Israel–Jordan Peace Negotiations", p. 410.

94 Meeting Sasson with al-Karmi, Foreign Office, 19 May 1950, ISA, 130.02/1/787; Nevo, *King Abdallah*, p. 197; Eli Podeh, *The Quest for Hegemony in the Arab World: The Struggle over the Baghdad Pact* (Leiden: E.J. Brill, 1995), p. 42.

95 W. W. Haddad and M. M. Hardy, "Jordan's Alliance with Israel", p. 45; Elpeleg, *The Grand Mufti*, p. 121.

96 Ne'eman, *Mamlekhet Abdallah Leahar Hasipoh*, p. 50.

97 Amman to Foreign Office, 18 January 1951, NA, FO 371/91367; Foreign Office: Research Department, 9 February 1951, ISA, 130.02/1/787.

98 Musa al-Alami received about 20,000 dunams in Jericho from the Jordanian government for his Arab Development Society. UNRAW's budget for the Jordanian government for the year 1950 was 2.7 million pounds. Ne'eman, *Mamlekhet Abdallah Leahar Hasipoh*, p. 49; Monroe, "The Arab–Israel Frontier", p. 445; Intelligence monthly review, no date, IDFA 600/580/1956.

99 Intelligence on the Middle East, 14 June 1950, IDFA 235/535/2004; Ne'eman, *Mamlekhet Abdallah Leahar Hasipoh*, p. 50; Gelber, *Palestine 1948*, p. 271.

100 The opposition in Jordan claimed that 14,000 people were held in prisons in 1951. IDF General Staff, intelligence branch, 12 May 1955, IDFA 117/535/2004.

101 Amman to Foreign Office, 2 January 1950, NA, FO 371/82703.

102 Morris, *The Birth of Palestinian Refugee*, p. 557.

103 Glubb, *A Soldier with the Arabs*, p. 281.

104 Podeh, *The Quest for Hegemony in the Arab World*, pp. 47–48; al-Alami, *Ibrat Filastin*, p. 42.

105 Intelligence review, November 1950, IDFA 38/43/1953; *Hamizrah Hehadash*, 2/3 (1951), p. 239.

106 *Al-Aharam*, 12 June 1951.

107 W. W. Haddad and M. M. Hardy, "Jordan's Alliance with Israel", p. 43; Podeh, *The Quest for Hegemony in the Arab World*, p. 50.

108 Foreign Office: News to Israeli delegations in the World, 24 July 1951, IDFA 40/68/1955.

109 Foreign Office: News to Israeli delegations in the World, 24 July 1951, IDFA 40/68/55; Foreign Office: Research Department, 31 August 1951, ISA 2565/11; Intelligence review, March–June 1951, IDFA 5/114/1957.

110 *Hamizrah Hehadash*, 2/6 (1951), p. 142; *The Jerusalem Post*, 30 July 1950.

111 Intelligence review, November 1950, IDFA 38/43/1953; Ne'eman, *Mamlekhet Abdallah Leahar Hasipoh*, p. 23. It should be mentioned that al-Khatib was considered a good mayor, who organized civil life in the city and thus increased the number of Jerusalem residents. In May, 1950, the Arab population in Jerusalem was approximately 60,000 in contrast to 20,000 in July 1949. *Al-Misri*, 5 May 1950.

112 Intelligence review, November 1950, IDFA 38/43/1953; *Hamizrah Hehadash*, 2/6 (1951), pp. 142, 145.

113 Shwadran, *Jordan: A State of Tension*, p. 308; *Hamizrah Hehadash*, 2/2 (1951), p. 145.

114 Intelligence review, 1 March 1951, IDFA 39/1431/1953; *Filastin*, 19 December 1950.

115 *Hamizrah Hehadash*, 2/6 (1951), pp. 143, 149.

116 *MEJ*, 3/3 (1949), p. 323.

117 *Hamizrah Hehadash*, 2/1 (1950), p. 39.

118 Intelligence review, November 1950, IDFA 38/43/1953; Vatikiotis, *Politics and the Military in Jordan*, p. 52; *Hamizrah Hehadash*, 2/4 (1951), pp. 332–333.

119 Gazit, "The Israel–Jordan Peace Negotiations", p. 409.

120 *Filastin*, 24 July 1951.

121 Glubb to Melville, 6 August 1951, NA, FO 371/91838; IDF General Staff, intelligence branch, 27 August 1951, IDFA 15/68/1955; Foreign Office: Research Department, 31 August 1951, ISA 2565/11.

122 Amman to Foreign Office, 25 July 1951, NA, FO 371/91838.

123 IDF General Staff, intelligence branch, 27 August 1951, IDFA 15/68/1955; Foreign Office: Research Department, 13 August 1951, ISA 2565/11; Foreign Office: Research Department, 31 August 1951, ISA 2565/11.

124 Amman to Foreign Office, 25 July 1951, NA, FO 371/91838; Musa and al-Madi, *Ta'arikh*, II, p. 556.

125 IDF General Staff, intelligence branch, 30 July 1951, IDFA

15/68/1955; Foreign Office: News to Israeli delegations in the World, 24 July 1951, IDFA 40/68/55.

126 Intelligence Report, 31 July 1951, IDFA 232/1559/1952; Ne'eman, *Mamlekhet Abdallah Leahar Hasipoh*, p. 30; *Ha'aretz*, 30 July 1951.

127 Foreign Office: News to Israeli delegations in the World, 6 August 1951, ISA 2565/11.

128 Glubb to Melville, 6 August 1951, NA, FO 371/91838.

129 *Ha'aretz*, 24 July 1951.

130 Foreign Office: Research Department, 24 August 1951, ISA 2565/11; Sasson to Shiloah, 31 August 1951, ISA 2565/11.

131 Mr. J. Chadwick to Mr. G. Furlonge, 24 July1951, NA, FO 371/91839.

132 Mr. J. Chadwick to Mr. G. Furlonge, 13 August1951, NA, FO 371/91839; Foreign Office: Research Department, 31 August 1951, ISA 2565/11.

133 Amman to Foreign Office, 25 July1951, NA, FO 371/91838.

134 Amman to Foreign Office, 25 July1951, NA, FO 371/91838; Foreign Office: Research Department, 31 August 1951, ISA 2565/11.

135 Amman to Foreign office (Eastern Department), 20 August1951, NA, FO 371/91839; Amman to Foreign Office, 11 August1951, NA, FO 371/91838.

136 Amman to Foreign Office, 11 August1951, NA, FO 371/91838; Intelligence Report, 31 July 1951, IDFA 232/1559/1952.

137 Foreign Office: Research Department, 18 August 1951, ISA 2565/11.

138 Walker to Morrison, 3 September1951, NA, FO 371/91838.

139 Foreign Office: Research Department, 18 August 1951, ISA 2565/11; *Ha'aretz*, 27 July 1951; Elpeleg, *The Grand Mufti*, p. 126; *al-Aharam*, 12 August 1951; Al-Tall, *Abdallah al-Tall*, II, pp. 886, 905; Glubb, *A Soldier with the Arabs*, p. 281.

140 *The New York Times*, 20 August 1951.

141 "Summary of Confessions and Evidence Given at the Trial", Kirkbride to Mr. Younger, 17 September1951, NA, FO 371/91839.

142 "King Abdullah's Assassins", *The World Today*, VII (1951), p. 411.

143 "Summary of Confessions and Evidence Given at the Trial", Kirkbride to Mr. Younger, 17 September1951, NA, FO 371/91839.

144 Foreign Office: Research Department, 31 August 1951, ISA 2565/11.

145 Glubb to Melville, 6 Agust1951, NA, FO 371/91838.

146 *Hamizrah Hehadash*, 2/6 (1951), p. 143; *Davar*, 24 August 1951.

147 Walker to Morrison, 3 September 1951, NA, FO 371/91838.

148 Foreign Office: Research Department, 31 August 1951, ISA 2565/11.

149 Al-Tall, *Abdallah al-Tall*, II, p. 691.

150 Elpeleg, *The Grand Mufti*, p. 126; "King Abdullah's Assassins", p. 419.

151 *Hamizrah Hehadash*, 2/6 (1951), p. 151; Shwadran, *Jordan: A State of Tension*, pp. 312–313.

152 *Hamizrah Hehadash*, 2/6 (1951), p. 151; IDF General Staff, intelligence branch, 27 August 1951, IDFA 15/68/1955.

153 *Al-Aharam*, 25 July 1951.

154 *Hamizrah Hehadash*, 2/6 (1951), p. 149.

155 Wilson, *King Abdullah*, p. 93; Article 22 (B).

156 Kamel, "The Legislature", p. 231.

4 In Exile in Egypt and Return to Jordan

1 Among the Jordanians, Tawfiq Abu al-Huda , who formed the first government after Talal was crowned as King, continued to be Prime Minister.

2 IDF General Staff, review intelligence half-year report, August 1951, IDFA 1311/922/1975; Shwadran, *Jordan: A State of Tension*, p. 313.

3 The only criticism he made toward King Talal was about the continued employment of General Glubb Pasha, but the Jordanian government refused to dismiss Glubb, arguing that if Jordan fired Glubb "Britain will appoint another Glubb". *Al-Jumhor al-msri*, 26 November 1951. Quoted in Select information of Arab World, IDFA 289/535/2004.

4 Foreign Office: Research Department, April 1952, ISA, 93.03/1.

5 "Recognize King Farouk as a King of Egypt and Sudan", Foreign Office: Research Department, 18 January 1952, ISA, 93.03/1.

6 For example, in *Filastin* newspaper "we congratulate Egypt and ourselves, because we feel that it has been liberated from slavery and constitutes a major turning point in all of Arab history", was written. *Filastin*, 11 October 1951.

7 Intelligence review, November 1950, IDFA 38/43/1953; Foreign Office: Research Department, April 1952, ISA, 93.03/1.

8 "Anti-British Activity", Cairo to Foreign Office, 18 December 1951, NA, FO 371/96858; Foreign Office: Research Department, 25 January1952, ISA, 93.03/1.

9 Panayiotis J. Vatikiotis, *The History of Modern Egypt: From Muhammad Ali to Mubarak* (Baltimore: Johns Hopkins University Press, 1991), p. 371.

10 Jean Lacouture, *Nasser: A biography* (London: Secker and Warburg, 1973), pp. 83, 117; Richard P. Mitchell, *The Society of the Muslim Brothers in Egypt* (London: Oxford University Press, 1969), p. 92; Be'eri, *Army Officers in Arab Politics*, p. 90.

11 Dayan, *Story of My Life*, p. 103.

12 *Ha'aretz*, 21 August 1951.

13 Ibid.; Asher Goren, *Haliga Ha'aravit* (The Arab League, Hebrew), Tel Aviv: Eynot, 1954, p. 99.

14 Al-Alami, *Ibrat Filastin*, pp. 49–50.
15 The six blocks were: Iraq; Greater Syria (Jordan, Syria, Lebanon and Israel); North Arabia (Hijaz and Najd to the Persian Gulf); South Arabia (Yemen); the Nile Valley (Egypt, Sudan and Libya); North Africa (Morocco, Algeria and Tunisia). Goren, *Haliga Ha'aravit*, p. 99; Taqi al-Din al-Nabhani, *Inqadh Filastin* (Salvation of Palestine, Arabic), Damascus, 1950, p. 187.
16 In addition to al-Qudsi, Shishakli and Nagib, the Iraqi politician Fadel al-Jamali also suggested in August 1952 to transfer the Arab League to the Commonwealth of Nations. Goren, *Haliga Ha'aravit*, pp. 97–98.
17 Intelligence Review, 17 August 1952, IDFA 215/642/1956.
18 IDF General Staff, review intelligence, August 1952, IDFA 113/535/2004.
19 Salibi, *The Modern History of Jordan*, p. 189; Avi Shlaim, *Lion of Jordan: The Life of King Hussein in War and Peace* (London: Allen Lane, 2007), pp. 62–63.
20 Lacouture *Nasser*, p. 127.
21 *Davar*, 29 May 1959.
22 Be'eri, *Army Officers in Arab Politics*, p. 81.
23 Lacouture, *Nasser*, p. 34.
24 Be'eri, *Army Officers in Arab Politics*, p. 78; Vatikiotis, *The History of Modern Egypt*, p. 347.
25 One of the meetings between al-Tall and Nagib took place on 8 June 1952. Al-Tall, *Abdallah al-Tall*, II, p. 691; Goren, *Haliga Ha'aravit*, p. 98.
26 Al-Tall, *Abdallah al-Tall*, II, p. 713.
27 *Davar*, 29 May 1959.
28 One of the important events in which al-Tall participated repeatedly, was the day marking the UN partition resolution of November 1947. Al-Tall, *Abdallah al-Tall*, II, p. 963.
29 Al-Tall, *Abdallah al-Tall*, II, p. 693.
30 *Davar*, 29 May 1959; Al-Tall, *Abdallah al-Tall*, II, pp. 693, 807.
31 Khalil Totah, *Dynamite in the Middle East* (New York: Philosophical Library, 1955), p. 74; al-Tall, *Abdallah al-Tall*, II, p. 718.
32 Charles B. Selak, "The Suez Canal Base Agreement of 1954", *The American Journal of International Law*, 49/4 (1955), pp. 487–505; Lacouture *Nasser*, p. 119; James P. Jankowski, *Nasser's Egypt: Arab Nationalism and the United Arab Republic* (Boulder: Lynne Rienner Publishers, 2002), p. 46.
33 Mitchell, *The Society of the Muslim Brothers*, pp. 136–137.
34 Jankowski, *Nasser's Egypt*, p. 23.
35 Lacouture, *Nasser*, p. 128; http://weekly.ahram.org.eg/2004/713/feature.htm.

36 The six leaders were: Hassan al-Hudaybi, Hindawi Duwayr, Ibrahim al-Tayyib, Yusuf Tal'at, Muhammaf Farghali and Abd al-Qadie Awda. Mitchell, *The Society of the Muslim Brothers*, p. 160.

37 Vatikiotis, *The History of Modern Egypt*, pp. 386–387.

38 On the relation between Abdullah al-Tall and the Muslim Brotherhood and the Mufti see: al-Tall, *Abdallah al-Tall*, II, pp. 791–796.

39 Jankowski, *Nasser's Egypt*, p. 64; Coet J. Campbell, *Defense of the Middle East: Problems of American Policy* (New York: Published for the Council on Foreign Relations by Harper and Brothers, 1962), pp. 50–51.

40 Podeh, *The Quest for Hegemony in the Arab World*, p. 72; Shlaim, *Lion of Jordan*, p. 77.

41 Campbell, *Defense of the Middle East*, p. 58; Anderson, *Nationalist Voices in Jordan*, p. 162.

42 Tal, "Jordan", pp. 111–112; George M. Haddad, *Revolutions and Military Rule in the Middle East: The Arab States* (New York: Robert Speller and Sons, 1971), II, p. 491.

43 Details on the arm deal see: IDF General Staff, review intelligence, 30 May 1956, IDFA 113/535/2004.

44 IDF General Staff, review intelligence, October 1955, IDFA 113/535/2004; Tal, "Jordan", p. 112; Haddad, *Revolutions and Military Rule*, III, p. 89.

45 IDF General Staff, review intelligence, 21 December 1955, 9 January 1956, IDFA 117/535/2004; IDF General Staff, review intelligence, 2 February 1956, IDFA 113/535/2004; Anderson, *Nationalist Voices in Jordan*, pp. 162–163.

46 The British officers who were also dismissed with Glubb Pasha were: Colonel W.M Hutton, Chief of Staff and Colonel P. Coghill, Director of General Intelligence. IDF General Staff, review intelligence, 4 March 1956, IDFA 117/535/2004; Tal, "Jordan", p. 112.

47 General Glubb Pasha preferred in the case of war with Israel that Jordan should abandon the West Bank and reinforce its forces in Jordan itself, while King Hussein thought that Glubb Pasha should send forces to the West Bank as well. Moreover, Glubb Pasha avoided promoting Arab officers, claiming they were unskilled, while the King wanted to see more Arab officers in the army. On the debate see: Shlaim, *Lion of Jordan*, pp. 98–99; Hasan N. Aruri, *Jordan: A Study in Political Development (1921–1965)* (The Hague: Martinus Nijhoff, 1972), pp. 129–130.

48 IDF General Staff, review intelligence, October 1955, IDFA 113/535/2004; Cohen, *Political parties in the West Bank*, pp. 95–96.

49 Uriel Dann, *King Hussein and the Challenge of Arab Radicalism* (New York: Oxford University Press, 1989), p. 58; Haddad, *Revolutions and*

Military Rule, II, p. 494; *MER*, 1 (1960), p. 327; Anderson, *Nationalist Voices in Jordan*, p. 167; Shlaim, *Lion of Jordan*, p. 73.

50 "Report on dismissal of Glubb Pasha", 4 March 1956, ISA, 130.02/1/786. According to Ahmad al-Tall, King Hussein updated Nasser on 23 February via his ambassador to Cairo about his intention to dismiss Glubb Pasha, but there is no other indication for this. Al-Tall, *Abdallah al-Tall*, II, p. 916; Jankowski, *Nasser's Egypt*, p. 89.

51 Al-Tall, *Abdallah al-Tall*, II, p. 917.

52 "Report on dismissal of Glubb Pasha", 4 March 1956, ISA, 130.02/1/786; IDF General Staff, review intelligence, 16 March 1956, IDFA 113/535/2004

53 The list of the Arab officers' appointment sees: IDF General Staff, review intelligence, 4 March 1956, IDFA 117/535/2004.

54 IDF General Staff, review intelligence, 24 May 1956, IDFA 113/535/2004; Salibi, *The Modern History of Jordan*, p. 189.

55 Vatikiotis, *Politics and the Military*, p. 107.

56 The alliance between Jordan and Iraq was signed in April 1956. IDF General Staff, review intelligence, 10 April 1956, IDFA 113/535/2004.

57 IDF General Staff, review intelligence, 23 July 1956, IDFA 113/535/2004; Aruri, *Jordan*, p. 137; Haddad, *Revolutions and Military Rule*, II, p. 496.

58 Party representation in Parliament see: Aruri, *Jordan*, p. 135.

59 Anderson, *Nationalist Voices in Jordan*, p. 162; *Davar*, 28 October 1956.

60 *Hamizrah Hehadash*, 8/2 (1957), 146.

61 Haddad, *Revolutions and Military Rule*, II, p. 496; Aruri, *Jordan*, p. 136; Salibi, *The Modern History of Jordan*, p. 191.

62 Review Arab press, 1952–1956, IDFA 341/535/2004; Aruri, *Jordan*, p. 137.

63 Ibid., p. 140. See also the Hussein order in IDF General Staff, review intelligence, 5 April 1957, IDFA 113/535/2004.

64 Cohen, *Political parties in the West Bank*, p. 37.

65 Lawrence Tal, "Jordan" in Yezid Sayigh and Avi Shlaim (eds.), *The Cold War and the Middle East* (Oxford: Clarendon, 1997), p. 114.

66 Salibi, *The Modern History of Jordan*, p. 192; Dann, *King Hussein and the Challenge*, p. 55.

67 Cohen, *Political Parties in the West Bank*, p. 38.

68 Anderson, *Nationalist Voices in Jordan*, p. 183.

69 Dann, *King Hussein and the Challenge*, p. 59; *MER*, 1 (1960), p. 327; Be'eri, *Army Officers in Arab Politics*, p. 233; Haddad, *Revolutions and Military Rule*, II, pp. 500–509.

70 Aruri, Jordan, p. 144. At the end of September, 1957, the military court sentenced Ali Abu Nuwar and Ali al-Hiyari to 15 years in prison,

Mahmud al-Musa to 10 years in prison and Ma'an Abu Nuwar was found not guilty and allowed to return to the army. Al-Tall, *Abdallah al-Tall*, II, pp. 923.

71 Al-Tall, *Abdallah al-Tall*, II, pp. 924, 949; Shaul Mishal, *West Bank/East Bank: The Palestinians in Jordan, 1949–1967* (New Haven: Yale University Press, 1978), p. 49; Anderson, *Nationalist Voices in Jordan*, p. 186.
72 *Davar*, 3 February 1958.
73 Tal, "Jordan", p. 115.
74 Al-Tall, *Abdallah al-Tall*, II, p. 931.
75 Mishal, *West Bank*, pp. 49–50; *MER*, 1 (1960), p. 328.
76 Ibid., p. 327; Dann, *King Hussein and the Challenge*, pp. 86–88; Haddad, *Revolutions and Military Rule*, II, pp. 509–511.
77 *MER*, 1 (1960), p. 327; Be'eri, *Army Officers in Arab Politics*, p. 233.
78 Tal, "Jordan", p. 116; Campbell, *Defense of the Middle East*, p. 149; Haddad, *Revolutions and Military Rule*, II, pp. 511–512.
79 *MER*, 1 (1960), p. 327; Be'eri, *Army Officers in Arab Politics*, p. 234.
80 Jankowski, *Nasser's Egypt*, p. 158; *MER*, 1 (1960), pp. 328–330.
81 Be'eri, *Army Officers in Arab Politics*, pp. 346–347.
82 Alistair Horne, *A Savage War of Peace: Algeria 1954–1962* (London: Macmillan, 1977), p. 23.
83 Benjamin Stora, *Algeria, 1830–2000: A Short History* (Ithaca: Cornell University Press, 2001), p. 38; Horne, *A Savage War of Peace*, p. 79.
84 Al-Tall, *Abdallah al-Tall*, II, pp. 768–770.
85 Stora, *Algeria, 1830–2000*, p. 38.
86 Horne, *A Savage War of Peace*, pp. 13–14.
87 Stora, *Algeria, 1830–2000*, p. 38.
88 Horne, *A Savage War of Peace*, pp. 521–534.
89 Tunisia, Morocco, Pakistan, Indonesia and Vietnam were also among the countries which recognized the government in exile.
90 Yezid Sayigh, *Armed Struggle and the Search for State: The Palestinian National Movement* (Oxford: Oxford University Press, 1999), p. 102.
91 *Davar*, 29 May 1959.
92 The article about Abdullah al-Tall is from *al-Musawar* newspaper (8 April 1960), was quoted in al-Tall, *Abdallah al-Tall*, II, p. 775; *Davar*, 31 March 1960.
93 *Davar*, 29 May 1959.
94 Al-Tall, *Abdallah al-Tall*, II, pp. 781–782.
95 *Davar*, 29 May 1959.
96 Sayigh, *Armed Struggle*, p. 78; *MER*, 1 (1960), p. 133; Lacouture *Nasser*, p. 292; Elpeleg, *The Grand Mufti*, p. 134.
97 *Al-Ahram*, 27 May 1959.
98 Elpeleg, *The Grand Mufti*, p. 135.
99 The meeting with Kamal Adwan took place in October, 1960, and the

meeting with Khalil al-Wazir took place in June, 1961. Al-Tall, *Abdallah al-Tall*, II, pp. 804–805, 966; Sayigh, *Armed Struggle*, p. 84.

100 Joshua A. Sherman, *Mandate Days: British Lives in Palestine, 1918–1948* (London: Thames and Hudson, 1997), p. 88; Martin Gilbert, *Exile and Return: The Struggle for a Jewish Homeland* (Philadelphia: Lippincott, 1978), p. 226; Yehoshua Porath, *The Emergence of the Palestinian-Arab National Movement 1918–1929* (London: Frank Cass, 1974), p. 38.

101 Morris, *The Road to Jerusalem*, p. 23.

102 About the relationship between Abdullah al-Tall and the Muslim Brotherhood and with the Mufti see: Al-Tall, *Abdallah al-Tall*, II, pp. 791–796.

103 Vatikiotis, *The History of Modern Egypt*, p. 320; Matthias Küntzel, *Jihad and Jew-hatred: Islamism, Nazism and the Roots of 9/11* (New York: Telos Press, 2007), p. 27.

104 David Dalin and John Rothmann, *Icon of Evil: Hitler's Mufti and the Rise of Radical Islam* (New York: Random House, 2008), p. 54; Küntzel, *Jihad and Jew-hatred*, p. 45.

105 Among the promises al-Tall made in his books were: "look from the place where you are, northward and southward and eastward and westward, for all the land which you sees, to thee will I give it, and to thy seed forever" (Genesis, 13: 14–15) to Isaac, God said: "Sojourn in this land, and I will be with you, and I will bless you . . . to your seed I will give all these lands" (Genesis, 26: 2–3). To Jacob, God said: "The land which I gave to Abraham and Isaac, to you I will give it, and to your seed after you . . . " (Genesis, 35: 12). Abdullah Y. al-Tall, *Khatar al-Yahudiya al-Alamiya Ala al-Islam wal-Masihiya* (The Danger of World Jewry to Islam and to Christianity, Arabic), Cairo, 1964, p. 15; Abdullah Y. al-Tall, *Judhur al-Bila* (Roots of the Evil, Arabic), Amman, 1970, p. 15.

106 Like the first biographer of the Prophet Muhammad, Ibn Ishaq, who claimed that the Jews knew that Muhammad would appear, even before he born. See: Abu Muhammad Ibn Hisham, *Sirat Sayidna Muhammad Rasul Allah* (The Biography of the Prophet Muhammad, Arabic) Cairo, 1911, I, pp. 13–15. More about the Jews in the Islamic tradition see: Muhammad ibn Ismail al-Bukhari, *Sahih al-Bukhari* (Prophetic Traditions of al-Bukhari, Arabic), Cairo, 1950, IX, Book 92, No. 461.

107 Al-Tall, *Khatar al-Yahudiya*, p. 13.

108 Porath, *The Emergence*, p. 40.

109 Al-Tall, *Judhur al-Bila*, p. 13.

110 Ibid., p. 311.

111 Harkabi, *Arab Attitudes*, p. 73; al-Tall, *Judhur al-Bila*, p. 311.

112 Al-Tall, *Khatar al-Yahudiya*, p. 15.

113 He presented these so-called "features of the Jews" mainly in his book *Judhur al-Bila*, pp. 10–67 and in his second book *Khatar al-Yahudiya*, pp. 53–68.

114 Ibid., pp. 53–54; al-Tall, *Judhur al-Bila*, pp. 59–60.

115 Al-Tall, *Khatar al-Yahudiya*, pp. 54–57.

116 Al-Tall, *Judhur al-Bila*, p. 44.

117 Ibid.

118 Al-Tall, *Khatar al-Yahudiya*, pp. 63–64.

119 Al-Tall, *Judhur al-Bila*, pp. 54–56.

120 Among them: denial of killing the prophets, arrogance and charging interest on loans.

121 Al-Tall, *Judhur al-Bila*, p. 93.

122 Ibid., p. 95.

123 Al-Tall, *Khatar al-Yahudiya*, pp. 66–68.

124 Ibid., p. 9.

125 Ibid., p. 171.

126 Ibid.

127 On the plot summary see: http://www.adl.org/ special_reports/ protocols/protocols_plot2.asp.

128 www.hayadan.org.il.

129 Al-Tall, *Khatar al-Yahudiya*, p. 20.

130 Al-Tall, *Khatar al-Yahudiya*, pp. 115–117; Harkabi, *Arab Attitudes*, p. 276.

131 The Arabic meaning of *fedayeen* is self-sacrifices.

132 Sayigh, *Armed Struggle*, p. 95.

133 Aryeh Yodfat and Yuval Arnon-Ohanah, *PLO Strategy and Politics* (London: Croom Helm, 1981), p. 22.

134 Moshe Shemesh, *Arab Politics, Palestinian Nationalism, and the Six Day War* (Brighton, Portland, Toronto: Sussex Academic Press, 2008), pp. 45–46.

135 Sayigh, *Armed Struggle*, p. 95; Yodfat and Arnon-Ohanah, *PLO Strategy and Politics*, p. 20.

136 Shemesh, *Arab Politics*, pp. 70–71; Elpeleg, *The Grand Mufti*, p. 146.

137 Elpeleg, *The Grand Mufti*, p. 148.

138 The latter was sent on 23 February, 1965. Al-Tall, *Abdallah al-Tall*, II, p. 919.

139 Shemesh, Arab Politics, p. 20; Asher Susser, *On Both Banks of the Jordan: A Political Biography of Wasfi al-Tall* (London: Frank Cass, 1994), p. 51.

140 Ibid., p. 75.

141 IDF Central Command, review intelligence, 14 May 1956, IDFA 1785/535/2004; *Filastin*, 4 April 1965, 9 April 1965.

142 *Filastin*, 7 April 1965.

143 Al-Tall, *Abdallah al-Tall*, II, pp. 919, 970; Susser, *On Both Banks of the Jordan*, p. 75.
144 On attempts to return Abdullah al-Tall to Jordan see: Ibid., pp. 912–914, 942–943; *Davar*, 29 May 1959.
145 Al-Tall, *Abdallah al-Tall*, II, p. 970; *Filastin*, 21 April 1965.
146 Al-Tall, *Abdallah al-Tall*, II, p. 977.
147 Ibid., I, p. 15.
148 Ibid., II, p. 971; *Davar*, 25 January 1967.
149 *Filastin*, 1 July 1966.
150 For his new claims, see: Al-Tall, *Abdallah al-Tall*, II, pp. 893–897.
151 *MER* (1968), pp. 367–368; Yodfat and Arnon-Ohanah, *PLO Strategy and Politics*, pp. 25, 28.
152 Shlaim, *Lion of Jordan*, p. 276; Salibi, *The Modern History of Jordan*, pp. 229–230.
153 Shlaim, *Lion of Jordan*, p. 313.
154 William B. Quandt (and other), *The Politics of Palestinian Nationalism* (Berkeley: University of California Press, 1973), p. 125; Salibi, *The Modern History of Jordan*, p. 232.
155 Mark Ensalaco, *Middle Eastern Terrorism: From Black September to September 11* (Philadelphia: University of Pennsylvania Press, 2008), p. 24; Quandt, *The Politics of Palestinian Nationalism*, p. 126; Yodfat and Arnon-Ohanah, *PLO Strategy and Politics*, p. 26.
156 The military government served its role until Dawud's resignation on 26 September, 1970 and he was replaced by Ahmad Tuqan, who headed the civilian government. Sayigh, *Armed Struggle*, pp. 259–264; Susser, *On Both Banks of the Jordan*, p. 138.
157 Quandt, *The Politics of Palestinian Nationalism*, pp. 127–128.
158 Wasfi al-Tall was appointed as Prime Minister on 28 October, 1970. Sayigh, *Armed Struggle*, p. 268.
159 Quandt, *The Politics of Palestinian Nationalism*, p. 131; Sayigh, Armed Struggle, pp. 278–279; Susser, *On Both Banks of the Jordan*, p. 154.
160 Sayigh, *Armed Struggle*, p. 281; Salibi, *The Modern History of Jordan*, p. 244; Yodfat and Arnon-Ohanah, *PLO Strategy and Politics*, p. 33.
161 Ensalaco, *Middle Eastern Terrorism*, p. 31; Yodfat and Arnon-Ohanah, *PLO Strategy and Politics*, p. 33.
162 Sayigh, *Armed Struggle*, p. 309.
163 Ensalaco, *Middle Eastern Terrorism*, pp. 37–39; Quandt, *The Politics of Palestinian Nationalism*, p. 211.
164 Susser, *On Both Banks of the Jordan*, p. 171.
165 Al-Tall, *Abdallah al-Tall*, I, p. 15.

Bibliography

I Archives

The National Archives (London).
Haganah Archives (Tel Aviv) .
Israel Defence Forces Archive (Tel Hashomer).
Israel State Archives (Jerusalem).

II Newspapers and Journals

Al-Ahram (Cairo).
Akhbar al-Youm (Cairo).
Arab al-Yawm (Amman).
Davar (Tel Aviv).
Al-Dustour (Amman).
Filastin (Jerusalem) .
Al-Ghad (Amman).
Ha'aretz (Tel Aviv).
Hamizrah Hehadash (Jerusalem).
Al-Liwaa (Amman).
MEJ (Washington).
MER (Tel Aviv).
Al-Misri (Cairo) .
Al-Nasr (Amman).
The Jerusalem Post (Jerusalem).
The Palestine Post (Jerusalem).
The New York Times (New York).
Yedioth Aharonoth (Tel Aviv).

III Books

Abdullah ibn Hussein, *Muzakarat al-Malik Abdallah* (Memoirs of the King Abdullah, Arabic), Amman, 1947.
Abu Diya, Sa'ad, *Ta'arikh al-Jayish al-Arabi 1921–1946* (The History of the Arab Legion 1921–1946, Arabic), Amman, 1987.
Abu Nowar, Ma'an, *The History of the Hashemite Kingdom of Jordan* (Oxford: St Antony's College, 1989).
Abu Nowar, Ma'an, *The Jordanian–Israeli War 1948–1951: A History of the Hashemite Kingdom of Jordan* (Reading: Ithaca Press, 2002).
Al-Alami, Musa, *Ibrat Filastin* (The Lesson of Palestine, Arabic), Beirut 1949.

Anderson, S. Betty, *Nationalist Voices in Jordan: The Street and the State* (Texas: University of Texas Press, 2005).

Antonius, George, *The Arab Awakening: The Story of the Arab National Movement* (Philadelphia: J.B. Lippincott, 1939).

Al-Arif, Arif, *Nakbat Filastin* (Palestine Disaster, Arabic), Amman, 1956.

Aruri, N. Hasan, *Jordan: A Study in Political Development (1921–1965)* (The Hague: Martinus Nijhoff, 1972).

Bailey, Clinton, *Jordan's Palestinian Challenge 1948–1983: A Political History* (Jerusalem: Studies in International Politics, The Hebrew University of Jerusalem, 1984).

Bar-Yoseph, Uri, *The Best of Enemies – Israel and Trans-Jordan in the War of 1948* (London: Frank Cass, 1987).

Be'eri, Eliezer, *Army Officers in Arab Politics and Society* (Jerusalem: Israel Universities Press, 1969).

Ben-Gurion, David, *Yuman Hamilhamh* (Ben-Gurion's War Diary, Hebrew), Tel Aviv, 1982.

Bernadotte, Folke, *To Jerusalem* (London: Hodder and Stoughton, 1951).

Bowker, Robert, *Palestinian Refugees: Mythology, Identity, and the Search for Peace* (Boulder: Lynne Rienner Publishers, 2003).

Al-Bukhari, Muhammad ibn Ismail, *Sahih al-Bukhari* (Prophetic Traditions of al-Bukhari, Arabic), Cairo, 1950.

Campbell, J. Coet, *Defense of the Middle East: Problems of American Policy* (New York: Published for the Council on Foreign Relations by Harper and Brothers, 1962).

Cohen, Amnon. *Political parties in the West Bank under the Jordanian Regime, 1949–1967* (Ithaca: Cornell University Press, 1982).

Cohen, Yona, *Yerushalyim Bematzur* (Jerusalem under Siege, Hebrew), Tel Aviv, 1976.

Dalin, David and Rothmann, John, *Icon of Evil: Hitler's Mufti and the Rise of Radical Islam* (New York: Random House, 2008).

Dann, Uriel, *King Hussein and the Challenge of Arab Radicalism* (New York: Oxford University Press, 1989).

Dayan, Moshe, *Story of My Life* (Jerusalem: Steimatzky, 1976).

Ensalaco, Mark, *Middle Eastern Terrorism: From Black September to September 11* (Philadelphia: University of Pennsylvania Press, 2008).

Eytan, Walter, *The First Ten Years: A Diplomatic History of Israel* (New York: Simon and Schuster, 1958).

El-Edroos, S. Ali, *The Hashemite Arab Army 1908–1979: An Appreciation and Analysis of Military Operation* (Amman: The Publishing Committee, 1980).

Elpeleg, Zvi, *The Grand Mufti: Haj Amin al-Hussaini, Founder of the Palestinian National Movement* (London: Frank Cass, 1993).

Ferro, Marc, *The Great War, 1914–1918* (London: Frank Cass, 1973).

Galili, Eliezer, *Tzvaot Ha'aravim Bedoreno* (Arab armies in our generation, Hebrew), Tel Aviv: Ma'archot, 1948.

Gelber, Yoav, *Palestine 1948: War, Escape and the Emergence of the Palestine Refugee Problem* (Brighton, Portland, Toronto: Sussex Academic Press, 2001).

Gelber, Yoav, *Jewish–Transjordanian Relations 1921–1948* (London: Frank Cass, 1996).

Gilbert, Martin, *Exile and Return: The Struggle for a Jewish Homeland* (Philadelphia: Lippincott, 1978).

Glubb, B. John, *A Soldier with the Arabs* (London: Hodder and Stoughton, 1957).

Glubb, B. John, *The Story of the Arab Legion* (London: Hodder and Stoughton, 1948).

Godfrey, Lias, *Glubb's Legion* (London: Evans Brothers Ltd., 1956).

Goren, Asher, *Haliga Ha'aravit* (The Arab League, Hebrew), Tel Aviv: Eynot, 1954.

Grainger, D. John, *The Battle for Palestine 1917* (Woodbridge: The Boydell Press, 2006).

Haddad, M. George, *Revolutions and Military Rule in the Middle East: The Arab States* (New York: Robert Speller and Sons, 1971).

Horne, Alistair, *A Savage War of Peace: Algeria 1954–1962* (London: Macmillan, 1977).

Hurewitz, J. C. *Diplomacy in Near and Middle East: A Documentary Record* (New York: Octagon Books, 1972).

Ibn Hisham, Abu Muhammad, *Sirat Sayidna Muhammad Rasul Allah* (The Biography of the Prophet Muhammad, Arabic), Cairo, 1911.

Jankowski, P. James, *Nasser's Egypt: Arab Nationalism and the United Arab Republic* (Boulder: Lynne Rienner Publishers, 2002).

Al-Khatib, N. Muhammad, *Min Athar al-Nakba* (Consequences of the Disaster, Arabic), Damascus, 1951.

Küntzel, Matthias, *Jihad and Jew-hatred: Islamism, Nazism and the Roots of 9/11* (New York: Telos Press, 2007).

Lacouture, Jean, *Nasser: A biography* (London: Secker and Warburg, 1973).

Lapierre, Dominique and Collins, Larry, *O Jerusalem* (London: Simon and Schuster, 1972).

Levi, Yitzhak, *Tish'a Kabin: Yerushalyim Bekravot Milhemet Ha'hatzmaot* (Jerusalem in independence war, Hebrew), Tel Aviv, 1986.

Lyman, Robert, *Iraq 1941: The Battles for Basra, Habbaniya, Fallujah and Baghdad* (London: Osprey Publishing, 2006).

Al-Majali, Hazza, *Muzakarati* (My Memoirs, Arabic), Amman, 1960.

Meir, Golda, *My Life* (Jerusalem: Steimatzky, 1975).

Mishal Shaul, *West Bank/East Bank: The Palestinians in Jordan, 1949–1967* (New Haven: Yale University Press, 1978).

Mitchell, P. Richard, *The Society of the Muslim Brothers in Egypt* (London: Oxford University Press, 1969).

Morris, Benny, *The Birth of Palestinian Refugee Problem, 1947–1949* (Cambridge: Cambridge University Press, 1987).

Morris, Benny, *The Road to Jerusalem: Glubb Pasha, Palestine and the Jews* (London: I.B. Tauris, 2003).

Al-Munim, Muhammad Abd, *Asrar 1948* (Secret 1948 War, Arabic), Cairo, 1968.

Musa, Suleiman, *Ayam la Tunsa: Al-Urdun fi Harb 1948* (Unforgettable Days: Jordan in 1948 War, Arabic), Amman, 1997.

Musa, Suleiman and al-Madi, Munib, *Ta'arikh al-Urdun fi al-Qarn al-Ishrin* (The History of Jordan in 20 Century, Arabic), Amman, 1997.

Al-Nabhani, Taqi al-Din, *Inqadh Filastin* (Salvation of Palestine, Arabic), Damascus 1950.

al-Nasser, Gamal Abd, *Falsafa al-Tawra* (The Philosophy of the Revolution, Arabic), Cairo, 1953.

Ne'eman, Zvi, *Mamlekhet Abdallah Leahar Hasipoh* (The Kingdom of Abdullah after the Annexation, Hebrew), Tel Aviv, 1950.

Nevo, Joseph, *King Abdallah and Palestine: A Territorial Ambition* (Basingstoke: Macmillan, 1996).

Pappe, Ilan, *The Making of the Arab–Israeli Conflict, 1947–51* (London: I.B. Tauris, 1992).

Parolin, P. Gianluca, *Citizenship in the Arab World: Kin, Religion and Nation-State* (Amsterdam: Amsterdam University Press, 2009).

Peak, G. Frederick, *A history of Jordan and its Tribes* (Coral Gables, Fla: University of Miami Press, 1958).

Phillips, John, *A Will to Survive* (New York: Dial Press, 1977).

Podeh, Eli, *The Quest for Hegemony in the Arab World: The Struggle over the Baghdad Pact* (Leiden: E.J. Brill, 1995).

Porath, Yehoshua, *The Emergence of the Palestinian-Arab National Movement 1918–1929* (London: Frank Cass, 1974).

Quandt, B. William (and other), *The Politics of Palestinian Nationalism* (Berkeley: University of California Press, 1973).

Rabinovich, Itamar, *The Road not Taken: Early Arab–Israeli Negotiations* (New York: Oxford University Press, 1991).

Rogan, Eugene, *Frontiers of the State in the Late Ottoman Empire: Transjordan, 1850–1921* (Cambridge: Cambridge University Press, 2002).

Al-Rusan, Mahmud, *Ma'arik Bab al-Wad* (The Battles of Bab al-Wad, Arabic), Amman, 1950.

Salibi, Kamal, *The Modern History of Jordan* (London: I.B. Tauris, 1998).

Sayigh, Anis, *Al-Hashemion Waqadiyat Filastin* (The Hashemite and Palestine Question, Arabic), Beirut, 1966.

Sayigh, Yezid, *Armed Struggle and the Search for State: The Palestinian*

National Movement (Oxford: Oxford University Press, 1999).

Sela, Avraham, *Haba'ath Hafalastini* (The Palestinian Ba'ath, Hebrew), Jerusalem, 1984.

Shealtiel, David, *Yerushalyim Tashah* (Jerusalem in 1948, Hebrew), Tel Aviv, 1981.

Shemesh, Moshe, *Arab Politics, Palestinian Nationalism, and the Six Day War* (Brighton, Portland, Toronto: Sussex Academic Press, 2008).

Sherman, A. Joshua, *Mandate Days: British Lives in Palestine, 1918–1948* (London: Thames and Hudson, 1997).

Shlaim, Avi, *Collusion across the Jordan: King Abdullah, the Zionist Movement, and the Partition of Palestine* (Oxford: Clarendon, 1988).

Shlaim, Avi, *Lion of Jordan: The Life of King Hussein in War and Peace* (London: Allen Lane, 2007).

Shwadran, Benjamin, *Jordan: A State of Tension* (New York: Council for Middle Eastern Affairs Press, 1959).

Stora, Benjamin, *Algeria, 1830–2000: A Short History* (Ithaca: Cornell University Press, 2001).

Susser, Asher, *On Both Banks of the Jordan: A Political Biography of Wasfi al-Tall* (London: Frank Cass, 1994).

Tal, David, *War in Palestine, 1948: Strategy and Diplomacy* (London: Routledge, 2004).

Al-Tall, Y. Abdullah, *Judhur al-Bila* (Roots of the Evil, Arabic), Amman, 1970.

Al-Tall, Y. Abdullah, *Karithat Filastin, Muthakart Abdullah al-Tall Qai'd Ma'arakat al-Qauds* (The Catastrophe of Palestine: Memoirs of Abdullah al-Tall Commander of the Battle on Jerusalem, Arabic), Amman, 1959.

Al-Tall, Y. Abdullah, *Khatar al-Yahudiya al-Alamiya Ala al-Islam wal-Masihiya* (The Danger of World Jewry to Islam and to Christianity, Arabic), Cairo, 1964.

Al-Tall, Y. Abdullah, *Rihla ila Britaniya* (Journey to Britain, Arabic), Jerusalem, 1947.

Al-Tall, Y. Ahmad, *Abdallah al-Tall Batal Ma'arakat al-Qauds* (Abdullah al-Tall: The Hero of the Battle on Jerusalem, Arabic), Amman, 1999.

Taqrir Lajnat at-Tahqiq al-Niyabiyya fi Qadiyyat Filastin (Report of the Parliamentary Committee of Enquiry into the Palestine Question, Arabic), Baghdad, 1950.

Totah, Khalil, *Dynamite in the Middle East* (New York: Philosophical Library, 1955).

Vatikiotis, J. Panayiotis, *The History of Modern Egypt: From Muhammad Ali to Mubarak* (Baltimore: Johns Hopkins University Press, 1991).

Vatikiotis, J. Panayiotis, *Politics and the Military in Jordan: A Study of the Arab Legion* (London: Frank Cass, 1967).

Wilson, C. Mary, *King Abdullah, Britain, and the making of Jordan* (Cambridge: Cambridge University Press, 1990).

Yodfat, Aryeh and Arnon-Ohanah, Yuval, *PLO Strategy and Politics* (London: Croom Helm, 1981).

Young, Peter, *The Arab Legion* (London: Osprey Publishing, 1972).

Zureiq, Constantin, *Ma'na al-Nakba* (The Meaning of the Disaster, Arabic), Beirut 1948.

IV Articles

Alexander, D. "Ezrat Ha'um Laplitim Ha'aravim" (U.N. Aid to Arab Refugees, Hebrew), *Hamizrah Hehadash: Quarterly of the Israel Oriental Society*, 5/1 (1953), pp. 1–13.

Bendman, Yona, "Haligion Ha'aravi Likrat Milhemet Ha'atzmaut" (The Arab Legion toward the War of Independence, Hebrew), *Ma'archot*, 294–295 (1984), pp. 36–45.

Coate, A. Winifred, "The Condition of Arab Refuges in Jordan", *International Affairs*, 29/4 (October 1953), pp. 449–456.

Cunningham, Alan, "Palestine – The last days of the Mandate", *International affairs*, 24/4 (October 1948), pp. 481–490.

Dann, Uriel, "The Beginnings of the Arab Legion", *MES*, 5/3 (October 1969), pp. 181–191.

Gazit, Mordechai, "The Israel–Jordan Peace Negotiations (1949–51): King Abdallah's Lonely Effort", *Journal of Contemporary History*, 23/3 (1988), pp. 409–424.

Gershoni, Israel, "King Abdallah's concept of a 'Greater Syria'", in Sinai, Anne and Pollack, Allen (eds.), *The Hashemite Kingdom of Jordan and the West Bank* (New York: American Academic Association for Peace in the Middle East, 1977), pp. 139–147.

Haddad, W. William and Hardy, M. Mary, "Jordan's Alliance with Israel and its Effects on Jordanian-Arab Relations", in Karsh, Efraim and. Kumaraswamy, P. R (eds.), *Israel, the Hashemites, and the Palestinians: The Fateful Triangle* (London: Frank Cass, 2003), pp. 31–48.

Heller, Mark, "Politics and the Military in Iraq and Jordan, 1920–1958: The British Influence", *Armed forces and society*, 4/1 (November, 1977), pp.75–99.

Kamel, S. Abu Jaber, "The Legislature of the Hashemite Kingdom of Jordan: A Study in Political Development", *The Muslim Word*, LIX (July–October 1968), pp. 220–250.

"King Abdullah's Assassins", *The World Today*, VII (1951), pp. 411–419.

Landis, Joshua, "Syria and the Palestine War: Fighting King Abdullah's 'Greater Syria Plan'", in Rogan, Eugene and Shlaim, Avi (eds.), *Rewriting the Palestine War: 1948 and the History of the Arab–Israeli Conflict* (Cambridge: Cambridge University Press, 2001), pp. 178–205.

Monroe, Elizabeth, "The Arab–Israel Frontier", *International Affairs*, 29/4 (October 1953), pp. 438–448.

Peak, G. Frederick, "Trans-Jordan", *Journal of the Royal Central Asian Society*, 26 (1939), pp. 375–396.

Peel, Earl, "The Report of the Palestine Commission", *International Affairs*, 16/5 (1937), pp. 761–779.

Porath, Yehoshua, "Abdallah's Greater Syria Programme", *MES*, 20/2 (1984), pp. 172–189.

Al-Qawuqji, Fauzi, "Memoirs, 1948" – Part 2, *Journal of Palestine Studies*, 2/1 (Autumn 1972), pp. 3–33.

Rudd, A. Jeffery, "Origins of the Transjordan Frontier Force", *MES*, 26: 2 (1990), pp. 161–184.

Sela, Avraham, "Transjordan, Israel and the 1948 War: Myth, Historiography and reality", *MES*, 28/4 (October 1992), pp. 623–688.

Selak, B. Charles, "The Suez Canal Base Agreement of 1954", *The American Journal of International Law*, 49/4 (1955), pp. 487–505

Shapira, Anita, "The Option on Ghaur al-Kibd: Contacts between Emir Abdallah and the Zionist Executive, 1932–1935", *Journal of Israeli History*, 1/2 (1980), pp. 239–283.

Shwadran, Benjamin, "Jordan Annexes Arab Palestine", *Middle Eastern Affairs*, 1/4 (April 1950), pp. 99–111.

Tal, Lawrence, "Jordan" in Sayigh, Yezid and Shlaim, Avi (eds.), *The Cold War and the Middle East* (Oxford: Clarendon, 1997), pp. 102–124.

Tell, Tariq, "Guns, Gold and Grain: War and Food Supply in the Making of Transjordan", in Heydemann, Steven (ed.), *War, Institutions, and Social Change in the Middle East* (California: University of California Press, 200), pp. 33–58.

"Trans Jordan's Army: The Arab Legion", *Palestine Affairs*, 3 (1948), pp. 44–45.

"Treaty of Alliance between His Majesty in Respect of the United Kingdom of Great Britain and Northern Ireland and His Majesty the King of the Hashemite Kingdom of Transjordan", *MEJ*, 2/4 (October, 1948), pp. 469–473.

Yitzhak, Ronen, "A Short History of the Secret Hashemite-Zionist Talks: 1921–1951", *Midstream*, LIII (May–June 2007), pp. 9–12.

Yitzhak, Ronen, "A Small Consolation for a Big Loss: King Abdallah and Jerusalem during the 1948 War", *Israel Affairs*, 14/3 (July 2008), pp. 398–418.

Yitzhak Ronen,"Jordanian Intelligence under the Rule of King Abdullah I (1921–1951)", *International Journal of Intelligence and Counterintelligence*, 23/4 (2010), pp. 647–662.

V Internet Websites

http://ezabadani.com/vb/showthread.php?t=83
http://weekly.ahram.org.eg/2004/713/feature.htm
http://www.adl.org/special_reports/protocols/protocols_plot2.asp
www.hayadan.org.il

Index

Arab League Summit (Cairo 1964), 140–41

Arab Legion
Arab officer appointments (1956), 122
Arab revolt in Palestine, 14
Arab–Israeli War (1948), 33, 36, 37–38, 39–47, 53–54, 55–56, 64, 86
Arava road incident (1950), 101
armistice talks (1949), 65, 72
assassination attempts on British officers, 20
becomes Jordanian army, 122
Bedouin recruitment, 13–14
British officers, ix, 25, 40, 53, 77–78, 83–4, 85–6, 101, 121, 132
British support, 14, 23, 24–25
capture of Rutbah Castel, 17
civil war in mandatory Palestine (1947–48), 26–33
Etzion Bloc attack, 29–33
expansion of, 14
formation of, 9
Glubb Pasha's appointment as deputy, 13–14
Glubb Pasha's appointment as leader, 16, 19
Glubb Pasha's dismissal (1956), 121–22, 131, 178*n*
invasion of Jerusalem (1948), 36, 41
Iraqi withdrawal from Triangle, 70–71
Israeli Operation *Uvda*, 70
military maneuvers in Iraq, 17–18
military maneuvers in Syria, 18–19
numbers on eve of 1948 war, 25
occupation of Arab Palestine, 34–35
officer military training in Britain, 24
Palestine truce (June–July 1948), 48–52
part of the British forces, 19
reductions, 12
Second World War, 16, 17–19
al-Tall's promotions, 23–24, 47, 80–81
al-Tall's recruitment, 23
al-Tall's resignation, 81
Wahhabi raid (1924), 10
West Bank annexation to Jordan, 95

Arab Liberation Army (ALA), 26–27, 29, 39, 41, 42, 44, 55–56
Arab Nationalist Movement, 23
Arab revolt (1916), 4, 9, 19
Arab revolt (1936-39), 14, 27
Arab–Israeli War (1948), 24, 33, 36–47, 52–61, 63–64, 74–75, 86, 150–51
Arabia, opposition to Hashemite rule, 6, 9
Arafat, Yasser, 132, 145–148
al-Arif, Arif, 44, 100
Ashu, Mustafa Shukri, 105, 107
Asian-African Conference (Bandung 1955), 120, 129
al-Askari, Ja'far, 152*n*
Atasi, Adnan, 88
Atasi, Hashem, 87
Ataturk, 2
Attlee, Clement R., 20, 104
Awda, Abd al-Qadie, 177*n*
al-Ayubi, Musa Ahmad, 105–6, 107, 108–9
Ayyad, Ibrahim, 105
Azcarate, Pablo de, 42
al-Azm, Khalid, 76, 104, 171–72*n*
Azzam, Abd al-Rahman, 26, 40, 48, 55

al-Ba'ath newspaper, 78–81
Ba'ath party
Iraq, 78, 168*n*
Jordanian purge, 81
Syria, 168*n*
and al-Tall, 78, 79
West Bank, 78
Badirkhan, Tahir, 21
al-Badr, Muhammad, 140, 142
Baghdad Pact, 119–21, 123
Balfour Declaration, x, 14–15
Bandung Asian-African Conference (1955), 120, 129
Bani Sakhr tribe, 8–10, 15
Bani Zayidan family, 21
al-Banna, Hassan, 133
Beaumont (British Consul to Jerusalem), 43, 45
Bedouins
Arab Legion, 13–14
raids, 2, 7
relations with Glubb, 13–14, 17–18
Be'eri, Eliezer, 75

Sharayri family, 21
Shealtiel, David, 47, 54–56
Shechem, 137
Shen Tahat Shen, Operation, 72
Shertok (Sharett), Moshe, 33, 68, 72
Shiloah, Reuven
  Abdullah's assassination (1951),
    105
  armistice talks (1949), 65, 68, 73
  Jordanian–Israeli negotiations
    (1949), 66
  Jordanian–Israeli peace negotiations
    (1949–50), 90, 92–93
Shishakli, Adib, 115
Shlaim, Avi, 145
al-Shuqairi, Ahmad, 141–142, 144
al-Shurayda, Kulayib, 6
Shurayqi, Muhammad, 100–101
Simeon, 137
Siri, Hussein Pasha, 82
Slim, William, 117
Socialist Party (Egypt), 113
Somerset, H.F.R., 152*n*
Soviet Union, 119
  diplomatic relations with Jordan,
    123
  Transjordan membership of UN,
    20
Sudan, 113
Suez, Anglo-Egyptian tensions,
  112–14, 117–18
Suez War (1956), 122–23
Sukenik (Yadin), Yigael, 54, 72, 91
Susser, Asher, 143
Syria
  Abdullah's assassination (1951),
    103–4, 109
  Abdullah's "Greater Syria" plan,
    19, 33, 35, 78
  Arab Collective Security Pact
    (ACSP), 98
  Arab League financial aid, 141
  Arab–Israeli War (1948), 36–37, 75
  armistice talks (1949), 74
  Ba'ath party, 168*n*
  British military maneuvers, 18–19
  coup (1949), 75–77
  Faysal's rule (1918-20), 1
  fedayeen (guerilla) organizations,
    140
  French mandate (1920-43), 1–3, 19
  "Greater Syria" plan, 103–4

independence, 19
Jerusalem issue, 89
Jordanian civil war (1970), 147
Lausanne Conference (1949),
  88–89
Palestine Conciliation Commission
  (PCC), 60–61
Palestinian refugees, 98
relations with Hussein's regime, 122
solidarity agreement (1957), 123
Syrian–Saudi invasion plan of
  Jordan, 104
Talal's regime, 110
al-Tall's coup-d'état plot, 77
al-Tall's visit (1950), 87–88
tripartite military alliance, 122
United Arab Republic (UAR), 126,
  140

Tabbara, Bahjat, 27, 123
Tafila tribes, 6
Talal bin Abdullah
  Abdullah's assassination (1951),
    103–104
  becomes King of Jordan, 109–10,
    112
  connections with Arab League
    countries, 112
  mental illness, 109–110, 115
  power struggle with Nayif, 109
  removal from power (1952), 115
  al-Tall's coup-d'état plot, 77,
    82–83, 87
Tal'at, Yusuf, 177*n*
Talhouni, Bahjat, 126
Tali, Rashid, 5
al-Tall, Abd al-Qadir, 21–22, 87
al-Tall, Abd al-Rahim, 21
al-Tall, Abd al-Rahman, 21
al-Tall, Abdullah Yousef, ix–xii
  Abdullah's assassination (1951),
    102, 105–7, 108–9, 112
  Algerian national movement,
    128–131
  Anglo-Egyptian tensions in Suez,
    114
  anti-British stance, 59, 76, 77–78,
    83–84
  anti-Semitism, 132–140
  Arab Legion membership, 23
  Arab Legion promotions, 23–24,
    47, 80–81